The Animal Experimentation Debate

Recent Titles in the
CONTEMPORARY WORLD ISSUES
Series

Books in the **Contemporary World Issues** series address vital issues in today's society such as genetic engineering, pollution, and biodiversity. Written by professional writers, scholars, and nonacademic experts, these books are authoritative, clearly written, up-to-date, and objective. They provide a good starting point for research by high school and college students, scholars, and general readers as well as by legislators, business-people, activists, and others.

Each book, carefully organized and easy to use, contains an overview of the subject, a detailed chronology, biographical sketches, facts and data and/or documents and other primary source material, a forum of authoritative perspective essays, annotated lists of print and nonprint resources, and an index.

Readers of books in the **Contemporary World** Issues series will find the information they need in order to have a better understanding of the social, political, environmental, and economic issues facing the world today.

The Animal Experimentation Debate

A REFERENCE HANDBOOK

David E. Newton

ABC-CLIO

Santa Barbara, California • Denver, Colorado • Oxford, England

Copyright 2013 by ABC-CLIO, LLC

Library of Congress Cataloging-in-Publication Data

Newton, David E.
   The animal experimentation debate : a reference handbook / David E. Newton.
      pages cm. — (Contemporary world issues)
   Includes bibliographical references and index.
   ISBN 978–1–61069–317–2 (hard copy : alk. paper) — ISBN 978–1–61069–318–9 (ebook) 1. Animal experimentation—Moral and ethical aspects. I. Title.
HV4915.N49   2013
179′.4—dc23   2012048845

ISBN: 978–1–61069–317–2
EISBN: 978–1–61069–318–9

17 16 15 14 13   1 2 3 4 5

This book is also available on the World Wide Web as an eBook. Visit www.abc-clio.com for details.

ABC-CLIO, LLC
130 Cremona Drive, P.O. Box 1911
Santa Barbara, California 93116-1911

This book is printed on acid-free paper ∞

Manufactured in the United States of America

x   Contents

Vivisection is a social evil because if it advances human knowledge, it does so at the expense of human character.
—George Bernard Shaw, Irish playwright and founder of the London School of Economics

Animal research and testing has played a part in almost every medical breakthrough of the last century. It has saved hundreds of millions of lives worldwide.
Joan Ryan, Home Office Minister, United Kingdom

Humans have always had mixed feelings about our animal cousins. On the one hand, our survival depends absolutely on animals. We hunt and domesticate animals for their meat and for the milk and blood that provides for our nutritional needs. We skin, shear, cut, and otherwise collect their hair, fur, and hide to provide for our clothing and other apparel needs and for the building materials from which we construct our homes. We share our homes with animals partly because of the protection they provide against human and animal marauders who attack and kill us and just for the companionship they provide. We use animal power to pull our wagons and plows, to turn our water wheels, and to supply many times the energy available from our own relatively puny human bodies. It is hardly surprising that most major religions acknowledge the crucial role that animals play in human civilization and approve our using them essentially as our slaves, to use as we choose to make our lives more healthy, safer, more comfortable, and more pleasurable.

Humans have also used animals for another purpose: scientific research. At first, this research was aimed primarily at better understanding humans themselves. In order to appreciate the inner workings of the human body, it is theoretically possible to cut open a human and see what is going on inside her or his body. But this approach is seldom practical. Instead, natural philosophers and scientific researchers have chosen to cut open nonhuman bodies—often while they were still alive—to look directly at the mechanisms that drive life, and then assumed, rightly or wrongly, that what they learned could be applied to human bodies also. Thus, over time, research on animals has expanded human understanding of human anatomy and physiology immeasurably.

Eventually, animal experimentation expanded to include a new mission: to discover ways of preventing and treating human disease and other disorders. Again, the principle has been that if one can find a substance to prevent a disease such as diphtheria in guinea pigs (as Emil von Behring did in the 1880s and 1890s), then that substance might also be used to prevent diphtheria in humans (which it did). The fundamental argument for more than two centuries has been, therefore, that experimenting on animals with the goal of preventing and curing human medical problems was a legitimate addition to the long list of ways in which animals are used for human benefit.

This philosophy has, however, always had its critics. For some individuals, animals should never be viewed simply as objects to be used for human purposes. These individuals have argued that animals have the ability to experience pain and suffering, just as do humans, and that they therefore deserve the same consideration as do humans. Over time, the idea of animal-as-object has been replaced in many minds by the concept of animal-with-value-of-its-own, a principle that has prompted questions about whether or to what extent animals should be subjected to experimentation that is generally not approved for human subjects.

Over the last century, that question has been focused even more sharply on the use of animals for the testing of cosmetics, household products, and other substances that have no role in saving human lives or protecting them from disease, and on instructional settings, in which animals are experimented on entirely for the sake of teaching the principles of biology, medicine, pharmaceuticals, or some other subject.

For much of the last 150 years, this debate has taken the form of a largely either/or argument: allow or do not allow researchers to use nonhuman animals in their research. Over time, that debate has become more sophisticated and more nuanced. Many people (but certainly not all) accept the fact that animal testing may sometimes be required to answer questions about human health and medical issues. But a wide variety of alternatives to animal testing are now available, and the number of occasions for which animal testing is the only available alternative appears to be becoming smaller and smaller. And the argument for causing pain and suffering among animals to produce a better lipstick or a more effective household wax has become even more problematic.

Animal Experimentation is intended as a resource guide for individuals who wish to learn more about this contentious and difficult topic. The first two chapters of the book provide a factual background on the history of animal testing and about current issues related to the topic. Chapter 3 provides an opportunity for individuals on all sides of the debate to express their personal view about the practice of animal experimentation and its contribution to human health and medical practice. The remaining chapters of the book provide a number of resources that will be useful in continuing a study of animal-testing issues, such as a chronology of animal experimentation, a list of sketches of individuals and organizations who have made important contributions to animal testing or efforts to limit or abolish vivisection, a glossary of important terms, and an annotated bibliography of print and electronic resources dealing with animal experimentation.

The Animal
Experimentation
Debate

Nkanti was in terrible pain. What is it that could be causing so much pain? He had felt fine this morning. But then the pain began after the midday meal. Perhaps an enemy had shot a magic dart into his side. Now Nkanti would have to see the mganga Sesubo. Sesubo always knew exactly what to do. Sometimes she would pray to the spirits. Sometimes she would sacrifice a goat. Sometimes they would both visit the graves of the ancestors. But she always knew how to make the cure. Well, almost always.

Vivisection in Ancient History

Throughout history, humans have been puzzled by many of the events that make up daily life. What is it that causes a baby to start growing inside a woman? What is it that causes a healthy child to suddenly become ill and die . . . or to suddenly become ill and then get better. Why do people lose their strength, their eyesight, their hearing, and other physical abilities as they grow older?

Detail from Joseph Wright's *An Experiment on a Bird in an Air Pump*, 1768. An avid chronicler of his era's interest in science, Wright depicts a scene in which a bird is deprived of air before an audience, recreating Robert Boyle's air pump experiments of the previous century. By Wright's time, such dramatic displays were commonplace; while some humane practitioners substituted an air-filled bladder, more typically live animals were a key part of the spectacle. (Corbis)

The basic problem that underlies most of these questions is that they involve a knowledge of what it is that takes place inside a human body when disease, injury, and death occur. What is going on inside Nkanti's belly to cause the terrible pain he feels? Perhaps the only way to really answer that question is to open a person up and look inside. Then it would be possible to see if there really is a magic dart there, or if Nkanti's appendix has burst.

But humans traditionally have seldom had the skills or the inclination to dissect a living human body to get the answers needed for questions like these. The term *dissection* refers to the process of cutting into a body for the purpose of study, diagnosis, or treatment. When dissection is performed on a living animal, the process is better known as *vivisection*, from the Latin terms *vivus*, for "living," and *sectio*, for "separation." (One of the challenges in reading history is to determine which procedure is actually being described prior to 1707 when the term *vivisection* was itself first introduced. Prior to that date, the term *dissection* could mean either simply cutting into tissue, whether alive or dead [today: dissection] or cutting into living tissue [today: vivisection].)

Dissection and Vivisection of Humans in Ancient Greece

One of the most remarkable points about the history of vivisection is that healers and physicians have essentially never practiced the dissection of living humans, although vivisection with other animals has been somewhat common throughout much of human history. The one glaring exception to that statement can be traced to the research of two Greek physicians in the third century BCE. The confluence of a number of cultural and personal factors appears to have made possible the vivisection of humans by two Greek physicians, Herophilus of Chalcedon and his younger contemporary Erasistratus of Ceos. The evidence is clear that these two men dissected human cadavers, and they almost certainly dissected living men also. The living subjects were apparently convicted criminals sent to the two physicians in their laboratory at Alexandria by the first two Ptolemys to rule Egypt in the third century BCE, Ptolemy I Soter and Ptolemy II Philadelphus. Both kings hoped to learn more about the way the human body works, and readily supplied both Herophilus and Erasistratus with the subjects they needed for their research (Williams and Williams 1904–1910, 195).

The Roman encyclopedist Celsus described the apparent theory behind the work of Herophilus and Erasistratus some four centuries later. He pointed out that it is not possible to determine the source of pain and disease in a human because these causes are essentially hidden from human sight. But by cutting open a living human body, a physician can see directly what is going on inside and find ways of relieving human suffering. People might object to the dissection of a living person, Celsus agrees, but in this case, the end justifies the means. Consider, he says, that "it is by no means cruel, as most people represent it, by the tortures of a few guilty, to search after remedies for the whole innocent race of mankind in all ages" (Celsus 1756, 7–8).

And there is little doubt that Herophilus and Erasistratus produced some remarkable achievements. They made a number of discoveries about human anatomy and physiology that would remain unmatched for at least two thousand years, such as the fundamental nature of the nervous system and the existence of at least seven pairs of cranial nerves; the gross anatomy of the eye; the existence of valves in the heart; the pump-like function of the heart; the difference between veins and arteries; the existence and structure of the liver and the pancreas; and the differences between the male and female reproductive organs (Von Staden 1992, 224).

In an essay on this phenomenon, Heinrich von Staden, emeritus professor of classics and the history of science at the Institute for Advanced Study, has attempted to understand the factors that led to this highly unusual foray into the vivisection of living humans in the third century BCE. He concludes that the disregard by Herophilus and Erisistratus of centuries of prohibitions against vivisection on humans was the result primarily of the strong personalities of the rulers of Alexandria at the time, Ptolemy I Soter and Ptolemy II Philadelphus. Both men were not only committed to expanding human knowledge about medicine in particular and science in general, but were also committed to making Alexandria "a glittering center of literary and scientific learning," an endeavor in which they were highly successful (Von Staden 1992, 231).

The even more interesting question, Von Staden notes, is not so much why Herophilus and Erisistratus broke through this new frontier of human vivisection, but why, after achieving such notable success with so many new and exciting discoveries, their new school of medicine began to disappear almost immediately upon their own deaths. Von Staden points out that the factors that originally led to the introduction of human vivisection remained in place, but that new factors also came into play. The most important of those factors was the rise of a new school of medicine called Empiricism. The Empiricists argued that it really did not make any difference what one did or did not know about the inner workings of the human body. What did matter was the physician's ability to recognize symptoms and devise a cure based on those symptoms. This new view of medical treatment, combined with the still powerful Greek proscriptions against vivisection of almost any kind, was responsible, Von Staden says, for the rapid decline of human vivisection.

However one explains this fascinating period in the history of medical research, human vivisection disappeared from the medical canon essentially forever, with only the rarest and often most inhumane efforts by rogue researchers ever employing living humans in medical experiments again. Perhaps the most important lesson to be drawn from this review of human vivisection is a principle that remains throughout all later human history: scientific practices such as dissection and vivisection do not exist in isolation from the rest of society. Whether a researcher in ancient Greece, eighteenth-century Germany, or modern-day United States decides to dissect or not dissect a dog, rat, or fruit fly depends on far more than her or his interest in the anatomy, physiology, and biochemistry of that organism. It is also dependent upon and even determined by the way that philosophers, church leaders, sociologists, politicians, educators, and common men and women think about animal life. Is life itself something fundamentally different from nonlife? Is human life somehow "special" in the grand scheme of the natural world? Is the life of a gorilla or a dog or a cat or a mouse of equal value to that of a human life?

These are, of course, profound questions about the most fundamental of issues. They are questions that the greatest minds in human civilizations—as well as the most ordinary lives of everyday life—ponder in every culture and every age. The answer to which people come regarding such questions, even though they may change over time, determines how scientific researchers design and conduct the experiments they carry out to learn more about the way humans are put together and the way they function, as well as the way human systems grow, develop, decay, break down, and eventually die.

Dissection and Vivisection of Animals

Although the dissection of living humans was largely proscribed in ancient Greece, the practice of using animals and cadavers for dissection was apparently not unknown among the leading natural philosophers of the day. Most historians suggest that the earliest known dissector may have been the philosopher Alcmaeon on Croton, best known for a book he wrote sometime between 450 and 500 BCE. Scholars are still uncertain as to how much dissection Alcmaeon actually did, what the purpose of his research was, and on what subjects he performed his experiments. It does seem clear, however, that by whatever means he made some important fundamental discoveries in human anatomy, including the first mention of the eustachian tube, discovery of the optic nerve, and association of the brain with nerve function in the body (Lloyd 1975; Huffman 2008).

Somewhat more is known about the activities of the greatest ancient scientist of them all, Aristotle, who apparently conducted many dissections during his lifetime. Although he may be better known for his studies of the heavens, physical motion, and other aspects of the inanimate world, he taught that the greatest opportunity for success for the natural philosopher was in the study of plants and animals. With regard to living objects, he observed, "We know more of them and we know them more fully . . . they are nearer to us and more of our own nature" (cited in Lennox 2011). Aristotle's two most famous books on animals were *The History of Animals* and *Parts of Animals*. In these books, he laid out a general scheme for the student of living organisms, a scheme in which dissection played an essential role because it allowed the investigator to look directly at the parts of which animals' bodies are made and how those parts are connected to each other. The two books also contain a vast amount of information on animal anatomy that Aristotle probably could have obtained only through the dissection of living and dead animals. The books apparently also contained drawings at one time (references to the drawings exist in the remaining texts), although the drawings themselves are now lost.

Another philosopher who may have been engaged in the dissection of animals was Democritus of Abdera, probably better known as the author of the ancient concept of atoms. In an attempt to learn more about the anatomy of animals, he apparently carried out a number of dissections. His fellow citizens had a somewhat different view of Democritus's studies, coming to the conclusion that they were a sign that he had gone mad. To confirm their view, they contacted the famous Greek physician Hippocrates and asking him to come to Abdera to examine Democritus. Hippocrates did so and found that, as he told the Abderites, Democritus was saner than the citizens themselves ("The Cult of Asclepius, God of Medicine" 2012).

Beyond these limited records, we have little information about the practice of dissection and vivisection in the ancient world. The next figure of any significance in the history of dissection is the Greek-born Roman physician Aelius Galenus (better known simply as Galen), who lived from about 130 CE to about 200 CE. Galen is of immense importance in the history of medicine because his texts (as erroneous as they might have been) were taken as the ultimate authority in medicine for nearly 1,500 years after his death. Galen based much of his information about the anatomy and physiology of the human body on the thousands of dissections he is said to have performed in his lifetime on animals ranging from mice, birds, and snakes to pigs, goats, and horses. Many of these dissections were done on dead animals, though Galen also used living animals extensively. Although he made enormous contributions to the procedures used in dissection and to the study of human anatomy, he introduced a number of errors into the latter field, at least partly because the knowledge gained from his animal models did not transfer directly to the human body. In fact, later researchers who, working with human cadavers, came up with information different from that of Galen often spent significant efforts trying to reconcile their own "incongruent" findings with those of the master (Von Staden 1995; "Galen Claudius" 2012; Gross 1998; Hankinson 2008).

The (Temporary) End of Vivisection

The decline of the Roman Empire was accompanied by a significant decrease in the pursuit of scientific questions, ranging from the structure of the universe to the composition and function of the human body. One notable history site has referred to the millennium after the fall of Rome as "Science's Siesta" ("History of Anatomy" 2012). The reason for this decline has been the subject of research by a host of scholars, but arguably the most important factor was the rise of Christianity. The new religion, which took root in Rome in the third century CE, placed a great deal of emphasis on the ephemeral nature of the real world around us, in general, and of human life, in particular. The Bible made it clear that the physical world is transient and that the goal of human endeavors must be to prepare individuals for life after death. The pursuit of knowledge was regarded not only as a waste of time but also as an absolute insult to the teachings of the Bible. If some type of scientific knowledge was truly necessary, such as the treatment of disease and injury, then there were classical authorities, like Aristotle and Galen, to whom one could turn for answers.

The great Flemish anatomist Andreas Vesalius described the status of dissection during the period when he was beginning his work:

> When all operations were entrusted to barbers, not only did true knowledge of the viscera perish from the medical profession, but the work of dissection completely died out. Physicians did not undertake surgery, while those to whom the manual craft was entrusted were too educated to understand what professors of dissection had written. (as quoted in Carrier 2010, an invaluable resource on this topic)

A number of factors lay at the basis of the Christian rejection of human dissection. Perhaps of greatest importance was the doctrine of the resurrection of the body at the end of the world. That event would be extremely difficult to achieve, theologians pointed out, if the body had been cut apart after its death. Perhaps more fundamentally was the notion that human life itself was of little long-term value, that illness and suffering were a normal part of the human condition, and that trying to prevent or cure those conditions was unnecessary and perhaps even evil. In any case, early Christians taught that disease and injury were not really natural events but occurrences caused by evil spirits and demons. The appropriate way to treat these events was with prayer and not with earthly medical treatments. The power of prayer and faith were illustrated over and over again in Christian literature by miracles, many of which involved the cure of a disease by no earthly means. All such arguments militated against efforts to better understand human anatomy and the causes and cures of disease during a period when Christian thought reigned supreme. (See, for example, "Christianity and the Medical Sciences" 2012; Curran 2012)

These factors also militated against the use of animals in medical experiments, since those experiments were in and of themselves regarded as unnecessary and inappropriate, no matter the animals on which they were performed. However, the Church did have a theological position on the at least *potential* use of animals other than humans as subjects of vivisection. The fundamental basis for that position was the Bible itself, which states clearly in Genesis that humans have dominion over the lower animals and maintain the right to use those animals for whatever purpose they choose. The relevant section of the Bible says:

And God said, Let us make man in our image, after our likeness: and let them have dominion over the fish of the sea, and over the fowl of the air, and over the cattle, and over all the earth, and over every creeping thing that creeps on the earth. (Genesis 1:26, King James Version)

Over the centuries, commentators have made it clear that there is no uncertainty about the meaning of this verse. As one such writer says,

The relation of man to the creature is now stated. It is that of sovereignty. Those capacities of right thinking, right willing, and right acting, or of knowledge, holiness, and righteousness, in which man resembles God, qualify him for dominion, and constitute him lord of all creatures that are destitute of intellectual and moral endowments. Hence, wherever man enters he makes his sway to be felt. (Genesis 1:26 2012)

As an aside, this view has not been restricted to the Middle Ages. For example, in 1982 James Watt, then secretary of the interior under President Ronald Regan, said:

The earth is merely a temporary way station on the road to eternal life. It is unimportant except as a place of testing to get into heaven. In this evil and dangerous world, one's duty is to pass through unspotted by the surrounding corruption. The earth was put here by the Lord for his people to subdue and to use for profitable purposes on the way to the hereafter. (Geering 2012; see also Watt 1982)

So what is the status of animals other than humans in the debate over vivisection? It appears that, because of the general rejection of scientific research by the Church, little dissection of animals took place either. However, an important precedent was being established by religious thinkers about the relative position of animals in a Christian world during the Middle Ages. The general principle was that humans were a little less than the angels but a little more than "beasts," other animals. For many historians, the person who best defined this position was the great Catholic theologian St. Thomas Aquinas (1225–1274). In his massive work *Summa Theologica*, Aquinas asked what the position of animals was in the worldly scheme of things. He concluded that only humans among the animals are rational and only they can have a soul. Nonhuman animals are irrational and have no soul, thus depriving them of a personality or any rights of their own. Their sole purpose on Earth is to serve humans and provide for their needs. If he were asked today whether they could be the subjects of vivisection for biomedical experiments (a fairly unlikely possibility), he would almost certainly say that they could honorably and morally be used for that purpose. Among his statements on the issue is the following, taken from his book *Summa contra Gentiles*:

Hereby is refuted the error of those who said it is sinful for a man to kill brute animals; for by the divine providence they are intended for man's use according to the order of nature. Hence it is not wrong for man to make use of them either by killing or in any other way whatever. (Pegis 1997, 222)

Dissection in Non-Western Cultures

For the historian of science, a plethora of written records exist, going back at least 2,000 years, that allows the scholar to discover the medical practices that have been performed throughout history, often with very specific comments about the philosophical or other bases for those practices. Such is often not the case with other cultures. Yet Western civilization is only a part of human history, which also includes the extended, and often very productive, civilizations of Islam, China, India, Africa, and South America. In general, scholars know far less about the history of science and medicine in these arenas than in Western civilization.

Islam provides an example. Historians do have an abundance of information about the transfer of knowledge from ancient Greek civilization in its golden era of the fifth to third centuries BCE, about the functions of many aspects of Islamic culture, and about the transfer of both Greek and Islamic knowledge back to Western civilization at the end of the Middle Ages. But a great deal less is known about some specific aspects of Islamic science and medicine, the practice of dissection being one.

It is well known that Islamic scholars were well aware of Greek science, including the practice of dissection both by the ancient Greeks and by Galen, who had become the repository of nearly all existing knowledge by the end of the second century CE. But to what extent were Muslims themselves engaged in the practice of dissection in the period between about the fourth and thirteenth centuries CE?

Answering that question is difficult for at least two reasons. In the first place, there appears to be a considerable gap between legal prescriptions with regard to the practice and actual medical procedures being carried out at the time. In general, Islamic law (shar_ah) forbids desecration of the human body, the most perfect example of God's creation (although a number of possible exceptions to that law exist). Numerous examples are available in Islamic legal and religious writings prohibiting the dissection of the human body for any but a limited number of reasons (such as the cutting up of military men whose armies have done that to Muslim fighters). Yet a review of the medical literature of the time suggests that dissection *may* have been practiced commonly during the time.

For example, perhaps the most famous of all early Muslim physicians, Abu Ali al-Husayn ibn Abd Allah ibn Sina (better known by his Latinized name of Avicenna), wrote in his most famous work, *The Canon of Medicine*:

> As for the parts of the body and their functions, it is necessary that they be approached through observation (hiss) and dissection (tashrih), while those things that must be conjectured and demonstrated by reason are diseases and their particular causes and their symptoms and how disease can be abated and health maintained. (quoted in Savage-Smith 1995, 92–93)

Much later in this period (the twelfth century), the most esteemed medical writers were (perhaps) still arguing for the importance of dissection in understanding the anatomy of human bodies and those of other animals. In his classical work *The Book of General Principles*, for example, the Spanish-Muslim physician, Abu l-Walid Muhammad bin 'Ahmad bin Rusd (better known by his Latinized name of Averroes), wrote that "whoever has been occupied with the science of anatomy/ dissection (tashrih) has increased his belief in God" (quoted in Savage-Smith 1995, 94). The problem in interpreting this passage is that the Arab word *tashrih* has a number of meanings, most commonly either "anatomy" or "dissection." It is impossible in most cases, then, to know whether a writer is speaking about the knowledge of the human body in general, as the term *anatomy* now means, or about the more specific technique of dissection, by which that knowledge is often gained.

In her definitive study of the possible place of dissection in Muslim medicine in the Middle Ages, Emilie Savage-Smith reviews the voluminous evidence against the practice of dissection from religious sources as well as some practical limitations (such as the unusually warm climate of Cairo, Baghdad, and other locations at which dissections would have been conducted). She then reviews the abundant evidence of human anatomy and that of other animals from numerous Muslim medical and scientific reports. In the end, she comes to the conclusion that "the evidence as to its [dissection's] actual practice, however, is conflicting and insufficient to allow one to draw definite conclusions" (Savage-Smith 1995, 105; also see Hehmeyer and Khan 2007; Shoja and Tubbs 2007).

Dissection in China during the Middle Ages and earlier appears to have been relatively uncommon for two reasons. First, the Confucian religion (like the Christian and Islamic religions) taught that the human body is sacred and that it could not be despoiled by procedures that involved cutting into it with a knife. Confucius himself wrote that "our body with skin and hair comes from our parents. We must not mutilate it" (Schnorrenberger 2008, 37). Second, the Chinese approach to the study of the human body depended less on the physical exploration of the body itself and more on a philosophical understanding of what the body represented and how it was associated with the view of nature in general. The Chinese approach to illness, diseases, and other medical problems has been described as a function of *systematic correspondence*, a belief that any system whatsoever is intended to exist in harmony, with all parts functioning smoothly with each other. This principle applied to every part of nature, ranging from the operation of the universe itself to the health of the human body to the functioning of the political state. Interestingly enough, this approach to human anatomy survived until fairly recent times. Out of this principle developed a view of human anatomy, health, and disease that did not really depend to any great extent on the actual location, appearance, and function of the internal organs nearly as much as it did on maintaining the smooth interaction of these organs, which could be controlled without ever knowing their structural details (see, for example, "Exploring Illness across Time and Space" 2012; Unschuld 1985, 78). Nonetheless, dissections were not entirely unheard of in ancient Chinese medicine. Probably the most famous example of dissection in ancient Chinese medicine occurred in 16 CE, when the emperor Wang Mang ordered the dissection of the body of a rebel by the name of Wang Sun-Ching. Wang may have felt that he could turn a political lesson into valuable medical information by having a skilled butcher cut open the rebel's body and make numerous measurements and observations with an eye toward finding ways to cure disease. The dissection resulted in the discovery of five organs (heart, liver, kidney, spleen, and gall bladder) that corresponded to the five planets, 12 tubes for the circulation of air and blood corresponding to the 12 great rivers of China, and an overall count of 365 parts of the body, corresponding to 365 days of the year (Matuk 2006, 6; Schnorrenberger 2008, 36). A second episode that is sometimes mentioned occurred in 1045 CE when a leader by the name of Tu Ch'i ordered the dissection of more than 70 rebels who had been captured in their effort to overrun Kwangsi province. The knowledge gained from these dissections became part of medical textbooks used in later times (Liu 1976, 298–299). Such events were apparently quite rare in Chinese history, and even as late as the nineteenth century, anatomy was still being taught in China primarily with the use of diagrams and models, rather than by performing dissections (Lyons 2012).

The history of dissection in India is similar to that of China. Religious prohibitions were even more severe in India and, as a result, dissection with a knife was forbidden. Indian physicians overcame that restriction with an imaginative approach. They placed a dead body in water until it began to decay and then peeled back the skin over a period of time to explore more and more deeply into the body. Throughout the ancient period, however, Indian physicians did understand the importance of exploring the insides of the human body—by one means or another—as made evident by the writings of probably the most famous of all Indian physicians of the period, Sushruta, who is thought to have lived sometime between 1000 and 600 BCE. One of the admonitions attributed to the physician was the need for exploring the inside of the body:

> Anyone who wishes to acquire a thorough knowledge of anatomy must prepare a dead body and carefully observe and examine all its different parts. One should select a body, which is complete in all its parts. Having removed all the excrementatious matter from it, the body should be wrapped in grass and placed in a cage. Having firmly secured the latter in a hidden spot in a river, the body should be allowed to decompose. After an interval of seven says, the thoroughly decomposed body should be taken out and very slowly scrubbed with a whisk made of grass roots (of kusa). At the same time every part of the body great or small, external or internal, beginning with the skin should be examined with the eye. (quoted in Rajgopal et al. 2002; also see Saraf and Parihar 2007)

In general, about the most that one can say about non-Western cultures prior to fairly recent times is that there is little reliable information about the use of animals for experimentation or about the use of living humans or cadaver dissection (see, for example, Singh et al. 2012).

The Renewal of Dissection

Toward the end of the twelfth century, religious attitudes toward dissection began to change. A confluence of theological, social, and political factors appears to have been responsible for a change in attitude among authorities that allowed physicians to begin once more to perform dissections without censure (Prioreschi 2001). Apparently the first public dissection to occur at the end of the long Middle Ages drought was conducted by the famous anatomist Mondino de Luzzi. Mondino is said to have personally dissected the body of a dead female criminal in January 1315 in Bologna before a group of medical students. As was customary at the time, the anatomist sat in a chair and lectured on anatomy while a barber performed the actual dissection. As an indication of changing attitudes, the dissection was apparently specifically authorized and approved by the pope (Lassek 1958, 63).

A renewed interest in vivisection was also without question associated with the growth of a new "scientific" approach to knowledge. This approach relied far more on experimentation than on ancient teachings and documents for determining what was and was not true about the natural world, including human beings. One could learn most reliably about human anatomy, according to the new philosophy, by dissecting a human being than reading about human anatomy in a textbook by Galen. One of the first and most famous spokespersons for this new philosophy was the English polymath Sir Francis Bacon (1561–1626). Bacon set forth his approach for the pursuit of knowledge in a classic work, *Novum Organum* (*New Method*), a rejoinder to Aristotle's original work of two thousand years earlier, the *Organon*.

Bacon's fundamental premise was that God had given humans control over nature in the Bible, as illustrated in the story of the Garden of Eden. Over time, however, humans had lost that control, and it was time that they reasserted their rightful place in command of plants, animals, and rest of nature. One way of achieving this objective, Bacon taught, was the use of experimentation, by which humans could almost literally "tear away the secrets of nature." One such method of experimentation was vivisection. As scholars had relied on dissection less and less over the centuries, Bacon said, they had been left with a view of humans only from their outer skin. It was time again, he asserted, to cut through the skin, look deep into the human body, and find once again what humans are really like ("Chapter 1: Meat Matters" 2008; Merchant 2012).

For Bacon, however, the problem was that he rejected the practice of dissecting humans. Fortunately (for him), Bacon regarded the dissection of animals as an adequate substitute for the dissection of humans. He believed that the structure and function of animal bodies were sufficiently similar to those of humans to allow vivisection of animals to produce reliable knowledge about human bodies. Perhaps more important, he regarded humans as being so far superior to other animals morally that there could be no ethical objection to the vivisection of animals for this purpose. Bacon most clearly states his position on vivisection in his work *The Advancement of Learning* (1605), in which he finds "much deficience" in the approach of classical scholars in studying human anatomy. One of the problems, he explains, is that much of the study of the human body has been done with dead bodies, where many fundamental functions have come to an end. What must be done, he says, is to study living bodies. He recalls that Celsus (see above) very correctly criticized the vivisection of living humans, but that Celsus need not have so completely given up on the use of vivisection; instead the practice might "have been well diverted upon the dissection of beasts alive, which notwithstanding the dissimilitude of their parts may sufficiently satisfy this inquiry" (Bacon 1893). In other words, vivisection and dissection of humans should be avoided, but use of the same procedures on lower animals is not only permitted but to be encouraged. As one of Bacon's early biographers noted, by means of this passage, "Bacon's position in the antivivisection controversy is here clearly defined" (Abbott 1885, 464).

Almost contemporaneous with Bacon, French scientist and philosopher René Descartes (1596–1650) introduced an even more radical concept into the debate over the use of animals in experiments. Descartes showed immense potential as a young student for the study of mathematics, and some of the achievements for which he is best known today were in that field. For example, he invented the science of analytic geometry, which is sometimes known as Cartesian geometry, and a number of mathematical terms carry his name, such as Cartesian coordinates, Cartesian circle, Cartesian diagram, and Cartesian product. It is hardly surprising then that he tended to think of the natural world in mathematical terms. In fact, he interpreted nature as a giant machine in which plants, humans, other animals, and all inanimate objects were simply masses of material that operated according to mathematical laws, like machines and their components.

Descartes recognized that humans and other animals were constructed similarly (but not identically) but that they differed in one important way: humans had souls and animals did not. In fact, Descartes liked to think of animals as automata without intelligence, memory, the ability to speak, and other human-like qualities that included the ability to feel pain and emotions. Given his own Christian background, it is not surprising that Descartes also saw service to humans as an essential role for the "lower" animals, thus justifying the use of vivisection with them. As to the possibility that animals might experience pain during vivisection, Descartes held a somewhat tangled view. On the one hand, he tried to make clear where he stood on the issue. In a letter to Marin Mersenne on July 13, 1640, he wrote that "we should have no doubt at all that the irrational animals are automata" (Jonas 1966, 56). In an earlier letter to Mersenne, however, he showed that this view was not quite so straightforward. He said that pain was a function of the soul, so humans could experience pain but animals (which had no soul) could not. Nonetheless, he said, all the "external motions" associated with pain that we observe (presumably screaming, crying, and trying to escape) "are found in the beasts," but for some reason, they are "not pain properly speaking" (Jonas 1966, 56).

Vivisection and the Rise of Modern Biology

The theoretical and philosophical imprimatur provided by the writings of Bacon, Descartes, and their colleagues provided a sound basis for the rise of a new approach to the study of living organisms, the modern science of biology. The one individual most commonly associated with this revolution was the English physician William Harvey (1578–1657). Harvey's most famous book, *De Motus Cordis* (*On the Motion of the Heart and the Blood*), was published in 1628. It provided an accurate and complete description of the process by which blood moves through the human body. In explaining the process, Harvey showed that Galen's theory of it, which had been taught for 1,500 years in all medical schools, was wrong.

In his book Harvey pointed out that his knowledge came from extensive vivisections of experimental animals (and a small number of human subjects), without which the information in *De Motus Cordis* could never have been obtained. Vivisections were also the source of many other data on human anatomy and physiology produced by Harvey during his lifetime. The physician was not unaware of the pain and suffering he brought to his subjects. Nonetheless, he was convinced that the knowledge gained from such experiments fully justified any discomfort the animals may have felt. As one observer has noted about Harvey's work, "Vesalius is perfectly clear that vivisection is a form of torture (the bitch is cruciata, crucified or tortured), but he delights in what it makes visible" ("Harvey and Vivisection" 2012).

Harvey's discoveries, as is often the case with revolutionary breakthroughs, were greeted with widespread and vigorous objection and disapproval. Many of these complaints simply pointed out that everything humans needed to know about anatomy was already contained in the beautifully illustrated texts of Galen. Others had problems with the experimental procedure followed by Harvey, that is, vivisection. For example, the French anatomist Jean Riolan II ("the younger"; 1577–1657) pointed out that the anatomy of the animals vivisected by Harvey was significantly different from that of humans, and it was not possible to draw conclusions from those experiments to the normal functions of the human body. The English physiologist Edmund O'Meara raised a somewhat similar objection. "The miserable torture of vivisection places the body in an unnatural state," he pointed out, with the result that information gained during the procedure had only limited value for the study of human anatomy, if even that (quoted in Maehle and Tröhler 1987, 22).

Finally, a number of critics objected to what they viewed as the unnecessary and inhumane cruelty visited upon the animals Harvey used in his experiments. A number of well-known English scientists who had undertaken experiments with animals, for example, either abandoned their research or continued it only under pressure from their colleagues. The physicist Robert Hooke, for example, designed an experiment in which an animal's normal respiration system was disrupted (by cutting its windpipe) and then maintained mechanically with a bellows. At the end of one set of experiments, he wrote to his colleague Robert Boyle that "I shall hardly be induced to make further trials of this kind, because of the torture to the creature." When he was persuaded to continue the research, one of his colleagues, John Evelyn, offered his own observation that the experience was "of more cruelty than pleased me" (quoted in Harrison 2004, 194).

Antivivisectionist complaints did not deter Harvey nor most of his peers, who saw significant progress to be gained from experiments on living animals, no matter the pain and suffering that might accompany such research. During the period when Hooke was performing (and agonizing over) his experiments in London, more than 90 experiments involving vivisection were reported to the Royal Society in the four-year period between 1644 and 1648, and 30 more were conducted as demonstrations for members of the society ("Harvey and Vivisection" 2012; see also Guerrini 2012). Vivisection also became widely popular in the Netherlands, where the center of research was the city of

Leiden. According to reports, students came from all over Europe to study under the masters of clinical dissection (Knoeff 2012).

Two of the best-known animal vivisectionists during the rise of modern biology were the French physiologist François Magendie (1783–1855) and his successor at the Collège de France, Claude Bernard (1813–1878). Both men made profoundly important discoveries in human anatomy, discoveries that depended to a large extent on their use of experimental animals. For example, one of Magendie's early discovery was that the dorsal and ventral spinal nerve roots have different functions. The former carries sensory information into the spinal cord and the latter carries motor information out of the spinal cord. Magendie depended entirely on animals for his discoveries in this field. He often worked with six-week-old puppies, whose vertebral column had not yet ossified, allowing him to expose the spinal cord and dissect the dorsal and ventral nerve roots very easily. It goes without saying that such a procedure

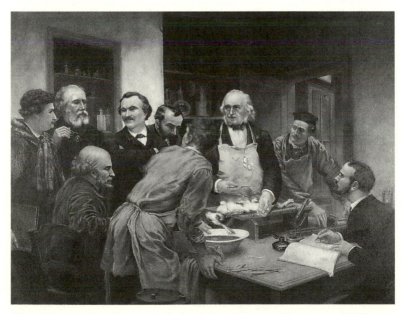

Claude Bernard and His Pupils, by Léon-Augustin Lhermitte. (Wellcome Library)

would have been extraordinarily painful to the subjects of the experiment (Tacium 2008/2009).

The Scottish anatomist Charles Bell (1744–1842) was performing similar experiments at about the same time and receives partial credit for the discovery of the function of spinal nerve roots. Somewhat ironically, he was not able to go as far as did Magendie in his studies, however, failing to recognize the difference between dorsal and ventral nerve roots. The irony comes from the fact that Bell had started his work more than a decade before Magendie and had made some fundamental breakthroughs prior to the work of the French anatomist. But Bell eventually discontinued his research because of a growing concern over the pain he was causing the animals with whom he worked. At one point, for example, he decided he could not continue to dissect living animals because of the obvious pain he was causing them. Instead, for one experiment, he decided to stun a rabbit that he planned to dissect by striking it behind the ear and essentially rendering it unconscious. The problem with this approach, of course, was that the procedure made it impossible for him to recognize motor functions of the nervous system (Tacium 2008/2009; see also Sechzer 1983).

In a letter written in 1822, Bell explained his feelings about animal vivisection:

> I should be writing a third paper on the nerves, but I cannot proceed without making some experiments, which are so unpleasant to make that I defer them. You may think me silly, but I cannot perfectly convince myself that I am authorized in nature or religion to do these cruelties. (Stephen and Lee 1885, 155)

(For a more detailed and lurid description of Magendie's experiments, see Leffingwell 1901.)

Claude Bernard began his scientific career as a "preparer" for Magendie and adopted his philosophical and experimental outlooks on research. Although he readily recognized the pain and suffering Magendie's research brought to animals, Bernard was apparently as committed to the use of animals for research as was his predecessor. He was absolutely convinced that the greater benefit brought to human health justified the harm caused to animals during his dissections. In his own masterwork on anatomy and physiology, *An Introduction to the Study of Experimental Medicine*, Bernard wrote:

> Have we the right to make experiments on animals and vivisect? . . . I think we have this right, wholly and absolutely. It would be strange indeed if we recognized man's right to make use of animals in every walk of life, for domestic service, for food, and then forbade him to make use of them for his own instruction in one of the sciences most useful to humanity. No hesitation is possible; the science of life can be established only through experiment, and we can save living beings from death only after sacrificing others. (Bernard 1865/1957, 102)

Bernard's plea for an understanding of his work, and the sacrifice of living animals that it required, was to set the agenda for untold numbers of researchers, not only in his own century but for the next 150 years. Perhaps needless to say, his justification for vivisection did not easily win over many individuals who saw more clearly the apparent horror of his work. Two such individuals were his wife, Françoise Marie (Fanny), and his daughter, Jeanne-Henriette (Tony), both of whom berated Bernard for what they regarded as his barbaric activities. In fact, his wife finally left Bernard in 1869, largely because of her inability to live any longer with a man who she deemed demonic in his research activities. (She was an active antivivisectionist both before and after the couple's separation and donated regularly to a variety of animal causes throughout her life; Kete 1994, chapter 1, especially n. 46).

Magendie and Bernard justified their use of living animals in their research because it produced valuable information (supposedly) about the structure and function of the human body that could be used to relieve human suffering. Yet it should be noted that much of the vivisection conducted before, during, and after their time was carried out for an entirely different purpose, the education of medical students and, in some cases, the delectation of the general public. An example that has been mentioned by more than one historian of vivisection concerns one of the earliest uses of vivisection in North America. In 1847, one Horace Nelson, a lecturer on anatomy at the Montreal School of Medicine and Surgery, carried out the vivisection of a dog to illustrate the effects of anesthetics, which had been discovered only a year earlier. His observers were other physicians, a dentist, a medical illustrator, and several medical students. Having anesthetized the dog, Nelson proceeded to remove one ear, cut the dog open from a hind leg to the ear, and amputate one foreleg. He was then called away to deal with a client, and when he returned, the anesthesia had worn off and the dog was in extreme distress. Nelson's colleagues thereupon strangled the dog to put it out of its misery. A repetition of the experiment with a second dog the next day resulted in even more horrible results, with a similar fate for the dog (Connor 1997, 39–40).

The Birth of the Antivivisectionist Movement

There can be little doubt that the rise of modern biology brought with it, probably without choice and sometimes with little enthusiasm among researchers, a much expanded role for vivisection in animal research. At the same time, opposition to the practice also began to blossom and soon became a full-blown force in opposition to vivisection. The motivation for this movement came from a number of sources.

One such source was formal religion itself, which in Western Europe meant Christianity. The irony was that the teachings of Aquinas, which were such a strong force in originally justifying the use of vivisection, had a more moderate component. After all, Christianity taught on the one hand that animals were created by God to serve humans and, as Aquinas pointed out, humans were therefore justified in using them for any purpose they chose. However, the Bible also taught compassion toward all living creatures, an attitude that obviously came into conflict with the actual practice of vivisection on at least some of God's creations. Recall that one of the great historical figures of the Middle Ages was Saint Francis of Assisi, who lived only a half century before Aquinas. Saint Francis is perhaps the ultimate Catholic embodiment of a love of animals, perpetuated today in the blessing of the animals that is conducted annually on October 4 around the world by members of the Franciscan Order, founded by the saint.

So it can hardly be surprising that many Christians were among the strongest critics of Vesalius, Magendie, Bernard, and their colleagues. One often-repeated story, which comes originally from Bernard's own accounts, is that Magendie was confronted on one occasion by an American Quaker who challenged the work the anatomist was doing:

> Thou performest experiments on living animals. I come to thee to demand of thee by what right thou actest thus and to tell thee that thou must desist from these experiments, because thou hast not the right to cause animals to die or make them suffer, and because thou settest in this way a bad example and also accustomest thyself to cruelty. (Olmsted 1944, 143)

A second factor that militated against the use of vivisection during the nineteenth century was, ironically, the very success of science itself. Many intellectuals argued that the scientific search for knowledge and truth had become a cold and dehumanized system in which the value of life for all animals, both human and nonhuman, had become so diminished as to be ignored or rejected. As such, a number of philosophers and writers added their arguments to those of religious leaders. One of the most famous of these comments came from the philosopher Jeremy Bentham (1748–1832). Bentham took the view that the division between humans and other animals was a false dichotomy. If one limits the concept of "rights" only to those organisms that have the right to reason, he asks, then what is the status of children, the very elderly, and individuals with various types of disabilities? These individuals are certainly "human" by most definitions, but they may not have the ability to reason and, thus, do not meet Descartes's dictum of "Cogito ergo sum" ("I think therefore I am"). And perhaps even more to the point, what is the status of someone whose skin color is different from the majority of Western Europeans (black, brown, or yellow), who are most certainly "human" but who have long been denied the rights of white "humans"?

Once having made this argument, Bentham is willing to extend his plea even more widely. And what about the rights of other animals?, he asks. It really does not make any difference whether they can reason or not; the real question is do they have feelings similar to human feelings? In perhaps his most famous passage, he writes:

> It may come one day to be recognized, that the number of the legs, the villosity of the skin, or the termination of the *os sacrum*, are reasons equally insufficient for abandoning a sensitive being to the same fate? What else is it that should trace the insuperable line? Is it the faculty of reason, or, perhaps, the faculty of discourse ? But a full-grown horse or dog, is beyond comparison a more rational, as well as a more conversible animal, than an infant of a day, or a week, or even a month, old. But suppose the case were otherwise, what would it avail? The question is not, Can they *reason*? nor, Can they *talk*? but, Can they *suffer*? (Bentham 1823, 236; italics in original)

Opposition to vivisection also came from another group of individuals who might generally be described as humanists, who argued for concerns not only for every class, race, and category of humans, as did Bentham, but also for other types of nonhuman animals. This group of individuals included some of the best known and most widely read literary giants of the time. In her superb history of the antivivisection movement, Debbie Tacium Ladry cites a number of quotations from these authors. Charles Dickens, for example, wrote:

> The necessity for these experiments I dispute. Man has no right to gratify an idle and purposeless curiosity through the practice of cruelty. (Tacium 2008/2009; most of these quotations are also found in a much earlier publication, Wilcox 1910)

Such comments were certainly not limited to England, but were also expressed in writers from lands as disparate as the United States, Russia, and China. For example, the American humorist Mark Twain wrote:

> I believe I am not interested to know whether vivisection produces results that are profitable to the human race or doesn't. To know that the results are profitable to the race would not remove my hostility to it. The pain which it inflicts upon unconsenting animals is the basis of my enmity toward it, and it is to me sufficient justification of the enmity without looking further. (Tacium 2008/2009)

Twain's contemporary, Russian writer and political activist Leo Tolstoy, echoed his thoughts:

> What I think about vivisection is that if people admit that they have the right to take or endanger the life of living beings for the benefit of many, there will be no limit to their cruelty. (Tacium 2008/2009; Wilcox 1910, 715)

And Chinese diplomat and politician Wu Ting-Fang added his own support to this position:

> You ask me for an opinion on the subject of vivisection. I believe the trend of public opinion is toward condemnation of recklessly killing animals without sufficient cause; and in my humble opinion it would require a very strong justification before I would allow an animal to be killed, even for physiological investigation. (Tacium 2008/2009; Wilcox 1910, 718)

Yet another force driving the development of the antivivisectionist movement in the second half of the nineteenth century was the rise of a women's/feminist movement. The evidence is now very strong that women who took the lead in educating and motivating their sisters about the need to become active in achieving rights equal to those of men saw a close corollary in achieving comparable rights for nonhuman animals. Throughout Western Europe and North America, many of the most outspoken and eventually most powerful antivivisectionist movements were formed and filled by women. Time after time, in their writing and speaking, these women saw striking parallels in the way that men in general, and particularly men in authority, treated both women and nonhuman animals as their chattel, with little or no say about the choices they could make about their own lives and, indeed often enough, their own deaths (see, for example, Adams and Donovan 1995; Birke 2000; Hamilton 2004; Kean 1995; for the situation in France, see Finn 2012).

One final factor in the growing antivivisectionist movement, especially in Great Britain, was a history of growing concern about the welfare of animals in general, whether those used for research or those employed by humans for a variety of other purposes. Legislation prohibiting the cruel treatment of various types of animals has a relatively long history in both Great Britain and the United States. For example, various types of legislative bills, ordinances, statutes, or other official statements had been issued against a variety of activities, such as bearbaiting, bullbaiting, cockfighting, and specific forms of fishing, fowling, hawking, horse racing, and hunting as far back as 1267 in Great Britain. As an example, King Edward III issued a writ in 1363 to his sheriffs asking them to prepare statements encouraging their subjects to become more interested in the practice of archery as a substitute for the popular sport of cockfighting. (See "Animal Rights Law" 2012, an excellent source for the history of vivisection and related laws. The original law cited here can be found at http://www.britishhistory.ac.uk/report.aspx?compid=33502&strquery=cockfighting.)

Early Antivivisectionist Legislation

During the first half of the nineteenth century, the British Parliament passed a number of bills dealing with cruelty to animals in a wide variety of circumstances. Perhaps the earliest attempt along these lines was a bill introduced in 1800 to ban the practice of bullbaiting, a "sport" that was very popular in communities throughout the kingdom. During the debate over the bill, some members suggested adding another popular "sporting" event, cockfighting, although that change was not made. Following debate, the bill was defeated by a vote of 43 to 41 (*The Parliamentary Register* 1800, 361–363; for a discussion of the "sport" of bullbaiting, see "History of Animal Fighting & Baiting" 2011). The bill was submitted again two years later and was defeated a second time, this time by a vote of 64 to 51 (*The Parliamentary History of England* 1820, 830–854). Bills to prohibit bullbaiting were introduced again in 1825, 1826, and 1828, sometimes with the inclusion of bans on cruelty to dogs, all of which also failed.

Some modern historians have called attention to the philosophical basis on which early animal legislation was based. They point out that early nineteenth-century society was very dependent on animals for its survival, and cruelty to animals and even between animals was something of a foregone conclusion. It would have been unheard of, then, for someone to propose legislation that was somehow "in the best interest of beasts." Almost no one would have understood what that position meant in practice. As a consequence, the bullbaiting and later acts were generally proposed with different stated objections. In the case of the 1800 bill, for example, proposers argued that bullbaiting was evil, not because of the harm, pain, or suffering it brought animals but because it demoralized those who watched the sport and made them unfit for work. Even that argument, at first, obviously did not carry the day (Harrison 1973, 786).

Another topic of cruelty laws was domestic farm animals, often subsumed under the general category of "cattle." The first act to criminalize the beating, abuse, or ill-treatment of "any Horse, Mare, Gelding, Mule, Ass, Ox, Cow, Heifer, Steer, Sheep, or other Cattle" was passed by the Parliament in 1822 (*The Statutes of the United Kingdom of Great Britain and Ireland* 1822, 403–405; "Animal Rights Law" 2012). The act was introduced by Colonel Richard Martin, member of Parliament from Galway, Ireland, and hence is generally known as Martin's Act. Martin was already well known for his concern about the welfare of animals because of a bill he introduced a year earlier, the Treatment of Horses bill. That bill was laughed off the floor of Parliament because his peers were concerned that adoption of the bill would soon be followed by protection for dogs, cats, cows, and other animals, an unheard of possibility at the time. (Martin's good works earned him the sobriquet of "Humanity Dick" by King George IV) ("Humanity Dick" 2012; Lynam 1975).

Finally, in 1835 Parliament passed an omnibus animal protection act, the Cruelty to Animals Act, which consolidated and vastly expanded all previous anticruelty acts by defining a whole range of animals as "cattle" and by banning a number of "sporting" activities, such as bearbaiting, cockfighting, and badger baiting. The main sections of the bill dealt with the prohibition of bouts of animal fighting (section I), ill-treatment of "cattle" (expanded to include a wide variety of animals; section II), keeping of any type of animal for fighting (section III), neglect of cattle (section VI), and slaughtering of horses (section VII) (*Statutes at Large* 1835 344–349).

In the half century following passage of the Animal Cruelty Act, Parliament continued to adopt legislation modifying and updating its 1835 bill. It accepted amendments to the original act in 1849, 1850, and 1854, and most significantly, in 1876. The Cruelty to Animals Act of 1876 was significant for a number of reasons, one of which was its massive updating and overhaul of the 1835 legislation dealing with all kinds of cruel treatment to a whole range of domestic and fighting animals. It also, for the first time in British law, included provisions for the humane treatment of animals used for "medical, physiological, or scientific purposes." The law starts out by clarifying that "a person shall not perform on a living animal any experiment calculated to give pain, except subject to the restrictions imposed by this Act." It then continues with a number of specific provisions for the use of animals in research, including:

- the experiment in question must be conducted with the purpose of adducing new knowledge that has application in saving or prolonging human life or alleviating pain;
- the experimenter must apply for and receive a government license to conduct the research;
- the animal must be under the influence of an anesthetic throughout the experimental procedure;
- the animal must be killed following the experiment if it is likely to continue to be in pain after the procedure has been completed; and
- the experiment can not be performed as a demonstration for medical students, the general public, or any other group of individuals or for the purpose of developing a manual skill. (*Public General Statutes* 1876 459–464; "Animal Rights Law" 2012)

Although the 1876 law was amended from time to time in the following century, its provisions for the treatment of experimental animals remained essentially the law of the land in Great Britain until it was replaced by the Animals (Scientific Procedures) Act of 1986.

Rise of Antivivisectionist Organizations

Efforts to form organizations for the protection of animals against cruelty in Great Britain date to the very early nineteenth century. Records exist suggesting that a meeting was held in November 1809 to form a Society for the Suppression and Prevention of Wanton Cruelty to Animals in Liverpool. Nothing is known, however, about the future of that organization other than that at least one more meeting was held (*Records of the Royal Society for the Prevention of Cruelty to Animals: Liverpool Branch* 2012).

A far more successful endeavor was launched on June 16, 1824, when a group of animal advocates met at Old Slaughter's Coffee House in London. The group consisted of a number of members of Parliament, including Richard Martin, William Wilberforce, Sir James Mackintosh, Sir Thomas Buxton, and Sir James Graham, along with other interested individuals, most notably the Reverend Arthur Broome. The meeting was called by Martin and his colleagues who were concerned that simply passing legislation prohibiting cruelty to animals was not sufficient to bring about changes in social attitudes and practices. The group decided to form an organization with the goal of monitoring real-life practices in the way people dealt with animals and then use the force of new legislation (Martin's act of 1822) to bring action against acts of cruelty. They proposed sending representatives into the community to monitor the way cattle, horses, and other animals covered under the act were being used. The name originally chosen for the group, the Society for the Prevention of Cruelty to Animals, was changed in 1840 by the addition of "Royal" when Queen Victoria, an ardent antivivisectionist herself, granted a royal charter to the group. The Royal Society for the Prevention of Cruelty to Animals (RSPCA) is thus the oldest continuous animal welfare organization in the world ("The History of the RSPCA" 1972).

Until the society received its royal charter, it struggled to survive and carry out the duties for which it was organized. In its early years, funds were always lacking and its efforts to carry out provision of Martin's act often met with resistance. On at least one occasion, an inspector hired by the society to check on the status of bullbaiting and cockfighting was attacked by participants in these events and injured so badly that he eventually died as a result. During the society's first few years, it seemed always to be in debt and survived only through the generous, albeit modest, contributions of its members and nonmember supporters. It was only with the grant of a royal charter that the association finally achieved financial stability and started to grow into the powerful organization for animal welfare it has since become ("The History of the RSPCA" 1972).

As the RSPCA grew stronger, it began to expand beyond its original goals and objectives. Not only did it open branches in other parts of Great Britain (Dublin, Wakefield, and Plymouth), but it also inspired the formation of similar organizations across the Continent—in Austria, Belgium, France, Germany, and the Netherlands—and in the United States. In France, for example, a member of the French Assembly, Jacques Philippe Delmas de Grammont, motivated by the creation of the RSCPA, formed the first animal protection society in France in 1845. The society was largely responsible for the adoption of the nation's first anticruelty law in 1850, a law named after Grammont, the Loi Grammont ("Philantrope Anglais Dans L'exercice De Son Sacerdoce" 1844).

In another turn of events, a special outreach to youth on issues of animal cruelty was established in 1875 with the formation of a group called Band of Mercy by antislavery activist Catherine Smithies. The group was modeled on a youth branch of the Temperance Society called Band of Hope. Just as the primary goal of Band of Hope was to teach children about the evils of drink, so Band of Mercy was originally designed to be an educational program about the evils of cruelty to animals. Somewhat unexpectedly, however, members of the Band of Mercy began to put the principles they had learned in the society into actions that sometimes turned violent. They are thought, for example, to have sabotaged hunters' guns, spread misleading scents in hunting fields, and distracted hunting dogs from their work in the fields ("Bands of Mercy" 2012; Li 2000). A modern animal welfare group that also takes an aggressive approach to dealing with cruelty to animals, Animal Liberation Front (ALF), began its operations in 1971 under the name Band of Mercy, changing its name five years later ("History of the Animal Liberation Movement" 2012).

As was the case elsewhere, the movement to ban cruelty against animals in the United States was inspired to a large extent by the formation of the RSPCA. In April 1866 one Henry Bergh, son of a successful businessman, called a meeting of like-minded individuals in New York City to establish an animal protection organization, to be given the name the American Society for the Protection of Cruelty to Animals (ASPCA). Bergh was motivated to take this action as the result of a long trip to Europe during which he saw the worst side of animal cruelty (bullfights in Spain) and the brightest hope for overcoming this problem (formation of the SPCA in London). At the original meeting of the organization, Bergh laid out its fundamental precept. "This is a matter purely of conscience," he told his audience. "It has no perplexing side issues. It is a moral question in all its aspects" ("History" 2012). The ASPCA continues to carry on its operations today as a privately funded 501(c)(3) not-for-profit corporation.

Another movement that grew out of the founding of the RSPCA was the animal rights movement. Prior to the mid-nineteenth century, campaigns and legislation against cruelty to animals were based largely on a sense of compassion; it was thought to be unkind, inhumane, and un-Christian to bring unnecessary pain and suffering to dumb animals. As such campaigns went forward, however, some individuals began to develop a very different basis for them. They began to argue that *all* animals have the same inherent rights as do humans. One such individual was Lewis Gompertz, an English inventor and one of the founders of the Society for the Prevention of Cruelty to Animals in 1824. In the same year, he published a book entitled *Moral Inquiries on the Situation of Man and of Brutes*, in which he suggested that the same moral principles that apply to humans apply equally to all other animals. He received patents for more than three dozen inventions, many of which were designed to relieve animal suffering. He was a vegan and refused to ride in horse-drawn carriages because of the suffering that mode of transportation produced in animals. Gompertz wrote a second animal rights book in 1852, *Fragments in Defence of Animals*, and founded the Animal Friends Society in 1832. He is regarded by some historians as being the father of the animal rights movement (Renier 2012).

The focus of early anticruelty organizations was, as was the case with early legislation, largely on domestic and work animals. Concerns about the use of animals in research came later, with the formation of the Victoria Street Society in December 1875 by Frances Power Cobbe. Cobbe was one of the most remarkable women of the late nineteenth century, a writer, suffragette, social reformer, and antivivisectionist. The story is told that Cobbe first became interested in the antivivisection movement in 1863 when she became acquainted with a medical man who was "among the inferior professors of medical knowledge" and was widely known for his indiscriminate use of animals in his research and teaching. She began to speak and write about the horrors of vivisection, a campaign that reached a climax in 1874 when she sent an appeal to the RSPCA for action against vivisectionists (Cobbe 1894; Williamson 2005).

Cobbe felt such action was needed because the Cruelty to Animals Act then under discussion in Parliament took what she thought was entirely the wrong approach to the use of animals in scientific and medical research. Her preference was to prohibit such practices entirely. Instead, the act took quite a different view of the issue: it provided for legalization of the practice of vivisection, provided that it be conducted under certain conditions and provisions (outlined above). Cobbe felt that the RSPCA was the appropriate organization through which to work for a complete ban on vivisection.

That hope, however, was soon dashed. Officials of the RSPCA decided that the proper approach to the problem was to interview the most prominent vivisectionists of the day for their views on the practice. Unsurprisingly, the result of these interviews was a decision to act no further on Cobbe's request (Coleridge 1918). At that point, Cobbe decided that she had to take matters into her own hands and called a meeting of like-minded individuals to be held on December 2, 1875, in Victoria Street, London. That meeting resulted in the formation of the first antivivisectionist association in the world, known at the time as the Victoria Street Society for the Protection of Animals from Vivisection (or, more succinctly, the Victoria Street Society). In October 1897, the organization changed its name to the National Anti-Vivisection Society (NAVS; "The History of the NAVS" 2012). The NAVS continues to be one of the most active antivivisectionist organizations in the world today.

The NAVS met with mixed success during the first two decades of its existence. While it boasted a significant membership and brought the issue of animal experimentation to the attention of the British public, it made little or no progress in achieving its primary goal, eliminating the practice of vivisection in scientific and medical research. This issue came to a head in 1897, when Francis Cobbe retired from her post as honorary secretary to be replaced by Stephen Coleridge, a longtime colleague of Cobbe's. In his new position, Coleridge expressed the view that the society perhaps should shift its emphasis from the abolition of vivisection back to its original goal of establishing strict standards by which the procedure was practiced. That view focused on the necessity of reducing the pain and suffering of animals used in research, rather than eliminating vivisection entirely.

Cobbe was outraged at the abandonment of an objective for which she had been working for more than 20 years. She chose, therefore, to create a new organization that retained the original goal of eliminating vivisection entirely. That organization was founded at a public meeting in Bristol on June 14, 1898, and given the name the British Union for the Abolition of Vivisection (BUAV). As with Cobbe's other creation, the NAVS, the BUAV remains an active opponent of vivisection in Great Britain today.

The NAVS, like the RSPCA, was to become a model for anti-vivisectionist organizations around the world. In the United States, for example, philanthropist Caroline Earle White formed the first antivivisectionist society in 1883. White had been involved in animal welfare activities and associations for most of her adult life. But, as was often the case at the time, she was not allowed to take a leadership role because of her gender. To resolve this problem, she and a group of her friends formed the Women's Pennsylvania Society for the Prevention of Cruelty to Animals (better known as the Women's Humane Society) in 1869. As part of their work, they opened the first animal shelter in the United States for abandoned cats and dogs, the Morris Refuge Association for Homeless and Suffering Animals ("Caroline Earle White" 2012).

This plan backfired to some extent as laboratory researchers began to appear at the shelter door, seeking animals that they could use in their experiments. White's response, made partially at the recommendation of Frances Cobbe, was to create yet another organization, the American Anti-Vivisection Society (AAVS), organized along the lines of Cobbe's British group. At first, the AAVS focused its efforts on lobbying for legislation that would control the way animals were being used in research. Before long, however, it decided to change this focus and to lobby instead for the complete abolition of vivisection in the United States. It continues to hold that stance and promote that objective today ("History of the American Anti-Vivisectionist Society" 2012).

A second antivivisectionist organization with a long history in the United States is the New England Anti-Vivisectionist Society (NEAVS), founded in Boston in 1895. The motivation for the creation of NEAVS was the introduction in 1871 at Harvard University of "the latest European methods for studying physiology," namely vivisection. While Harvard president Charles William Eliot was delighted with the idea of using the most up-to-date procedures in science, some of his faculty were less enthusiastic. In particular, Henry Bigelow, a well-known surgeon and teacher at the Harvard Medical School and Massachusetts General Hospital, was outraged at the use of animals in such procedures. He took his case to the editor of the prestigious Boston newspaper, *The Transcript*, who passed this news on to the general public ("A Brief History of NEAVS" 2012).

The debate over vivisection at Harvard simmered until the 1890s, when a group of citizens met in Boston to found the NEAVS. The organization continues to operate today with an impressive list of achievements in the elimination or reduction of the use of animals in scientific and medical research. It has also established a number of sanctuaries for animals who had previously been used for or were rescued from research programs.

As the nineteenth century drew to a close, then, the battle lines were set for a conflict that was to last throughout the new century and into the present era. Scientific and medical researchers had, by 1900, become thoroughly convinced of the value of using nonhuman animals in research. They argued that the benefits to human health and medical treatments were so great as to easily justify any harm that animals might suffer as a result of experiments in which they were used. Opponents to vivisection were of two minds. On the one hand, a number of critics said that the horrors visited upon experimental animals were so great that no benefit could justify such inhumane treatments. On the other hand, others argued that vivisection was clearly undesirable but that there might be circumstances under which some forms of the procedure could be used to the benefit of humankind. How that debate was to play out and the issues that it creates for today's world are the subject of the next chapter.

Bibliography

Abbott, Edwin Abbott. *Francis Bacon, an Account of His Life and Works*. London: Macmillan, 1885. http://books.google .com/books?id=lCWEPJ3dUpkC&pg=PA507&lpg=PA507 &dq=francis+bacon+vivisection&source=bl&ots=qUa Vr8r4Ac&sig=LRYkVSxpDRK7e0Joh8CL6oR14Qc&hl =en&sa=X&ei=qVr8T9niOeKe2AWB6ZjNBg&ved =0CFYQ6AEwCDgU#v=onepage&q=francis_bacon _vivisection&f=false. Accessed July 10, 2012.

Adams, Carol J., and Josephine Donovan, eds. *Animals and Women: Feminist Theoretical Explorations*. Durham, NC: Duke University Press, 1995.

Allen, Colin. "Animal Consciousness." In Edward N. Zalta, ed. *The Stanford Encyclopedia of Philosophy*. Edited by Edward N. Zalta. Winter 2011. http://plato.stanford.edu/archives/ win2011/entries/consciousnessanimal/. Accessed July 10, 2012.

"Animal Rights Law." Animal Rights History. http://www .animalrightshistory.org/animal-rights-law.htm. Accessed July 17, 2012.

Aristotle. *On the Parts of Animals*. Trans. William Ogle. Internet Classics Archive. http://classics.mit.edu/Aristotle/ parts_animals.mb.txt. Accessed July 9, 2012.

Bacon, Sir Francis. *The Advancement of Learning*. Trans. David Price. London: Cassell, 1893 edition of the original 1605 work. Available at http://www.gutenberg.org/dirs/etext04/ adlr10h.htm. Accessed July 10, 2012.

"Bands of Mercy." be kind: A Visual History of Humane Education, 1880–1945. http://bekindexhibit.org/exhibition/bands-of-mercy/. Accessed July 17, 2012.

Bentham, Jeremy. *An Introduction to the Principles of Morals and Legislation*. London: W. Pickering, 1823. http://ia700401.us.archive.org/33/items/introductiontopr02bent/introductiontopr02bent.pdf. Accessed July 16, 2012.

Bernard, Claude. *An Introduction to the Study of Experimental Medicine*. New York: Dover, 1957. Reprint of 1865 edition. http://books.google.com/books?id=MIx8D61JlboC&pg=PA102&lpg=PA102&dq=%22have+we+the+right+to+make+experiments+on+animals%22&source=bl&ots=cOXbZQ3n5J&sig=seWs6wJ5r5YxBmKnX_Huuk YYKPg&hl=en&sa=X&ei=gkwEUN_dBsbAqQHh9Sx DA&ved=0CDAQ6AEwAQ#v=onepage&q=%22have%20we%20the%20right%20to%20make%20experiments%20on%20animals%22&f=false. Accessed July 16, 2012.

Birke, Lynda. "Supporting the Underdog: Feminism, Animal Rights and Citizenship in the Work of Alice Morgan Wright and Edith Goode." *Women's History Review* 9, no. 4 (2000): 693–719.

"A Brief History of NEAVS." New England Anti-Vivisectionist Society. http://www.neavs.org/about/history/brief. Accessed July 18, 2012.

"Caroline Earle White." National Museum of Animals & Society. http://www.museumofanimals.org/#/caroline-earle-white/3788770. Accessed July 17, 2012.

Carrier, Richard. "Flynn's Pile of Boners." 2010. http://richardcarrier.blogspot.com/2010/01/flynns-pile-of-boners.html. Accessed July 9, 2012.

Celsus, A. Cornelius. *Of Medicine*. In 8 books. London: D. Wilson and T. Durham, 1756. http://ia700801.us.archive.

org/7/items/acorneliuscelsus00cels/acorneliuscelsus00cels
.pdf. Accessed July 3, 2012.

"Chapter 1: Meat Matters." Chapter outlines for Ron Broglio, *On the Surface: Thinking with Animals and Art*, Minneapolis: University of Minnesota Press, 2008. http://www.lcc.gatech .edu/~broglio/animals/draft_with.Hirst.art.doc. Accessed July 10, 2012.

"Christianity and the Medical Sciences." The Rejection of Pascal's Wager. http://www.rejectionofpascalswager.net/ medicine.html. Accessed July 9, 2012.

Cobbe, Frances Power. *Life of Frances Power Cobbe*. Boston: Houghton Mifflin, 1894.

Coleridge, Stephen. *Great Testimony against Scientific Cruelty*. London: John Lane, 1918. http://www.readcentral.com/ chapters/Stephen-Coleridge/Great-Testimony-against -scientific-cruelty/003. Accessed July 18, 2012.

Connor, J. T. H. "Cruel Knives? Vivisection and Biomedical Research in Victorian English Canada." *Canadian Bulletin of Medical History* 14, no. 1 (1997): 37–64.

"The Cult of Asclepius, God of Medicine." Kickoff. http://fx .damasgate.com/the-cult-of-asclepius-god-of-medicine/. Accessed July 9, 2012.

Curran, Stuart. "Contexts—Science—Biology—Anatomy— Dissection." Frankenstein—or the Modern Prometheus. http://knarf.english.upenn.edu/Contexts/dissect.html. Accessed July 9, 2012.

"Exploring Illness across Time and Space." http://www.sas .upenn.edu/~rogert/chinawv.html. Accessed July 12, 2012.

Finn, Michael R. "Dogs and Females: Vivisection, Feminists and the Novelist Rachilde." *French Cultural Studies* 23, no. 3 (2012): 190–201.

"Galen Claudius." http://www.mlahanas.de/Greeks/Galen .htm. Accessed July 9, 2012.

Geering, Lloyd. "The World to Come: From Christian Past to Global Future." http://www.religion-online.org/show chapter.asp?title=2735&C=2468. Accessed July 9, 2012.

Genesis 1:26. Biblos. http://bible.cc/genesis/1-26.htm. Accessed July 9, 2012.

Gross, Charles G. "Galen and the Squealing Pig." *The Neuroscientist* 4, no. 3 (1998): 216–221.

Guerrini, Anita. "The Ethics of Experimentation in Seventeenth-Century England." http://www.nd.edu/~kbrading/Classes/Phil%2043713/The%20Ethics%20of%20Animal%20Experimentation%20in%20the%2017th%20century%20England-Newlands.pdf. Accessed July 10, 2012.

Hamilton, Susan. *Animal Welfare & Anti-vivisection 1870–1910: Nineteenth Century Woman's Mission.* London: Routledge, 2004.

Hankinson, R. J., ed. *The Cambridge Companion to Galen.* Cambridge: Cambridge University Press, 2008.

Harrison, Brian. "Animals and the State in Nineteenth-Century England." *The English Historical Review* 88, no. 349 (1973): 786–820.

Harrison, Peter. "Reading Vital Signs: Animals and the Experimental Philosophy." In *Renaissance Beasts: Of Animals, Humans, and Other Wonderful Creatures.* Edited by Erica Fudge, 186–207. Urbana: University of Illinois Press, 2004.

"Harvey and Vivisection." Kickoff. http://fx.damasgate.com/harvey-and-vivisection/. Accessed July 10, 2012.

Hehmeyer, Ingrid, and Aliya Khan. "Islam's Forgotten Contributions to Medical Science." *CMAJ* 176, no. 10 (2007): 1467–1468.

"History." ASPCA. http://www.aspca.org/about-us/history.aspx. Accessed July 17, 2012.

"History of Anatomy." History World. http://www
.historyworld.net/wrldhis/PlainTextHistories.asp
?historyid=aa05. Accessed July 9, 2012.

"History of the American Anti-Vivisectionist Society."
American Anti-Vivisectionist Society. http://www.aavs.org/
site/c.bkLTKfOSLhK6E/b.6452353/k.F40F/History_of
_the_American_AntiVivisection_Society.htm#.UAcn
N7TDA1I. Accessed July 18, 2012.

"History of Animal Fighting & Baiting." January 6, 2011.
http://www.lb7.uscourts.gov/documents/ILSD/game-bred
.pdf. Accessed July 17, 2012.

"History of the Animal Liberation Movement." North
American Animal Liberation Press Office. http://web
.archive.org/web/20080611140821/http://www.animal
liberationpressoffice.org/history.htm. Accessed July 17,
2012.

"The History of the NAVS." July 24, 2012. National Anti
-Vivisectionist Society. http://www.navs.org.uk/about_us/
24/0/299/. Accessed July 17, 2012.

"The History of the RSPCA." 1972. Animal Legal & Historical
Center. http://www.animallaw.info/historical/articles/
arukrspcahist.htm. Accessed July 17, 2012.

Huffman, Carl. "Alcmaeon." In *The Stanford Encyclopedia of
Philosophy* (Winter 2008 ed.). Edited by Edward N. Zalta.
http://plato.stanford.edu/archives/win2008/entries/
alcmaeon/. Accessed July 9, 2012.

"Humanity Dick." National Museum of Animals & Society.
http://www.museumofanimals.org/#/humanitydick/
3745671. Accessed July 18, 2012.

Jonas, Hans. *The Phenomenon of Life: Toward a Philosophical
Biology*. New York: Harper & Row, 1966.

Kean, Hilda. "The 'Smooth Cool Men of Science': The
Feminist and Socialist Response to Vivisection." *History
Workshop Journal* 40 (1995): 16–38.

Kete, Kathleen. *The Beast in the Boudoir: Petkeeping in Nineteenth-Century Paris*. Berkeley: University of California Press, 1994. http://publishing.cdlib.org/ucpressebooks/view?docId=ft3c6004dj;brand=ucpress. Accessed July 16, 2012.

Knoeff, Rina. "Dutch Anatomy and Clinical Medicine in 17th-Century Europe." http://www.ieg-ego.eu/de/threads/modelle-und-stereotypen/das-niederlaendische-jahrhundert17.-jhd/rina-knoeff-dutch-anatomy-and-clinical-medicine-in-17th-century-europe. Accessed July 10, 2012.

Lassek, A. M. *Human Dissection: Its Drama and Struggle*. Springfield, IL: Thomas, 1958. http://ia600308.us.archive.org/7/items/humandissectioni00lassrich/humandissectioni00lassrich.pdf. Accessed July 10, 2012.

Leffingwell, Albert. *The Vivisection Question*. New Haven, CT: Tuttle, Morehouse, & Taylor, 1901. http://www.archive.org/stream/vivisectionquest00leffuoft/vivisectionquest00leffuoft_djvu.txt. Accessed July 16, 2012.

Lennox, James. "Aristotle's Biology." In *The Stanford Encyclopedia of Philosophy* (Fall 2011 ed.). Edited by Edward N. Zalta. http://plato.stanford.edu/archives/fall2011/entries/aristotle-biology/. Accessed July 9, 2012.

Li, Chien-hui. "Union of Christianity, Humanity, and Philanthropy: The Christian Tradition and the Prevention of Cruelty to Animals in Nineteenth-Century England." *Society & Animals* 8, no. 3 (2000): 265–285. http://www.societyandanimalsforum.org/sa/sa8.3/chien.shtml. Accessed July 17, 2012.

Liu, Cunren. *Selected Papers from the Hall of Harmonious Wind*. Leiden, Netherlands: Brill, 1976. http://books.google.com/books?id=AsQUAAAAIAAJ&pg=PA72&lpg=PA72&dq=sung+1045+dissection+rebels&source=bl&ots=h7gDdVPauz&sig=u6vprLucOyrqvE9aUuKjEzNzL7c&hl=en&sa=X&ei=lFgAUI3pEsrQqAHA3sjIBw&ved=0C

EUQ6AEwAA#v=snippet&q=%22tu%20ch'i%22&f=false. Accessed July 13, 2012.

Lloyd, Geoffrey. "Alcmaeon and the Early History of Dissection. *Sudhoffs Archive* 59, no. 2 (1975): 113–147.

Lynam, Shevawn. *Humanity Dick*. London: Hamish Hamilton, 1975.

Lyons, Albert S. "Ancient China." Health Guidance. http://www.healthguidance.org/entry/6333/1/Ancient-China.html. Accessed July 13, 2012.

Maehle, Andreas-Holger, and Ulrich Tröhler. "Animal Experimentation from Antiquity to the End of the Eighteenth Century: Attitudes and Arguments." In *Vivisection in Historical Perspective*. Edited by Nicolaas Rupke, 14–47. London: Croom Helm, 1987.

Matuk, Camillia. "Seeing the Body: The Divergence of Ancient Chinese and Western Medical Illustration." *Journal of Biocommunication* 32, no. 1 (2006): 1–8.

Merchant, Carolyn. "Environmentalism: From the Control of Nature to Partnership." http://nature.berkeley.edu/departments/espm/env-hist/Moses.pdf. Accessed July 10, 2012.

Olmsted, J. M. D. *François Magendie, Pioneer in Experimental Physiology and Scientific Medicine in XIX Century France*. New York: Schuman's, 1944.

The Parliamentary History of England from the Earliest Period to 1803. Vol. 36. London: T. C. Hansard, 1820. http://books.google.com/books?id=CLgTAAAAYAAJ. Accessed July 17, 2012.

The Parliamentary Register: or an Impartial Report of the Debates. Vol. 2. London: T. Gillet, 1800. http://books.google.com/books?id=ulYxAAAAIAAJ. Accessed July 17, 2012.

Pegis, Anton Charles, ed. *Basic Writings of Saint Thomas Aquinas*. Indianapolis, IN: Hackett, 1997.

"Philantrope Anglais Dans L'exercice De Son Sacerdoce."
1844. Brandeis Institutional Repository. https://bir
.brandeis.edu/handle/10192/1664?show=full. Accessed
July 18, 2012.

Prioreschi, P. "Determinants of the Revival of Dissection of the
Human Body in the Middle Ages." *Medical Hypotheses* 56,
no. 2 (2001): 229–234.

*The Public General Statutes Passed in the Thirty-Ninth and
Fortieth Years of the Reign of Her Majesty Queen Victoria,
1876.* London: George Edward Eyre and William
Spottiswoode, 1876. http://books.google.com/books
?id=EwMUAAAAYAAJ. Accessed July 17, 2012.

Rajgopal, L., G. N. Hoskeri, P. S. Ghuiyan, and K.
Shyamkishore. "History of Anatomy in India." *Journal of
Postgraduate Medicine* 48, no. 3 (2002): 243–245. http://
www.jpgmonline.com/article.asp?issn=0022-3859;
year=2002;volume=48;issue=3;spage=243;epage=5;
aulast=Rajgopal#ref7. Accessed July 15, 2012.

*Records of the Royal Society for the Prevention of Cruelty to
Animals: Liverpool Branch.* The National Archives. http://
www.nationalarchives.gov.uk/a2a/records.aspx?cat
=138-179ani&cid=0#0. Accessed July 17, 2012.

Renier, Hannah. "An Early Vegan: Lewis Gompertz." London
Historians. March 15, 2012. http://www.londonhistorians
.org/?s=articles. Accessed July 17, 2012.

Saraf, Sanjay, and Rav S. Parihar. "Sushruta: The First Plastic
Surgeon in 600 B.C." *The Internet Journal of Plastic
Surgery* 4, no. 2 (2007). http://www.ispub.com/journal/the
-internet-journal-of-plastic-surgery/volume-4-number-2/
sushruta-the-first-plastic-surgeon-in-600-b-c.html. Accessed
July 15, 2012.

Savage-Smith, Emilie. "Attitudes toward Dissection in
Medieval Islam." *Journal of the History of Medicine and Allied
Sciences* 50, no. 1 (1995): 67–110. http://jhmas.oxford

journals.org/content/50/1/67.full.pdf. Accessed July 11, 2012.

Schnorrenberger, Claus C. "Anatomical Roots of Chinese Medicine and Acupuncture." *Journal of Chinese Medicine* 19, nos. 1 and 2 (2008): 35–63. Available at http://tedpriebe .com/documents/Anatomical_Foundations_of_Chinese %20Med.pdf. Accessed July 12, 2012.

Sechzer, Jeri A. "The Ethical Dilemma of Some Classical Animal Experiments." *Annals of the New York Academy of Sciences* 406 (1983): 5–12.

Shoja, Mohammadali M., and R. Shane Tubbs. "The History of Anatomy in Persia." *Journal of Anatomy* 210, no. 4 (2007): 359–378.

Singh, J., M. S. Desai, C. S. Pandav, and S. P. Desai. "Contributions of Ancient Indian Physicians—Implications for Modern Times." *Journal of Postgraduate Medicine* 58, no. 1 (2012): 73–78. http://www.jpgmonline.com/article .asp?issn=0022-3859;year=2012;volume=58;issue=1; spage=73;epage=78;aulast=Singh. Accessed July 15, 2012.

Statutes at Large. A Collection of the Public General Statutes, 1833–1869. 37 vols. London: George Eyre and Andrew Spottiswoode, 1835. http://books.google.com/books/about/ Statutes_at_Large_37_v_A_collection_of_t.html? id=45tKAAAAMAAJ. Accessed July 17, 2012.

The Statutes of the United Kingdom of Great Britain and Ireland. London: His Majesty's Statute and Law Printers, 1822. http://books.google.com/books?id=6LsuAAAAIAAJ. Accessed July 17, 2012.

Stephen, Sir Leslie, and Sir Sidney Lee. *Dictionary of National Biography.* Vol. 4. London: Smith, Elder & Company, 1885. http://archive.org/details/dictionaryofnati04stepuoft. Accessed July 16, 2012.

Tacium, Debbie E. 2008. "A History of Antivivisection from the 1800s to the Present." *Veterinary Heritage.* In 3 parts. 31, no.1 (May 2008): 1–9; 31, no. 2 (November 2008): 21–25; 32, no. 1 (May 2009): 1–5. Available at http://brebisnoire. wordpress.com/a-history-of-antivivisection-from-the-1800s -to-the-present-part-i-mid-1800s-to-1914/. Accessed July 16, 2012.

Unschuld, Paul U. *Medicine in China: A History of Ideas.* Berkeley: University of California Press, 1985.

von Staden, Heinrich. "Anatomy as Rhetoric: Galen on Dissection and Persuasion." *Journal of the History of Medicine and Allied Sciences* 50, no. 1 (1995): 47–66.

von Staden, Heinrich. "The Discovery of the Body: Human Dissection and Its Cultural Contexts in Ancient Greece." *Yale Journal of Biology and Medicine* 65, no. 3 (1992): 223–241.

Watt, James. "Ours Is the Earth." *Saturday Evening Post*, January/February 1982, 74–75.

Wilcox, Ella Wheeler. "The Madness of Vivisection." *Cosmopolitan Magazine* 48 (1910): 713–718. http://books .google.com/books?id=WK8xAQAAMAAJ&pg=PA714 &lpg=PA714&dq=%22Man+has+no+right+to+gratify+an +idle+and+purposeless+curiosity+through+the+practice+of +cruelty%E2%80%9D+dickens&source=bl&ots=EBx7ew P9T&sig=AT5aONxyoF0c9yMumNPZYNKx6u0&hl =en&sa=X&ei=No0FUNKG4Tm2gWtuayiBQ&ved=0CF EQ6AEwAw#v=onepage&q=%22Man%20has%20no %20right%20to%20gratify%20an%20idle%20and%20 purposeless%20curiosity%20through%20the%20practice %20of%20cruelty%E2%80%9D%20dickens&f=false. Accessed July 17, 2012.

Williams, Henry Smith, and Edward H. Williams. *A History of Science.* 5 vols. New York: Harper, 1904–1910. https://play .google.com/store/books/details?id=chNLAAAAYAAJ&rdid =book-chNLAAAAYAAJ&rdot=1. Accessed July 6, 2012.

Williamson, Lori. *Power and Protest: Frances Power Cobbe and Victorian Society.* London: Rivers Oram Press, 2005.

2 Problems, Controversies, and Solutions

I believe I am not interested to know whether Vivisection produces results that are profitable to the human race or doesn't. To know that the results are profitable to the race would not remove my hostility to it. The pains which it inflicts upon unconsenting animals is the basis of my enmity towards it, and it is to me sufficient justification of the enmity without looking further. ("Mark Twain on Scientific Research" 2012)

This letter, written by Mark Twain to the editor of *Animals' Friends Magazine* in 1900, probably reflected the views of many well-known men and women of the day, as well as that of the ordinary "man on the street." For all of their efforts to win over the general public in their campaign for increased use of animals in biomedical and scientific research, scientists still struggled against a strong antivivisectionist feeling in the United Kingdom, the United States, and other parts of Western Europe. Typical of the battle being fought is the now-famous case of "the brown dog."

Electrodes, used to detect neurological activity, protrude from the brain of a Japanese macaque immobilized in a laboratory in Japan. Despite the scientific gains from such research, subjecting primates to medical experimentation is a highly controversial and ethically charged practice. (Yann Arthus-Bertrand/Corbis)

The Tide Turns: The Brown Dog Affair
and the Decline of Antivivisectionism

The controversy was initiated in 1903 when William Bayliss and
Ernest Starling, two of the world's leading physiologists at the
time, conducted a demonstration in front of 60 medical students
using a brown mongrel dog that had been picked up wandering
the streets of London. Unbeknownst to Bayliss and Starling,
two members of the Anti-Vivisection Society of Sweden had infil-
trated the lecture and spread word of the event to their colleagues
in the antivivisectionist movement in England. The dog had
apparently suffered through at least two dissections—anesthetized
according to Bayliss and Starling, but not according to the Swedish
women—before he was finally euthanized when the experiment
failed in its objectives.

Reports of the demonstration inspired widespread objections
among the growing antivivisectionist movement in London and
other parts of the country, objections that eventually grew into a
movement that lasted for more than four years. Eventually, a
statue of the brown dog (who was never known by more than
that sobriquet) was erected in the Battersea region of London in
1906 with a plaque that read "Men and women of England,
how long shall these Things be?" The statue and plaque soon
became a rallying point not only for antivivisectionists but also
for those (primarily medical students) who were convinced of
the absolute necessity of vivisection to advance medical knowledge and the training of new physicians. The controversy between
the two groups finally reached its conclusion in 1907, when more
than a thousand supporters of vivisection (called "anti-doggers")
marched through the streets of London attacking anyone (including police) who attempted to stand in their way. The event
eventually became known as the day of the Brown Dog riots
(Lansbury 1985; Mason 1997).

Although certainly not obvious at the time, it appears that
the Brown Dog riots represented the peak of the antivivisectionist movement. Only a decade before the riots, there were

more than 100 antivivisection societies in the world, apparently riding a wave of discontent against the use of animals in biomedical and scientific experiments. (See one estimate from the time at *Annual Report* 1895, 55.) Shortly after the turn of the century, however, medical and scientific societies began to gain the upper hand in the debate over vivisection. Almost certainly, the factor most responsible for this change of view among the general public was the amazing success of biomedical researchers in finding cures or methods of prevention for a wide variety of disease, as well as the development of new treatments for diseases that had once ravaged the world. The pain and suffering caused to a few experimental animals in the accomplishments of these breakthroughs seemed, to most individuals, a small price for the miracles that had come to be part of modern medicine.

The earliest of these breakthroughs, of course, came with the discoveries of Harvey, Magendie, Bernard, and their colleagues. These breakthroughs produced no immediate improvements in health care or medicine, so it was the agony of the experimental animals by which they were best known to the public, not their contribution to scientific knowledge. By 1900, however, that situation had begun to change, and proponents of animal experimentation could point to any number of discoveries that had a direct effect on people's everyday lives. One of the earliest of these developments came in 1909 when German physician and medical researcher Paul Ehrlich announced a new way of treating syphilis, one of the oldest scourges of human health. In the research that led to this discovery, Ehrlich had relied heavily on the use of laboratory animals (usually mice), a fact not unnoticed by the general public. An article in the January 28, 1912, edition of the *New York Times*, for example, described in great detail how the use of animals was leading to research in which "the fate of mankind was being settled." To make its point clear, the paper inserted a large sketch of Ehrlich at work in his laboratory (but with no animals present) (Metz 1912).

Nor was syphilis by any means the only disease that was conquered through the use of animal experimentation. For example, the development of an antitoxin for diphtheria in 1894 had an almost immediate and dramatic effect on infant mortality. Just to make clear the role that animals played in this kind of research, many medical workers specifically told this story for the general public. In a 1909 article in the *New York Times*, for example, William H. Park, professor of bacteriology and hygiene at New York University, explained that development of the diphtheria antitoxin "would have been absolutely impossible without animal experimentation," which involved primarily guinea pigs and horses. As a result of these experiments, Park noted, 90 percent of all cases of diphtheria were being treated with the newly developed antitoxin, resulting in a savings of more than 100,000 lives in Europe and the United States (Park 1909, SM10).

Perhaps the most notable and widely reported use of animals in medical research occurred in the early 1920s during research on the cause of diabetes by Canadian researchers Frederick Grant Banting and Charles Best. Banting and John J. R. Macleod were awarded the 1923 Nobel Prize in Medicine or Physiology for this discovery (although the exclusion of Best from the award is a topic of some debate even a century later). Banting and Best depended heavily on the use of dogs in proving that insulin was produced in the islets of Langerhans in the pancreas and that damage to that tissue was responsible for the development of at least some types of diabetes. Senior researcher Banting was well aware of the issues involved in vivisecting dogs in this line of study, but had no doubt that the eventual results would well justify his approach. His beliefs were ultimately justified when the general public soon learned that the treatment developed for the treatment of diabetes— developed through animal experimentation—was ultimately responsible for saving the lives of untold numbers of humans (Bliss 1993, 149–155).

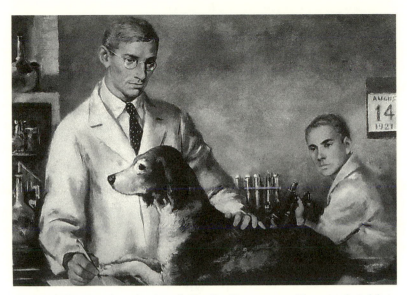

Frederick Banting (standing) and Charles Best, pictured here in their lab in 1921, won acclaim for their discovery of insulin, a direct result of their canine research, which involved the removal of the pancreas of many test dogs to induce diabetes. (National Library of Medicine)

In any case, the last decade of the nineteenth century and the first decade of the twentieth century saw a significant increase in the use of animals for scientific research, at least in the United Kingdom, and probable elsewhere as well. The only reliable statistics on this trend come from the United Kingdom, where the collection of data on animal experimentation was required as part of the 1876 Cruelty to Animals Act. According to those annual surveys (which are still conducted today), the number of procedures that involved the use of animals in the country increased from 311 in 1880 to more than 95,000 in 2010 (Monamy 2009, 12–13).

During the same period, some fundamental changes in the nature of experimentation were taking place. Perhaps most significant of these was the availability of anesthetics, such as ether, first used by American physician Crawford Long in 1842. The availability of anesthesia made it possible, at least in theory, to dramatically reduce the pain and suffering experienced by animals during experiments conducted on them (although the extent to which researchers actually took advantage of this new development is subject to some debate). In addition, researchers began to be more selective about the animals they used for research. Prior to 1900, most researchers used a very wide variety of animals in their studies, often selected for a host of reasons. Quite commonly, a researcher would use whatever animals were most readily available, which accounts for the popularity of dogs in many instances. But researchers also tried to match the species they selected for their studies according to its suitability for that particular line of research. In experiments that required the collection of large quantities of blood, for example, larger animals such as cows and horses were likely to be preferred over smaller animals, such as mice and rats.

In a review of the two most popular physiological journals of the late nineteenth century, Cheryl A. Logan of the departments of psychology and biology at the University of North Carolina at Greensboro found that the most common subject of animal research reported between 1885 and 1900 was, in one journal, humans, accounting for a quarter of all test organisms. After humans, the most popular animals were dogs, frogs, and rabbits. The same four animals were most widely reported on in the second journal, with the exception that dogs replaced humans as the most commonly used subjects.

The more important finding in Logan's research was the philosophical assumptions adopted by researchers before and after 1900. During the earlier period, researchers generally took the stance that the greater the variety of animals they could study, the more reliable the information about human physiology they could obtain. After 1900, however, the science of physiology matured in a variety of ways, one of which was the "industrialization of the life sciences," which included the selective breeding of certain species of animals (such as rats and mice) specifically for the purpose of carrying out scientific research. That approach has evolved to the point today that researchers can purchase almost any number of very specific lines of specific species for their research studies. The philosophy underlying this approach to animal experimentation is that life systems tend to be much the same from animal species to animal species. As a result, the information gained by studying a specific line or rat or mouse is likely to produce information that is generally applicable to human systems and that, therefore, can be used for specific medical and health applications. (See a more detailed discussion of this point in Logan 2002.)

The increasing success of animal-based research in the early decades of the twentieth century was mirrored by a corresponding decrease in the popularity of the antivivisection movement. By the 1920s, a number of previously outspoken and aggressive antivivisection organizations were having second thoughts about the goals they could hope to achieve and the aggressiveness with which they could work toward those goals. As noted in chapter 1, the British National Anti-Vivisection Society (NAVS) had abandoned its original goal of working for the complete abolition of vivisection and directed its efforts to developing stricter standards for its use in research (a move that had prompted Francis Power Cobbe to form a new group that maintained NAVS's original objective of complete abolition of vivisection, the British Union for the Abolition of Vivisection [BUAV]).

In 1926, Major Charles W. Hume founded an organization reflecting the new view of antivivisectionists about animal research, the University of London Animal Welfare Society (ULAWS). In 1938, the organization changed its name to the Universities Federation for Animal Welfare (UFAW) to reflect the wider range of individuals and institutions involved. Hume later wrote the he formed the organization in order to "compensate the harm done to the cause of animal welfare by animal-lovers of the unbalanced kind, and to form an intelligently humane body of opinion" (Hume 1962, 202, as quoted in Monamy 2009, 26). The initial aims of the organization were:

- To enlist the influence of university men and women on behalf of animals, wild and domestic;
- To promote, by educational and other methods, interest in the welfare of animals in Great Britain and abroad;
- To lessen, by methods appropriate to the special character of a university organisation, the pain and fear inflicted on animals by man;
- To obtain and disseminate accurate information relating to animal welfare;
- To further and promote legislation for the protection of animals. ("A History of Improving Animal Welfare" 2012)

The major difference between ULAWS and earlier antivivisection groups, such as the original NAVS and BUAV, were, Hume suggested, that protection of animals used in research should be based "on facts rather than sentimentality." His goal, then, was to work *with* scientific researchers, veterinarians, and others engaged in animal studies rather than battling *against* these individuals (Thompson 1990). In a 2001 review of the history of the antivivisection movement, one observer has said that "relative to previous years, the period between 1920 and 1960 was characterised by little or no change in the protection of animals, and efforts to overturn vivisection were greatly reduced on both sides of the Atlantic." The writer ascribed this change to two factors primarily. The first was the passage of two world wars in which "the concern for animal pain [was rendered] somewhat ridiculous," in addition to distracting national resources to rebuilding their economies. The second fact, he said, was "the phenomenal success of medicine in the eradication of smallpox and polio, and the development of intensive farming mechanisms that made meat and dairy products affordable to almost everybody" (Derbyshire 2001; some of the alleged accomplishments attributed to animal experimentation are listed in Cohen and Regan 2001, 122–123). As a consequence, he points out, by the early 1960s even the ASPCA was selling off excess shelter animals for use in scientific and biomedical experiments (Derbyshire 2001; also see Stephens, Goldberg, and Rowan 2001, 122).

The Antivivisection Movement in the United States Hits Bottom

As mentioned in chapter 1, the antivivisection movement was not entirely absent from the United States in the late nineteenth century. However, the movement had much less energy on this side of the Atlantic than in the United Kingdom. In his superb outline of the history of animal experimentation, Vaughan Monamy points out a number of reasons for this relative lack of interest among ordinary people (although less so than among the elite) for animal issues, including the huge success of government-supported scientific research in the United States (especially compared to the case in Great Britain), the relative economic success of the United States (especially compared to European nations that had been wracked by two world wars on their own soil), and the relatively few experiments conducted in the United States in which animals were used for study (Monamy 2009, 26–27).

All of which is not to say that there was *no* opposition to vivisection in the United States. Indeed, many progressive associations, such as the Women's Christian Temperance Union and the American Humane Association, saw antivivisectionism as a natural fit for their generally humane philosophies. The interest engendered for antivivisection among these groups was stoked to a significant extent, Monamy points out, by the reports of visitors from Europe who had actually witnessed the use of vivisection themselves. One such individual was Henry Bergh, an American who had traveled extensively throughout Europe in the late 1860s. During a visit to England, he made the acquaintance of the Earl of Harrowby, who was then president of the RSPCA. So impressed was Bergh by the work of the RSPCA that he vowed to devote the rest of his life to the protection of "dumb animals" ("Death of Henry Bergh" 1888). One of his first acts upon returning home for an extended visit to Europe was the formation of the ASPCA in 1866, a cause to which he did, indeed, devote the rest of his life.

As in Europe, the antivivisection movement in the United States appears to have reached its zenith at the end of the nineteenth century. The defining event in this history was the filing of a bill in the U.S. Senate for strengthening provisions for the protection of animals used in scientific experiments in the District of Columbia. Proponents of the bill were, at first, optimistic about their chances of having the bill adopted. One observer wrote to the English journal *The Zoophilist* that "our speakers were very strong and our opponents very weak. They hardly knew what to say" (*The Animals' Defender and Zoophilist* 1896, 52).

That optimism was premature, however, as the Senate committee considering the bill was flooded with objections from a variety of medical and scientific organizations, including the American Medical Association (AMA), the National Academy of Sciences (NAS), the Surgeon General of the United States, the Congress of American Physicians and Surgeons, the Joint Commission of the Seven Scientific Societies of Washington, the Association of Military Surgeons, the Entomological Society of Washington, the Pennsylvania Medical Society, the Association of American Physicians, the Detroit Medical and Library Association, and numerous other professional organizations. The committee also received more than a hundred personal communications both for and against the bill (*Congressional Serial Set* 1896, 1–159). The bill was eventually defeated on the floor of the Senate, was reintroduced again in 1900, and was once more defeated in the Senate.

Vaughan Monamy (and a number of other observers) suggest that the defeat of the antivivisection bill in 1896 and 1900 "took the wind out of the sails" of the movement in the United States for most of the next 60 years. Another element that contributed to that downfall was the split between antivivisectionist organizations and other animal welfare groups. In 1877, a coalition of 27 "humane" organizations, concerned about the welfare of animals and children, had been formed under the name of the American Humane Association (AHA). Although supposedly interested in issues of welfare of all animals, the AHA was never entirely comfortable with fighting the battle for research animals. Finally, in 1900, at an international conference of "human" organizations, all antivivisectionists groups were expelled from the parent organization, and the AHA and its component groups focused instead on the welfare of farm animals, pets, and stray cats and dogs (Phelps 2007, 145–146; Liddick 2006, 30). Without the support of even its fellows in arms, the antivivisectionist groups in the United States faced a relatively hopeless future. Their position was made crystal clear in 1914 when an attendee at the AHA conference told a lobbyist for the research industry that the association simply wanted to "leave vivisection alone" (quoted in Monamy 2009, 28).

Resurgence of the Antivivisection Movement

By the mid-twentieth century, medical researchers were beginning to become a victim of their own success with regard to the use of animals. Following the conclusion of World War II, scientific research in general and medical research in particular began to mushroom in size and scope. Nearly any topic that one could imagine studying, ranging from the structure of molecules to the social behavior of humans and other animals, was considered fair game for researchers. And there seemed to be more money available for research than could easily be spent.

One of the side effects of this boom in research was a rapidly increasing demand for animals for research. And a ready supply of animals that would otherwise "go to waste" appeared to be available: abandoned dogs and cats in local animal shelters ("pounds"). By early 1950, a number of states had passed laws permitting the use of such animals for scientific and biomedical research. The first such law was adopted in Minnesota in 1948, requiring unclaimed animals at publicly funded shelters to be released to researchers. A year later, Wisconsin passed a similar but more stringent law, requiring unclaimed animals at *all* shelters, both public and private, to be made available for research. Before long a number of other states, including Connecticut, Iowa, Massachusetts, New York, Ohio, Oklahoma, and South Dakota, had passed similar laws (Rowan 1984, 52; for a summary of current pound laws, see Perry 2009, 5).

Although pleased with the general tone of the public's attitude toward animal experimentation, researchers were nonetheless understandably concerned about possible backlashes against the increased use of "Fido" and "Spot" for experimental purposes. In anticipation of a possible backlash against the use of lost and stray pets for research, three physicians at the University of Illinois Medical School, Andrew C. Ivy, Ralph G. Carlson, and George E. Wakerlin, established the National Society for Medical Research (NSMR) in 1945 with the purpose of "improv[ing] public understanding of the principals methods and needs of the biological services" (Rowan 1984, 52). The first goal of the new society was to push for the adoption of pound seizure laws like those described above, an effort in which they were obviously very successful.

The overall strategy of the association was described in considerable detail in a memorandum written by Clarence Dennis, a member of the organization in 1966. In his "Suggested Program for the National Society for Medical Research," Dennis warned that efforts by antivivisectionists to play on "the almost universal human instinct of kindliness toward all domesticated animals" placed the welfare of American people, "indeed of all people everywhere," in jeopardy. He was especially concerned about the influence of the "humanistic mystic" Albert Schweitzer, who had "no experience whatsoever with the scientific research aspects of medicine" ("The Clarence Dennis Papers" 2012).

In order to combat this threat, Dennis proposed an extensive program that would inform the general public of the great advances in medicine resulting from animal experimentation and tell them that animals never suffered from such experiments "except when important information could not otherwise be obtained." Some elements of the program included a speakers bureau with scientists who could address lay groups on animal experimentation; inspections of science laboratories by congressmen and state legislators; special regional programs for science writers; special press releases on advances resulting from the use of animals in research; special outreach to radio, television, newspapers, and magazines; and enlistment of nonscientists through varsity clubs, veterans groups, service clubs, labor unions, farm groups, churches, sports groups, hospitals, and other lay organizations ("The Clarence Dennis Papers" 2012). (In 1985, the NSMR merged with the Association of Biomedical Research to form the National Association for Biomedical Research, which still exists today.)

Dennis's proposal appeared at just about the time that two events occurred that many historians mark as the resurgence of the antivivisection movement in the United States: the theft of a Dalmatian dog named Pepper from a farm in Pennsylvania, and an exposé of dog farms by *Life* magazine. Pepper had been rescued from a rundown kennel in rural Pennsylvania in the summer of 1965 by Julia Lakavage, an animal lover who had already taken in a number of stray dogs. Pepper rapidly became a regular member of the family who accompanied Julia to work at her job as a nurse in a local hospital—except for the night of June 22, 1965, when Pepper was, unusually, nowhere to be found on the Lakavage farm.

Warned by animal welfare groups that unmarked vans were picking up stray dogs, Julia and her children set out to track down their lost dog. They eventually tracked Pepper to a notorious dog farm in upstate New York, known for its dealings with scientific researchers. The family enlisted the aid of Representative Joseph Resnick (D-NY), who was also refused access to the dog farm. The search for Pepper finally came to an end when her family learned that the dog had been sold to Montefiore Hospital in New York City, where she was to be used in tests of a new pacemaker. Something had gone wrong (no one knows what) during the procedure, and Pepper died on the operating table. As one chronicler of the story has written, "The loss of a single Dalmatian meant little to the pacemaker program at Montefiore. The new prototypes would be tested on another dog, and another, and many more," with the eventual development of one of the most useful medical devices ever produced for humans, the heart pacemaker (Engber 2009; the original story about Pepper was reported in Phinizy 1965).

Representative Resnick was outraged when he learned of Pepper's death, and he promised the Lakavage family that he would not let the issue die. Seven days after Pepper died, he filed a bill, H.R. 9743 (now known as "Pepper's Law"), calling for licensing of individuals who dealt in the sale of cats and dogs and for penalties for dog- and cat-napping. The bill was hardly the first effort by animal welfare groups to get Congress to pass stronger protections for animals; that battle had been going on for two decades, with no success. Pepper's story made the difference, however, and in 1966 the Congress passed a much enhanced version of Pepper's Law, the Laboratory Animal Welfare Law of 1966 (LAWA). (The act was amended in 1970 and renamed the Animal Welfare Act.) That law vastly changed the landscape of animal experimentation and other animal welfare issues in the United States ("Legislative History of the Animal Welfare Act" 2012).

Supporters of the Animal Welfare Act also owed their success to a second event, the publication of a photo-article published in the February 4, 1966, issue of *Life* magazine, only months after the Pepper case had caught the nation's attention. The article, entitled "Concentration Camp for Dogs," described conditions under which dogs were being kept by dealers, most of whom were trying to meet researchers' demand for 2 million dogs a year for their experiments. The most compelling aspects of the feature were a number of photographs that showed dogs in extreme physical and emotional distress ("Concentration Camp for Dogs" 1966).

Animal Welfare Legislation

In some regards, the United States was about a century behind the United Kingdom in efforts to protect animals from abuse. A number of states adopted such ordinances in the nineteenth century, but no federal legislation was adopted until 1966. The first such legislation at the state level was a New York State law passed in 1828 providing for the conviction of anyone who mistreated horses, oxen, cattle, or sheep (Liddick 2006, 28). Of those states that did adopt anticruelty laws, 14 specifically exempted animal experiments. Overall, such laws were generally fairly weak, applied only to farm animals, and, in any case, resulted in only two prosecutions for animal experimentation during the century. (The best available review of this topic is probably Leavitt 1990.)

The Laboratory Animal Welfare Act of 1966 was a huge step beyond the somewhat limited bill originally offered by Representative Resnick. That act was aimed primarily at the care of cats, dogs, nonhuman primates, rabbits, hamsters, and guinea pigs in the custody of animal dealers or preresearch laboratories. Agents who transferred dogs and cats across state lines were required to have a license to do so. The act was not in force very long before regulators realized that the original bill had some serious shortcomings. For example, U.S. Department of Agriculture (USDA) inspectors were allowed to visit animals only prior to the research experience itself, but not to see the actual experimental conditions ("Legislative History of the Welfare Act" 2012; also see "Animal Welfare Act: Historical Perspectives and Future Directions" 2012).

In an effort to deal with these deficiencies, the U.S. Congress adopted a number of amendments to the 1966 act in 1970. (It was at this point that the name of the act was also simplified to the Animal Welfare Act.) Among the major changes in the 1970 amendments was an expansion of the definition of *animal* to include a much wider range of species than in the original act, an extension of the law to in-state facilities and transactions as well as to cross-state transactions, and additional requirements for the use of anesthetics and other materials and procedures for sedating animals used in research. The 1970 amendments specifically stated that animal welfare rules were to be applied to "all warm-blooded animals," but that provision did not survive the rule-making process that followed adoption of the law. In 1971, the secretary of agriculture ruled that rats, mice, and birds were to be exempted from the provisions of the act. This decision, which remains in effect today, means that roughly 95 percent of all animals used in research (those mice, rats, and birds specifically bred for research) are not covered by animal protection laws in the United States ("Animal Experiments: Overview" 2012).

Over the next four decades, the Animal Welfare Act was amended six more times. The major feature(s) of each action are summarized here:

- 1976: Provisions of the 1966 and 1970 act are "fine-tuned," with more detailed requirements for the housing and transportation of animals. Restrictions are placed for the first time on animal fighting, such as cock- and dog-fighting events.

- 1985: The Improved Standards for Laboratory Animals Act made a number of changes in existing law, perhaps the most important of which was creation of the Institutional Animal Care and Use Committees (IACUCs). Every institution that uses animals for research and that receives funds from a federal agent must establish an IACUC, whose responsibility it is to review research protocols and evaluate the care and housing of research animals. IACUCs have become a key element in the nation's efforts to provide research animals with safe, healthy, and compassionate care. The act also provided more details about the humane care of animals, including provisions for ventilation, sanitation, feeding, and housing. It made more stringent requirements for avoiding pain and suffering among laboratory animals and more clearly defined the meaning of these conditions. The act also limited the number of experiments to which an animal could be subjected.

- 1990: The Protection of Pets Act established requirements for the handling of pets (limited to dogs and cats) at animal shelters. Animals must be kept for a period of at least five days to allow owners an opportunity to recover their pets. After that time, shelters are required to keep detailed records as to the disposition of any unclaimed animals with penalties of $5,000 per animal for whom such records are not kept.

- 2002: Title X, Subtitle D of the Farm Security and Rural Investment Act amended the Animal Welfare Act of 1966 to change the definition of animals covered by that act. It exempted all birds, rats of the genus *Rattus*, and mice of the genus *Mus*, bred for use in research. The act also placed restrictions on the shipment of animals across state lines for the purpose of "sports," such as cockfighting and dog fighting.

- 2007: A short bill strengthened the provisions of the animal-fighting legislation currently on the books.

- 2008: The Food, Conservation, and Energy Act included provisions for strengthening the prohibitions against and penalties for dog fighting, with a change in the maximum fine for violation of the 1966 Animal Welfare Act from $2,500 to $10,000 per violation. (Animal Welfare Act 2012)

(A summary of current laws and regulations dealing with animal welfare can be found at http://www.gpo.gov/fdsys/pkg/USCODE-2009-title7/html/USCODE-2009-title7-chap54.htm and http://www.gpo.gov/fdsys/pkg/CFR-2009-title9-vol1/xml/CFR-2009-title9-vol1-chapI-subchapA.xml.)

Issues of Violence and Morality

Adoption of the Animal Welfare Act of 1966 and its amendments in 1970 marked the beginning of a historic change in the question of animal experimentation in the United States and a number of other developed nations around the world. That change took two quite different directions, the first involving a far more aggressive and sometimes violent approach to the misuse of animals by their human supporters and the other a revolutionary new view of the moral status of animals that underlies much of the antivivisection argument that dominates the modern debate over animal experimentation.

Animal Liberation

Until the 1960s, antivivisectionists tended to make use of a traditional and relatively moderate approach to their campaign against the use of animals in research. This approach involved the formation of societies (like NAVS in the United Kingdom and the United States) that attempted to raise people's consciousness about animal concerns with pamphlets, letters to the editors, public speeches, peaceful marches, lobbying of legislators, and other largely peaceful forms of protest. Such efforts were sometimes successful (as evidenced by the passage of the Cruelty to Animals Act of 1876 and the Animal Welfare Act of 1966), but peaceful protest was also ineffective on a number of occasions in the face of continued medical success against human illness and disease.

One of the earliest groups to consider more aggressive ways of protesting ill use of animals was the Band of Mercy, described in chapter 1. First active in the early 1970s, the modern group of that name decided to forgo public pleadings for their cause and to act as strongly as they thought necessary to make their case. As an example, members of the group heard in late 1973 that Hoechst Pharmaceutical was planning to build a new laboratory near Milton Keynes, England. In considering the options available for preventing the abuse of laboratory animals at the facility, the Band decided to forgo what they regarded as the too-mild efforts of their animal welfare predecessors and take direct action against the proposed facility. On the night of November 10, 1973, two members of the

Band gained access to the partially completed building and set it afire. Members returned six days later to make sure their project was a success by setting a second fire. The two actions resulted in more than £46,000 in damage to the facility. To make certain that their point was understood, the Band members left a note at the building's remains saying:

> The building was set fire to in an effort to prevent the torture and murder of our animal brothers and sisters by evil experiments. We are a non-violent guerrilla organization dedicated to the liberation of animals from all forms of cruelty and persecution at the hands of mankind. Our actions will continue until our aims are achieved. (Molland 2012)

Members of the Band executed a number of similar attacks in succeeding years, one of which resulted in the imprisonment of two of its members, Ronnie Lee and Cliff Goodman. Shortly after their release, Lee decided to rename the small, decentralized, but very effective organization Animal Liberation Front (ALF), a name it has retained to the present day ("History of the Animal Liberation Movement" 2012).

The United States was not far behind the United Kingdom in the development of an aggressive animal liberation movement. According to the North American Animal Liberation press office, the first such attack took place in 1977 when a group calling itself Undersea Railroad released two porpoises from a Hawaii research station. Two years later, the first group calling itself the Animal Liberation Front in the United States staged a raid on a laboratory at a New York University research laboratory, releasing two dogs, two guinea pigs, and one cat ("25 Years of Saving Lives with the Animal Liberation Front" 2012).

Among the activities carried out over the years by the ALF are firebombing of department stores in London that sell fur clothing; bombing of the cars of a number of animal researchers in the United Kingdom and United States; release of cats, dogs, and guinea pigs from breeding facilities; an attack on an independent filmmaker producing a documentary on the activities of the ALF; and a variety of arson attacks on laboratories, meat-processing plants, lumber facilities, and other locations that pose a threat to animals in one way or another. Throughout its history, animal liberation front organizations have insisted that they do not approve of violent action. Such action, however, may be necessary under certain circumstances, they say. For example, following an attempt to place a Molotov cocktail on the front steps of the home of an animal researcher at the University of California at Los Angeles (UCLA), a representative of ALF said that "force is a poor second choice, but if that's the only thing that will work . . . there's certainly moral justification for that" ("Terror at UCLA" 2006).

ALF groups have faced widespread and fervent opposition throughout their history. Such opposition first appeared only a year after the organization was first formed in England. A group that would normally have been like-minded—the Hunt Saboteurs Association (HSA)—noted that while it approved of the goals of the ALF group, it was opposed to its methods. It offered a £250 reward for information that could be used against the original Band of Mercy. (The HSA had been formed to take direct action against people who were engaged in blood sports, such as fox hunting. They thus had similar goals to those of ALF, but preferred to use less treacherous actions, such as tire slashing and flushing of birds prior to a hunt) (Molland 2012).

A survey conducted of participants in the 1990 and 1996 March for Animals held in Washington, D.C., attempted to determine the attitudes of animal rights advocates about the most effective methods for achieving their goals. Respondents placed education, boycotts, and legal actions as the most effective ways of reaching the goals of enhanced animal welfare, while direct tactics such as the release of laboratory animals and harassment and intimidation of researchers to be least effective (Galvin and Herzog 1998, 1). The U.S. government finally reached the end of its rope in attempting to deal with the ALF and other direct-action groups when it passed the Animal Enterprise Terrorism Act of 2006. That act provides any individual from "damaging or interfering with the operations of an animal enterprise" (Public Law 109-374 2006). According to the bill's original author, Representative Thomas Petri (R-WI), the bill was designed to provide law enforcement officers with "the necessary authority to apprehend, prosecute, and convict individuals committing animal enterprise terror" ("S. 3880 [109th]: Animal Enterprise Terrorism Act" 2012).

A Moral Code for Animals

Historically, antivivisectionists have based their campaign against animal experimentation primarily on two arguments. First, they say that animal testing is an unreliable biomedical procedure since the anatomy and physiological of test animals is likely to be very different from that of humans. Thus results obtained from animal experimentation are likely to be invalid and unreliable. Second, they point out that animal testing causes pain, suffering, long-term damage, and, generally, death to the subjects of such experiments. One might characterize the second argument as an emotional reaction: most people like some or animal kinds of animals and feel sorry for them when they are subjected to painful laboratory procedures. It is only human, critics say, to want to protect some or all species of animals from such experiences. One can hardly read the complaints of early antivivisectionists in the United Kingdom and United States and not be very conscious of the passion with which antivivisectionists cared about the animals they were trying to defend.

In the 1960s and 1970s, a very new response to antivivisection arose, based on the argument that all living creatures—not just humans—have certain inalienable rights to a life free from pain and suffering. The first person to present this viewpoint in a clear and cohesive way was Australian philosopher

Peter Singer. Singer applied to the debate of vivisection a field of philosophy known as *utilitarianism*, a branch of philosophy first developed by English philosopher Jeremy Bentham (see chapter 1) who suggested that the fundamental test of the morality of any action is the extent to which it contributes the greatest good to the greatest number of individuals. While that philosophy had long been applied by some thinkers to humans, Singer suggested that it should actually be applied to all animals. He further argued that the application of utilitarianism to humans *without regard* to other animals was a form of *speciesism*, a term first suggested by English psychologist Richard D. Ryder to describe the exclusion of nohuman animals from the rights, privileges, and protections generally available to humans.

Singer codified his ideas about the treatment of animals in a now classical work, *Animal Liberation*, written in 1975. The circumstances under which the book was produced are somewhat unusual. In 1973, Singer had written a review for *The New York Review of Books* of *Animals, Men, and Morals*, by philosophers and animal rights advocates Rosalind and Stanley Godlovitch. In his review, Singer wrote that the Godlovitches' book was a "manifesto for an Animal Liberation movement" (Singer 1973). Editors at *The New York Review of Books* were intrigued as to what Singer meant by that comment and ask him to write a book on the concept, a book that eventually became *Animal Liberation* (Singer 1986).

In his book and in a number of other publications, Singer has laid out the fundamental philosophy on which the concept of animal liberation is based. He has written:

> If a being suffers there can be no moral justification for refusing to take that suffering into consideration. No matter what the nature of the being, the principle of equality requires that its suffering be counted equally with the like suffering—insofar as rough comparisons can be made—of any other being. (Singer 2012)

Singer's position on animal rights has by no means been lacking in critics. According to some opponents, for example, one simply could not say that the health and well-being of a frog intended for use in an animal experiment was of equal value to the life of an autistic or physically handicapped child. If the frog had to be sacrificed in a medical experiment to save or improve the life of the child, they said, there could be no debate as to what the appropriate action would be. Other critics have been even more outspoken, arguing that Singer denies the very obvious fact that humans are, in fact, superior to other animals in all regards, including their moral standing. And some philosophers have expressed concerned that Singer's extension of moral rights to nonhuman animals threatens the very foundations of ethical thought itself. As one critic has written, Singer's point of view portends "the death of ethics and of every human value" (Loftis 2002; Gensler 1999).

Whatever objections his critics may have raised, Singer unquestionably transformed the debate over vivisection throughout the world. As Vaughan Monamy said in his classic book on animal experimentation:

> Although the majority of animal researchers did not subscribe to Singer's arguments, *Animal Liberation* was pivotal in rekindling debate (which had lain dormant for much of the twentieth century) over the relative worth (costs versus benefits) of animal experimentation. (Monamy 2009, 33)

The Impact of *Animal Liberation*

One area in which Singer produced his greatest impact was in the proliferation of new perspectives about the fundamental nature of animals. Recall that throughout history animals have largely been regarded as a Supreme Being's gift to humans for their own use: as food, for clothing, for recreation, as helpmates, and so on. Within that perspective, as Descartes observed, animals were probably nothing more than nonthinking, nonsentient tools for humans. Singer made people think about animals in very different ways. For example, American philosopher and advocate for animal rights Tom Regan published a book in 1983, *The Case for Animal Rights*, in which he offered a slightly different perspective on the issue than Singer's. Regan argued that nonhuman animals have a consciousness about themselves just as do humans. Not only do they feel pain and suffering (as Singer had proposed), but they also experience an awareness of themselves, a consciousness that Regan called "subjects of a life," which he defined as referring to any creature who has a complex mental life such as perception, desire, belief, memory, intention, and a sense of the future among other attributes. He is confident of this position because of what he believes is extensive scientific research confirming a form of consciousness among a vast expanse of animal species. The existence of a subject-of-life-condition means, Regan wrote, that animals have "an inherent value of their own" (Regan 2012).

The consequences of Regan's philosophy re profound. It means that he is opposed to all forms of commercial animal agriculture, all forms of commercial and sport hunting and trapping, and the complete abolition of the use of all animals for scientific research (Regan 2012). As one might expect, many professional philosophers and laypersons have many of the same objections to Regan's philosophy of animal welfare as they do to Singer's. They worry that valuing animals so highly means valuing humans less highly. In one classic incident, Regan was asked if he had to save a baby or a dog when a boat capsized in the ocean, what would he do? His reply was that "if it were a retarded baby and a bright dog, I'd save the dog" ("Animal Wrongs" 2012). Thus even though he has specifically and repeatedly disavowed any rejection of the importance of human rights, Regan stands accused by his opponents of placing less value on humans than they are worthy of. One critic, for example, has emphasized the importance of *personhood* (which extends beyond just *human rights*) as a major difference between humans and nonhuman animals. He writes:

No animals can be said to have such "person-rights" as "freedom of worship," or a "right to a college education," not because we humans are tyrants, but simply because these animals lack the capacities to exercise such rights. (Partridge 1999)

Like Singer then, Regan has had a profound impact on the animal welfare movement, although a considerably lesser impact on most animal researchers.

Another perspective on the nature of animals was first offered by philosopher Bernard E. Rollin in his 1981 book *Animal Rights and Human Morality*. Rollin differs from both Singer and Regan in that he argues for animal welfare not from the standpoint of sentience (Singer) or consciousness (Regan) but from a position that he calls the animal's *telos*, from the Greek word for "goal" or "purpose." Rollin defines *telos* as being "a nature, a function, a set of activities intrinsic to it, evolutionarily determined and genetically imprinted." An animal's life, Rollin continues, consists of "a struggle to perform these functions, to actualize this nature, to fulfill these needs, to maintain this life" (Rollin 1992, 75–76). Rollin more simply describes an animal's telos as being its "pigness," "dogness," or "ratness," and an animal's struggle to live out that state is nothing more than the phenomenon represented in the line of the old song, "Fish gotta swim and birds gotta fly" (Rollin 1990, 3459).

The significance of this philosophy is that any actions taken by humans to interfere with this inherent quality of animals are immoral. Once one acknowledges that animals have an inherent telos that directs their lives (which not everyone does), it then becomes inevitable that all animals deserve the same ethical treatment as do humans. Rollin concludes his argument by insisting that his philosophy "attempts to apply the moral notion we all share about people to animals, and to encode basic protection for fundamental aspects of animals' natures into law" (Rollin 1990, 3459).

One of the most influential books on animal welfare ever written actually appeared more than 15 years before Singer's *Animal Liberation* was published. That book was *The Principles of Humane Experimental Technique*, written by W. M. S. Russell and R. L. Burch and published in 1959. The book had an even longer history, dating to the publication in 1947 of a laboratory guide, *Handbook on the Care and Management of Laboratory Animals*, by the UFAW. During the 1950s, the view of the UFAW about the care of laboratory animals evolved from one focused primarily on issues such as housing and feeding to one more concerned with the potential pain and suffering experienced by animals used in research. In 1954, Major Charles Hume, founder and president of the UFAW, announced that his association was undertaking a more ambitious review of the way in which experimental animals should be treated. This review was to be under the direction of Russell and Burch and resulted in the publication of *Principles* in 1959.

The key chapter in the new book was chapter 4, "The Sources, Incidence, and Removal of Inhumanity." After a discussion of the factors most likely to lead to inhumane treatment of animals in a laboratory setting, Russell and Burch set forth a new program, which they called "the three Rs": replacement, reduction, and refinement. Replacement referred to the practice of using alternative methods of testing wherever possible in a laboratory setting, thus obviating the use of animals in research entirely. In recognition that the first R might not always be possible, Russell and Burch then recommended using fewer animals in an experiment, certainly using no more than were absolutely necessary to obtain the data needed for valid and reliable results. Finally, when both replacement and reduction had been instituted to the degree possible, researchers should, according to Russell and Burch, consider refinement of their experimental methods, that is, making whatever changes in the experimental condition are possible to eliminate or reduce the pain and suffering experienced by animals (Russell and Burch 1959, chapter 4).

Publication of the three Rs principle of animal welfare marked a turning point in the history of the debate over animal experimentation. Throughout most of history, individuals and organizations had been either *for* or *against* vivisection. Over time, that debate became more nuanced with an increasing number of researchers adopting the view that they needed to give more serious attention to the health, care, and potential suffering of their animal subjects, and antivivisectionists beginning to understand that animal testing *had* resulted in huge steps forward in medical science and that there might indeed be conditions under which no adequate substitute was available for the use of animals in research. Today, even the most diehard supporters of animal research tend to support the principles of the three Rs, while strong antivivisectionists may agree to the use of animals in experiments provided that researchers abide by the three Rs principle. This statement by no means suggests, however, that a vigorous and sometimes acrimonious debate over the use of animals in research does not continue to the present day.

Another manifestation of the growing interest in animal welfare was the founding of a number of groups with the protection of animals as their primary goal. Some of these groups predated the writings of Singer, Regan, and Rollin, such as the International Fund for Animal Welfare (IFAW), founded in 1969, and Animal Rights International (ARI), established in 1974. IFAW was established by a small group of men and women, including Brian Davies, for the purpose of interfering with the annual hunt of baby harp seals in Newfoundland, a campaign that has continue ever since. The group grew to a membership of more than 200,000 in the first decade, and has since expanded its efforts to include the saving of animals in a wider variety of settings, including the relocation of polar bears in Canada, the rescue of elephants and hippos from wildlife parks in Africa, action against European Union (EU) directives that would have expanded the range of cosmetics testing on animals, and campaigns to ban whaling of many species.

As of the end of 2012, the organization had active projects continuing in 40 countries around the world.

ARI was founded in 1974 by Henry Spira, a Belgian-born American political activist who was engaged in a variety of political activities throughout his life. He formed ARI in 1974 after having heard a lecture by Peter Singer about animal welfare issues. In 1976, Spira and ARI conducted a campaign against the American Museum of Natural History urging them to end a 20-year-old research program in which cats were mutilated to determine the effect on their sex lives. ARI next mounted a campaign against the Revlon corporation in an attempt to have it discontinue Draize testing on rabbits. The tests involved dropping chemicals into the eyes of rabbits to determine whether and at what point they were toxic. ARI's aggressive campaign finally forced Revlon to reconsider its activities and, in the end, to become a financial supporter of a new research program, the Center for Alternatives to Animal Testing. Revlon was joined in this support by most other large cosmetics companies, including Avon, Bristol Meyers, Estée Lauder, Max Factor, Chanel, and Mary Kay Cosmetics. After Spira's death in 1998, Peter Singer became chair of the organization, although he was unable to provide the time and energy required to keep ARI strong and healthy. After struggling for a decade, it discontinued operations in 2010 and distributed its assets to other animal welfare groups.

The Animal Legal Defense Fund (ALDF) was founded in 1979 by a group of lawyers interested in shaping the evolving field of animal law, ensuring the enforcement of existing laws, and, in general, advancing the interest of animals through the legal system. The organization currently claims to have in excess of 100,000 members. Some of its most important accomplishments include preventing a research dealer from importing more than 71,000 monkeys for laboratory experiments (1983–1984); bringing to a halt the trophy hunting of California mountain lions (1987); suing the USDA for failing to set adequate standards for dogs and primates used in laboratory experiments (199);

initiation of a Zero Tolerance for Cruelty campaign (1993); aiding in the defeat of legislation that would have allowed the U.S. Air Force to purchase 148 chimpanzees for space research (1996); obtaining actions against humans who "hoard" large numbers of animals (various years); and contributing to the passage of Proposition 2 in California, which bans a variety of confinement systems for animals used in agriculture, research, and other settings.

People for the Ethical Treatment of Animals (PETA) was founded in March 1980 by a small group of people living in the Washington, D.C., area, led by Ingrid Newkirk and her partner at the time, Alex Pacheco. Newkirk had worked at a variety of animal shelters in the Washington area and had become appalled at the treatment received by animals from workers at those shelters. In 1980 she, Pacheco, and a small number of other young men and women decided to form PETA for the purpose of working against animal cruelty. The organization first became famous with regard to the so-called Silver Spring monkeys case. In that case, Pacheco got a job as a laboratory assistant in the laboratory of researcher Edward Taub. Taub was studying therapeutic procedures that could be used to help human stroke victims recover partial use of damaged limbs. In his research, Taub severed sensory nerves in 17 wild-born macaque monkeys such that they were no longer able to experience feeling in one or more of their limbs. The monkeys were then bound in such a way that they were forced to use their damaged limbs.

After observing Taub's work, Pacheco began to return to the laboratory after hours, taking pictures of the procedures being used and the filthy conditions in which the monkeys were forced to live. When local police were shown Pacheco's photographs, they raided Taub's laboratory, arrested him, and charged him with cruelty to animals. He was eventually convicted on six counts of cruelty to animals. In addition, PETA sued for custody of the animals, intending to find a safe environment to which they could be assigned. The case worked its

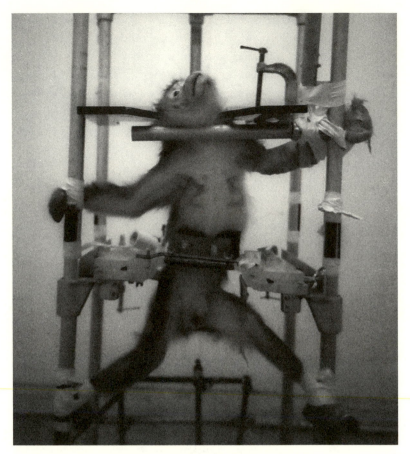

Domitian, one of the Silver Spring monkeys, in a restraint chair in 1981 inside the laboratory of Edward Taub at the Institute of Behavioral Research in Silver Spring, Maryland. Taken undercover by Alex Pacheco of People for the Ethical Treatment of Animals (PETA), the image has become an iconic symbol for the movement against scientific testing of animals. (Alex Pacheco/PETA)

way through the courts, eventually reaching the U.S. Supreme Court, which issued its decision in July 1991. At that point, only two of the monkeys were still alive, and they were killed a few days after the Supreme Court's decision. In one sense, PETA lost in its battle to save the Silver Spring monkeys, but in the larger scheme of things, it may have come out a winner. The case made PETA's name and reputation known throughout the United States and worldwide. It now claims to have more than 2 million members with an annual operating budget of more than $37 million in 2011 (Pacheo and Francione 1985).

Yet another organization that was formed as part of what is sometimes called the modern animal rights movement was the Farm Animal Reform Movement (FARM). FARM grew out of an older group, the Vegetarian Information Service, which itself had been founded in 1976 to help people who wanted to eliminate or reduce the role of meat eating in their diets. FARM has sponsored a number of actions during its 30-year history, including World Farm Animals Day, Great American Meatout, Gentle Thanksgiving, Pay-Per-View, Letters From FARM, Sabina Fund, Vegan Earth Day, Meatout Mondays, and Live Vegan.

One of the most common activities of the young animal welfare organizations has been an "action" or campaign for some specific objective. As an example, NAVS (Great Britain) initiated a World Lab Animal Day in 1979 to bring to public attention the plight of animals being used in research. That activity has eventually evolved into a World Lab Animal Week, which is recognized by the United Nations and celebrated, according to NAVS, in every country of the world. Each year, the campaign has a somewhat different theme. For example, the theme in 2008 was "Kick Animal Testing out of the House," an effort to get support for the NAVS campaign to get a ban on the use of animals for the testing of household products ("World Lab Animal Week 21–27 April" 2012).

The growing sensitivity to animal welfare issues also had some perhaps less-expected consequences. For example, in 1987 a California high school student, Jennifer Graham, objected to the dissection of a frog that was a part of her biology class (as it was a part of the vast majority of high school biology classes in the United States at the time). Graham was a vegetarian who also refused to purchase products that had been tested on animals. As a matter of principle, she declined to participate in the dissection exercise even though she was told that she would receive a lower grade in the class for not participating. Graham explained her position by saying that she was "not squeamish. I'm just against the idea of raising pigs, crawfish, frogs or any animals for use in high school biology class" ("A Teen Fights for Frog Rights and Bio May Never Be the Same" 1987). Eventually, Graham and her parents sued the school board at Victor Valley High School in Victorville, California, over the issue. They won the case, and Graham's grade of "C" in biology was changed to an "A" ("Jennifer Graham" 2012).

As of late 2012, 10 states have laws that allow high school students to decline to participate in dissections and to use alternative exercises in their place. Those states are California, Florida, Illinois, New Jersey, New York, Oregon, Pennsylvania, Rhode Island, Vermont, and Virginia. In addition two other states, Maine and Louisiana, have other types of provisions that allow students to opt out of dissection exercises. According to the website Animalearn, even students who live in states with no legislation on the issue have ways of avoiding dissection exercises. For more details, see http://www.animalearn.org/highSchoolLaws.php.

Industries Respond

One of the most fundamental debates in the field of animal experimentation involves the use of animals in testing for cosmetics and other nonmedical products. One might very well argue that animal testing is essential for the development of medical products and procedures that save human lives. But are the same arguments applicable to the development of products designed to make men and women more attractive or simply more comfortable with their own physical appearance? Until relatively recently, virtually all cosmetics, health care, household, and other commercial products were tested for safety on animals such as rabbits, rats, mice, and guinea pigs. How did this practice begin?

Prior to the 1930s, companies were allowed to market virtually any such product and make virtually any claims it chose to without government intervention of any kind. In the United States, the Pure Food and Drug Act of 1906 provided general guidelines for the marketing of safe pharmaceutical products, but that act had almost nothing to say about nonmedical products, such as hair dye, face powder, toothpaste, hair renewal products, and the like. A number of events occurred in the 1930s that changed that situation.

One such event involved the use of a type of mascara that could be used on a relatively permanent basis. A woman shaved off or plucked her eyebrows and then painted on the permanent mascara. One of the most popular brands of this permanent mascara had the trade name Lash Lure. The active ingredient in the product—the ingredient that provided the black color for the mascara—was a chemical known as p-phenylenediamine, a derivative of coal tar. Today, p-phenylenediamine is known as an allergen (a substance that produces allergic reactions), although it has not been found to be toxic, carcinogenic, or harmful to human health in any way. In the 1930s, however, a number of women who used the product had severe reactions to the product, partly because the manufacturer used up to 30 times the amount of p-phenylenediamine known to be safe to use. These reactions resulted in the formation of blisters and abscesses on the face that in some cases were so severe as to cause blindness and, in at least one case, death ("Mrs. Brown's Sad Story" 2012; "Lash Lure" 2012).

Lash Lure was by no means the only mascara-type product for whom reactions were observed. Nor was mascara the only cosmetic for which medical problems were being reported. For example, a product containing the heavy metal thallium called Koremlu was being marketed in the 1930s as a treatment for ringworm and as a depilatory (a product for the removal of hair). Although thallium had long been known for its toxic and carcinogenic effects, the U.S. Food and Drug Administration (FDA) had no authority to control its production and sale. As of 1934, 692 cases of thallium poisoning, including at least 31 deaths, had been attributed to the use of Koremlu ("Mrs. Brown's Sad Story" 2012; Daubert 2012).

By the mid-1930s, health problems associated with the use of untested cosmetic and household products had reached such a level that the U.S. Congress decided it had to deal with the issue. In 1938, it adopted the Federal Food, Drug, and Cosmetic Act (FFDCA) to replace the 30-year-old Pure Food and Drug Act of 1906. The FFDCA made a number of fundamental changes to the nation's testing laws for a wide range of products. With regard to cosmetics and household products, the law authorized the FDA to conduct inspections of factories at which such products were being made and to adopt such regulations as were necessary to ensure that products reaching the marketplace were both safe and efficacious ("Food, Drug, and Cosmetic Act of 1938" 2012).

One of the steps taken by the FDA, as authorized by the FFDCA, was the development of a standard test for the allergic or toxic effect of a substance on the human body. In 1944 an employee of the FDA, Dr. John H. Draize, developed such a test, now known as the *Draize test*. The Draize test involves the insertion of a measured amount of the substance being tested (usually 0.5 gram of 0.5 milliliter) into the eye of a test animal. The test animal most commonly used is the rabbit, although other animals also have been used in tests. Rabbits are the animal of choice because they tend not to produce very many tears, so the inserted substance is not washed out during the test. The test most commonly uses albino rabbits that are specially bred for this type of research.

The animal remains conscious during the test and is restrained during the experiment. The eye is then washed out and the animal is observed over some period of time (anywhere from a few hours to 14 days) to determine any redness, swelling, discharge, ulceration, hemorrhaging, cloudiness, blindness, or other abnormality in the tested eye. Researchers assign a score to the amount of damaged caused by the substance being tested to indicate its degree of allergenicity or toxicity. If no effect is observed, the animal may be used again for additional tests. If damage to the eye or surrounding skin is observed, the animal is euthanized (Wilhelmus 2001).

The Draize test was one of the first laboratory procedures targeted by animal rights groups in the 1970s and 1980s, partly because of questions about its applicability to humans, partly because of the pain and suffering it caused animals, and (probably) partly because the rabbit was viewed by most people as a soft and cuddly animal, one that should not be exposed to experimentation. Indeed, animal rights groups have selected a stylized rabbit as the logo for so-called cruelty-free commercial products that have been tested without the use of live animals. The first company to disavow the use of the Draize test in testing its products was Avon, famous for its "Avon calling" slogan of the time. The organization PETA picked up on that slogan and began a new campaign against Draize testing called "Avon killing." Largely as the result of that campaign, Avon announced in 1989 that it would discontinue the use of animals in its testing program. Avon was soon followed by two other cosmetics giants, Estée Lauder and Mary Kay, and, after a somewhat longer period of time, nearly all of the major cosmetic producers in the world. Only recently, however, the success of the PETA campaign has come into question, as all of these companies appear once more to have reverted to the use of animals in their product testing, apparently in response to requirements by the Chinese government for the testing of commercial products sold in that country ("Avon, Mary Kay, Estée Lauder Paying for Tests on Animals" 2012).

Over time, certain other manufacturers have also decided to eschew the use of animals in the testing of their products. In some ways, one of the most significant of those decisions was made by General Motors in 1993, when they decided not to use live animals any longer in their crash tests ("The Impact of Crash Test Dummies in Automobile Safety" 2010). Prior to that time, the company had used thousands of animals to determine the effects on an animal by crashing it into a barrier at various rates of speed. The most common animal used in these experiments was the pig because of its similarity in anatomy and physiology to the human ("19,000 Animals Killed in Automotive Crash Tests" 1991).

Today, the laws on using animals in product testing differ from region to region. The controlling agency in the United States, the FDA, notes that it "does not specifically require the use of animals in testing cosmetics for safety," and neither does it have any restrictions that prevent the use of animals, provided that the conditions of the Animal Welfare Act are observed ("Animal Testing" 2002). Three states have adopted cruelty-free laws: California (2000), New Jersey (2007), and New York (2008). A number of other states have considered but not yet adopted such laws. In general, these laws tend to require companies to use alternative other than animals except in those cases where no suitable alternative are available ("Laws on Product Testing" 2012).

Legislation in Europe for the development of animal-free product testing dates to 1976 with the adoption of Council Directive 76/768, the so-called Cosmetics Directive. The goal of that directive was to ensure the free circulation of safe cosmetics within the European marketplace. That directive has now been amended seven times, in each case with somewhat more severe restrictions on the use of animals in testing procedures. In 2004, one of those amendments placed a ban on the production and sale of any finished cosmetic that had been tested on animals, while another amendment in 2009 extended that ban to any ingredient used in the manufacture of a cosmetic. The regulatory process in Europe has been determined to a considerable extent by the technology available. Bans on testing have not been adopted (or have been adopted but not enforced) simply because alternatives to animal testing have not been available. The most recent amendment, adopted in August 2009, foresees a period probably no more than a few years into the future, when sufficient alternatives will be available to permit a complete and effective ban on all use of animals in product testing in Europe. Thus far, no country or region anywhere in the world has progressed to this point in dealing with animal testing of cosmetic and household products (Abbott 2009).

Researchers Fight Back

As the above discussion illustrates, the 1960s, 1970s, and 1980s were a difficult time for researchers who wished to use animals in their experiments. Both public opinions and legislative actions were making their lives and work more difficult. They did not sit idly by, however, and ignore the threat posed to their work by animal welfare and animal rights organizations. An example of the type of action taken by researchers and the organizations that supported them was revealed in 1989, when a plan of action developed within the AMA was leaked to a number of animal rights groups. The plan outlined a program for redefining the ground rules of the debate between researchers and animal rights groups and an action plan designed to carry out the new initiative. The basic principle of the plan was "to peel away the outermost layers of support and isolate the hardcore activists from the general public and shrink the size of the sympathizers." Researchers need to show that animal activists are "not only anti-science but also a) *responsible for violent and illegal acts* that endanger life and property and b) a threat to the public's freedom of choice" ("AMA Animal Research Plan" 1989; italics in original).

The 11-page plan then went into great detail explaining how the AMA and its allies could carry out this program. The General Strategy portion of the plan consisted of 13 objectives, such as:

- Change the public agenda from "Animals in Research" to "Advancing Biomedical Research"

- Combat emotion with emotion (e.g., "fuzzy" animals contrasted with "healing" children)
- Mobilize physicians and federation of medicine [*sic*] with AMA in the lead role *Identify animal rights activists as antiscience and against medical progress.* ("AMA Animal Research Plan" 1989; italics in original)

The more than 70 specific objectives were divided into about a half dozen general categories, such as enhancement of public education programs to counter animal welfare and animal rights "propaganda"; educational programs aimed especially at children and teachers; education and mobilization of physicians, biomedical researchers, scientists, and other stakeholders; development of legal strategies to use against animal welfare and animal rights groups and individuals; and creation of multidisciplinary coalitions to promote the benefits of animal experimentation ("AMA Animal Research Plan" 1989).

The AMA action plan, although not originally planned for public disclosure, was hardly a surprise to anyone who was familiar with the medical association's view on animal experimentation. In just the previous year, for example, the AMA had conducted a survey of its members to determine their attitudes about animal research. In that survey, 99 percent of respondents have agreed with the statement that animal experimentation had contributed to medical progress, 96 percent supported the use of animals for drug testing, and 93 percent supported the use of animals in programs of medical education (Loeb et al. 1989). Nor did this survey represent a change of heart by American physicians. A similar survey conducted a half century earlier in 1948 produced essentially the same results, with almost unanimous approval of all aspects of animal testing in research (Resolution 109 2012).

The AMA put the opinions expressed in its 1989 survey in more formal terms during its annual meeting held in June 1990. At that meeting, members of the House of Delegates unanimously adopted a resolution strongly supporting the "appropriate and humane" use of animals in research and encouraging physicians to educate their patients, community groups, and legislators about the need for additional animal experimentation (Merz 1990).

At the same meeting, the members of the House of Delegates also adopted a second resolution, condemning the efforts of an organization called Physicians Committee for Responsible Medicine (PCRM). PCRM was founded in 1985 by Neal D. Barnard, a psychiatrist employed by the George Washington University School of Medicine for the purpose of promoting a plant-based (vegan) diet and the elimination of animals in scientific and biomedical research. PCRM has been the subject of intense criticism from the medical community and other organizations since its founding, with some observers pointing out that fewer than 5 percent of its members are actually physicians ("Physicians Committee for Responsible Medicine" 2012). The 1990 AMA resolution registered "strong objections" to the PCRM's implications that physicians who support the use of animals in research are "irresponsible," for misrepresenting the critical role that animals play in the evolution of new biomedical knowledge, and for obscuring the "overwhelming support" that animal research had among physicians in the United States (Resolutions 1990, 392). PCRM continues to operate today with a membership of 150,000 "health care professionals and concerned citizens." Dr. Barnard continues to serve as chair of the organization, and the battle between PCRM and animal-testing advocates continues unabated in the first decade of the twenty-first century ("State Sen. Chip Rogers and PCRM" 2010).

Of course, physicians were by no means the only group who reacted to the aggressive attack of antivivisectionists in the 1980s and beyond. Another organization that began to speak out strongly in support of animal experimentation during the period was the National Association for Biomedical Research (NABR). The NABR was founded in 1979 as the Research Animal Alliance (RAA) in response to proposed legislation offered by Representative Frederick W. Richmond (D-NY). Representative

Richmond's bill would have allocated up to half of all the research money allotted by the U.S. Congress annually to be spent on the search for alternatives to animal testing (H.R. 4805). Faced with a devastating loss of revenue from the federal government, animal researchers and their supporters banded together to defeat Richmond's bill and to educate members of the U.S. Congress about the benefits of animal research and the need to continue funding research that uses live animals. The RAA was established with that goal in mind.

In 1981, the RAA changed its name to the Association for Biomedical Research (ABR), and in 1984 it moved its offices from Boston to Washington, D.C., to facilitate its lobbying activities. A year later, in 1985, ABR merged with a much older organization, the NSMR (see above), which had been in existence since 1945, fighting for the use of animals in scientific and biomedical research. The new organization took the name of the National Association for Biomedical Research. Since its founding, the NABR has been remarkably successful in making its case for animal testing before the U.S. Congress and various regulatory agencies. One of its first accomplishments was its support of the Animal Enterprise Protection Act of 1992, which criminalized the interference of any "animal enterprise." NABR was also an important force in the adoption of the Animal Enterprise Terrorism Act of 2006, an updating and expansion of the 1992 act.

The NABR has also made its influence felt in preventing the adoption of laws that it feels would interfere with the use of animals in research. For example, it was largely responsible for the defeat of the Consumer Products Safe Testing Act of 1989 and the Information Dissemination and Research Accountability Act of 1989, both of which would have placed what the NABR considered to be onerous restrictions on the use of live animals in research. It also spearheaded efforts by the research committee to obtain an exemption for rats, mice, and birds from the Animal Welfare Act that controls the housing, care, and use of experimental animals (National Association of Biomedical Research 2012, 7).

Another successful group lobbying in support of the use of animals in research is Americans for Medical Progress (AMP), founded in 1991 for the purpose of "protecting society's investment in research by nurturing public understanding of and support for the humane and necessary use of animals in medicine." The organization offers news and information to the general public and the scientific community on animal experimentation issues, lobbies governmental agencies on all levels on animal use issues, attempts to change public opinion about animal testing, and issues an electronic newsletter and other print and electronic publications on animal experimentation issues.

In addition to national organizations like the NABR and AMP, a number of state and regional organizations have been established to promote the case for the use of animals in scientific and biomedical research. In virtually all cases, these organizations were formed in the early 1980s in response to a perceived threat that public and legislative action would impose intolerable restrictions on animal testing. The statement of purpose of the Michigan Society for Medical Research (MISMR), founded in 1981, provides an example. The organization was created, its website says, in order to better educate the general public about the nature of biomedical research and the essential role of animal testing in that research. MISMR attempts to carry out its mission primarily through the development and publication of a newsletter that focuses on specific issues, such as medical devices, diabetes, cancer, and pain management (Michigan Society for Medical Research 2012). Other states and regions with active pro-animal testing programs include California, Connecticut, Massachusetts, New Jersey, North Carolina, Ohio, Pennsylvania, Texas, Wisconsin, and the Northwest and Southwest regions.

The International Scene

Partially for reasons of space, this book has focused on developments in the field of animal experimentation in the United

Kingdom and United States. However, similar movements can be traced to other countries, many of which have strong and active antivivisectionists and pro-animal-testing groups today. To cite just a few examples of the former:

- ADDA, la Asociación Defensa Derechos Animal, was the first animal welfare organization founded in Spain in 1976. Its headquarters are currently in Barcelona.
- The Finnish association, Animalia, was established in 1961.
- The German organization, Deutscher Tierschutzbund, is one of the oldest animal welfare organizations in the world, having been founded in 1881. Today, it consists of 16 state associations and more than 700 individual animal societies.
- The Danish group Forsøgsdyrenes Værn was created in 1963 and now has about 18,000 members.
- The Czech association, Svoboda zvírat, was founded in 1998 and currently has about 200 members in five regional groups.
- One Voice is a French animal welfare organization devoted to the abolition of animal experimentation. It was founded in 1995 and currently has about 15,000 members.
- Djurens Rätt is the largest animal welfare organization in Scandinavia, founded in 1882 with the mission of ending animal testing. Today it has a membership of about 36,000 and has its headquarters in Älvsjö.

The seven organizations listed here are about a third of the total membership of the European Coalition to End Animal Experiments (ECEAE), which was created in 1990 to work for the banning of animal testing of cosmetics and household products. Today, the organization has a somewhat broader campaign with the fundamental goal of eliminating animal testing in virtually all forms of scientific and biomedical research.

Animal welfare groups are considerably less common, but not unheard of, in most other parts of the world. For example, the Asian Animal Protection Network (AAPN) was created by physician John Wedderburn, who retired to Hong Kong from his original home in Scotland in 1987. Influenced by his vegan son, Wedderburn went on to develop a network of individuals who were interested in animal welfare issues and formally incorporated AAPN in 2000. The organization remains a somewhat loose confederation of like-minded individuals concerned about a host of animal welfare issues, include animal testing, zoos, vegetarian and vegan issues, wildlife habitats, traditional medicine, and general education about animal rights issues.

One of the most influential animal rights organizations in Africa is Animal Rights Africa (ARA), formed in 2008 through the consolidation of three older animal welfare groups, Justice for Animals, Xwe African Wild Life and South Africans for the Abolition of Vivisection. ARA has a somewhat different and broader focus than do most animal welfare groups, working on topics ranging from the abolition of animal experimentation to abuses of the ivory trade to the use of animals for circuses and zoos to the trophy-hunting industry. As of late 2012, the organization's main campaigns deal with issues such as an end to whaling, protection of captive elephants, animal-testing policies, ethical conservation, and poaching.

Animal-Testing Statistics

Statistics on the number and kind of animals used in research are collected annually in both the United Kingdom and the United States. These data are required by prevailing animal welfare laws in both countries.

In the United States, the total number of research animals as counted by the USDA Animal and Plant Health Inspection Service (APHIS) has fallen from a total of 1,653,345 in 1973 (the first year for which data were collected) to 1,101,958 in 2004 (the last year for which data have been published). An important caveat about these data is that they do not include numbers for rats, mice, and birds, which are not covered by the Animal Welfare Act and are, therefore, not counted by APHIS. This number is of some consequence because experts estimate that anywhere from 90 to 95 percent of all animals used in research fall into this "not counted" area (Cohen 2006). The numbers for all species tabulated by APHIS fell significantly during the period from 1973 to 2004 with the exception of the number of primates, which rose from 42,298 in 1973 to 54,998 in 2004 (*Animal Care Annual Report of Activities* 2008, 45). (For a complete report of statistics over this period, see chapter 5, table 5.4.)

Data from the United Kingdom are not directly comparable to those from the United States because of the systems of classification used in each country. According to the most recent data from the British Home Office (2008), by far the most popular animals used in scientific and biomedical research are those species not counted in the United States: rats, mice, and birds. The numbers of such animals used for research have fallen from about 860,000 for rats in 1998 to 355,000 in 2008, and for birds from 269,000 in 1998 to 123,000 in 2008. By contrast, the number of mice used during the same period rose from 1,850,000 in 1998 to 2,418,000 in 2008. The overall number of research animals used in the United Kingdom during this period rose slightly from 3,480,300 in 1998 to 3,563,100 in 2008 (British Home Office 2008, table 20).

Statistics from the EU also differ from those from both the United States and United Kingdom for a variety of reasons, two of which include the method of classifying animals and the number of nations reporting data over the years. In general, the trends indicate that, as elsewhere in the world, rodents are by far the most common subjects of experimentation with mice accounting for 59.3 percent of all research subjects in the most recent reporting year (2008), followed by rats (17.7%), cold-blooded animals (9.2%), rabbits (2.8%), and guinea pigs (1.8%). Carnivores (such as cats and dogs) accounted for about 0.26 percent of all research subjects, and nonhuman primates,

0.08 percent ("Commission Staff Working Document" 2010, 10, figure 1.1). The totals for rodents has remained about constant from 1996 to 2008, while the percentage of cold-blooded animals used in research has decreased slightly, matched by a slight corresponding increase in the number of birds used in research ("Commission Staff Working Document" 2010, 11). The total number of animals used in research in the 27 reporting states of the EU in 2008 was 12,001,022, a small decrease of 116,559 over numbers reported from the same countries three years earlier in 2005 ("Commission Staff Working Document" 2010, 12, table 1.0).

Statistics on the number of experimental animals used in Canada are tabulated and released annually. These reports date to 1996 and are available on the Internet at http://www.ccac.ca/ en_/publications/audf/stats-aud/data-2010/analysis-2010. In the most recent report (2010), the largest number of animals used in research were fish, with 1,416,042 having been used for research in the preceding year. A major contribution to that number was the more than half million fish used in invasive-cod studies in the country. The next most commonly used animals were mice, rats, domestic birds, and wild Canadian animals. These species accounted for 93 percent of the 3,311,083 animals used in research in Canada in 2010 ("Animal Use Statistics" 2012).

Statistics for Australia and New Zealand comparable to those provided are available from Humane Research Australia (http:// www.humaneresearch.org.au/statistics/) and National Animal Ethics Advisory Committee (http://www.biosecurity.govt.nz/ files/regs/animal-welfare/pubs/naeac/naeac-ar-10.pdf; appendix 7). Data from most other countries are difficult to obtain or nonexistent.

Alternatives to Animal Testing

One of the most enduring contributions of the Russell and Burch book on the three Rs of animal experimentation was the emphasis on developing alternatives to the use of animals in research. In its simplest form, that argument was that the most direct way of resolving the debate over the use of animals in research was to find other ways to test chemicals that did not require the use of animals at all. The approach was significant because it involved individuals and organizations *opposed* to animal experimentation beginning to work *with* researchers to find ways of reducing the number of animals used in research. Only three years after *The Principles of Humane Experimental Technique* was published, an important first step in that direction occurred with the establishment of the Lawson Tait Trust in the United Kingdom. The trust was formed through the joint efforts of three antivivisection groups, the BUAV, the NAVS, and the Scottish Society for the Prevention of Vivisection. (The Lawson Tait Trust eventually evolved into its modern-day counterpart, the Humane Research Trust.)

The concept of finding alternatives for animal testing grew slowly in the United Kingdom (as it did elsewhere in the world). In 1965, a special commission appointed to study the status of the 1876 Cruelty to Animals Act (the Littlewood Committee) was not optimistic about finding alternatives for animal testing. It said in its final report that it had received reports about the search for such alternatives, but it was not convinced that they were observing a trend. "Discoveries of adequate substitutes for animal tests have, however, so far been uncommon," the report concluded, "and we have not been encouraged to believe that they are likely to be more frequent in the future" (Stephens, Goldberg, and Rowan 2001, 124).

And indeed, the next few years appeared to confirm that belief. In 1969, a bored London housewife, Dorothy Hegarty, and a research biologist, Charles Foister, founded a charity whose goal it was to find alternatives to animal testing (AATs). The organization the Fund for the Replacement of Animals in Medical Experiments (FRAME) got its beginning with a £100 grant that allowed Hegarty and Foister to work on their project out of the living room in Hegarty's home. Today, FRAME continues to operate with a budget of nearly a million pounds annually ("Financial Review" 2012). At about the same time, a comparable foundation was established by NAVS in the name of Air Chief Marshall the Lord Dowding, who was at the time president of NAVS. The fund is now part of a consortium that also consists of NAVS and Animal Defenders International. It claims to have made grants of about £2 million over its lifetime ("The Lord Dowding Fund for Humane Research" 2012).

Antivivisectionists in the United States followed their British counterparts in the search for alternatives to animal research. The first scientific meeting sponsored by a major governmental agency on the topic was held in Washington, D.C., on October 22–23, 1975, hosted by the Institute of Animal Resources of the U.S. National Academy of Sciences (Schneider 1976). One consequence of this early history of interest in alternatives to animal research was the filing of H.R. 4805, the Research Modernization Act, in the U.S. House of Representatives in 1979. As noted above, research institutions mounted pressure against the act, which was never reported out of committee.

By the early 1980s, both government and industry had begun to see the handwriting on the wall: the search for AATs was not an ephemeral fringe activity undertaken by a handful of emotional researchers and laypersons. It was likely to be the wave of the future in which everyone with a stake in the research process needed to become involved. Reflecting this change in mood, the Cosmetic, Toiletry, and Fragrance Association made a $1 million grant in 1981 to Johns Hopkins University for the creation of a Center for Alternatives to Animal Testing (CAAT). The mission of the new institute was "to develop basic scientific knowledge necessary to create innovative non-whole animal methods for evaluating the safety and efficacy of commercial and therapeutic products" ("CAAT History" 2012). CAAT has grown to become the preeminent center of research on alternative testing procedures in the United States with European branches at CAAT-Europe and the Transatlantic Think Tank of Toxicology (t^4).

At the same time, the federal government finally began to act to force industry to think more seriously about AATs. Mention of the topic begins to occur in amendments adopted to the 1966 Animal Welfare Act and, more specifically, in the Health Research Extension Act of 1985 in which funds are provided for research on the identification and development of AAT (U.S. Congress. Office of Technology Assessment. 1986, 291).

Again, the emphasis on developing AATs was not restricted to the United Kingdom and the United States. In 1977, for example, the Animal Protection Law adopted in the Netherlands provided funds for research on the development of alternatives to animal experimentation, the Swedish government allocated funds for research in the field in 1979, the Swiss government allocated 2 million Swiss francs for research in 1983, and the government of West Germany enacted new laws requiring research on AATs in 1986. More comprehensively, various divisions of the EU have adopted resolutions dating as far back as 1971 urging or requiring member states to take more aggressive action in the development of alternative for animal testing (Stephens, Goldberg, and Rowan 2001, 125–129).

Progress in AATs

So what can be said about progress in the search for AATs after more than three decades of research on the topic? The answer is, a very great deal, indeed! A number of organizations interested in alternatives to animal testing now maintain websites that provide information to and extensive examples of AATs for researchers in particular as well as for the general public. One such resource is Altweb, the global clearinghouse for information on alternatives to animal testing, maintained by the Centers for Alternatives to Animal Testing. The clearinghouse provides an extensive database in which researchers can search for specific alternatives to existing animal-based tests, as well as information about AATs in educational settings from kindergarten through college (Altweb Resources 2012). Another resource that focuses on alternatives in the field of cosmetic and household product testing is the European Centre for the Validation of Alternative Methods (ECVAAM; http://ihcp .jrc.ec.europa.eu/our_activities/alt-animal-testing/). The U.S. National Library of Medicine also has an excellent searchable database at http://toxnet.nlm.nih.gov/altbib.html. And a general, global clearinghouse for virtually all databases on AATs is available from the Norwegian Reference Centre for Laboratory Science Animal Science & Alternatives at http:// oslovet.norecopa.no/databasesintro.html.

The many databases of information that are available are organized in different ways, depending on target audiences and an organization's own predilection for arranging the available data. In many cases, they may be arranged to conform with the principle of the three Rs, with available resources categorized as animal *replacement, reduction,* or *refinement* procedures. In the first category are all those procedures in which no animal— or at least no sentient or no nonhuman animal—is used in an experiment. The most obvious approach for such alternative is to use in vitro rather than in vivo procedures. The expression *in vitro* refers to procedures that take place outside the bodies of living organisms, such as in test tubes or flasks, and comes from the Latin words for "in glass." By contrast, the term *in vivo* refers to procedures that take place within a living organism and comes from the Latin term for "in life."

An example of in vitro technology currently in use is the EpiSkin test, developed the L'Oréal company as a replacement for animal testing of cosmetics. The test takes advantage of extensive advances in the field of tissue engineering, in which tissues found in living organisms are reproduced or replicated in a laboratory setting. Tissue engineering has been the subject of scientific research for many decades and has now become a very sophisticated technology. The synthetic skin produced by the L'Oréal process can be modified to produce forms that are similar to young human skin, older human skin, skin that has been exposed to sunlight, and other special forms of human skin. These synthetic skins can then be exposed to chemicals being considered as components of skin creams, powders, makeup, and other types of cosmetics. Not only does this form of testing save animal lives, but it also tends to produce more reliable and valid results than does animal testing (Jacquot 2007).

Another example of an in vitro substitution for animal testing is the so-called IC_{50} test. This test replaces a very old laboratory procedure used to predict the toxicity of some substance. A group of experimental animals is exposed to the substance in some way (is fed the substance or has the substance applied to its skin, for example), and the amount of substance used is gradually increased over time. The amount of the substances required to kill half of the laboratory animals is called the LD_{50} ("lethal dose" for 50% of the population) value. This measure provides an indication of the potential risk posed by the substance. The problem is, of course, that large numbers of animals must be killed to obtain this number.

A different approach is to test the substance on cells or tissues grown on a petri dish, in a test tube, or in some other "glass" environment. The results obtained from such tests is known as the IC_{50} value for the substance, an acronym that stands for the "inhibitory concentration" of a substance, the amount of that substance that will reduce the growth of some material (cells, tissue, or microorganism, for example) by half. Some studies have shown that IC_{50} not only offers the advantage of saving animals lives but is actually a better predictor of the risk posed by a substance to human cells and tissue than is the traditional LD_{50} based on experiments with rats, mice, guinea pigs, and other animals (Paris et al. 2012).

At an even more distant remove from live-animal testing is the use of computer programs to simulate the behavior of living systems. Such systems are sometimes called in silico, meaning "in the silicon chips that make up computing systems." An example of such systems is the PhysioLab program developed by the Entelos Corporation of San Mateo, California. This program can be adapted to model human anatomical and physiological systems with a high degree of precision. The models can then be used to determine the changes that will occur if certain substances are added to the human body. This process completely obviates the need for living organisms of any kind and has been shown to be at least as valid, if not more so, in predicting the use of drugs, cosmetics, and other substances on the human body as are animal tests. (See the Entelos website at http://www.entelos.com/.)

Another computerized approach to the testing of substances is sometimes called *toxicogenomics*. This process attempts to answer questions such as what effect will a given substance have on the way a gene is expressed (or not expressed) in humans and how do variations in dosage affect gene expression? In principle, computer models of gene expression in humans can answer such questions far more precisely and accurately than can the use of experimental animals. (See, for example, Wills and Mitchell 2009.)

One of the most promising uses of computer models as a replacement for animal testing is in education. A number of programs are now available that allow students to follow and/ or take part in the process of animal dissection without ever encountering a live or dead mouse, rat, guinea pig, worm, or other organism. A computer program can display all the components of the organism to be studied, and students can carry out essentially the identical procedures traditionally involved with dissection. One of the best known examples of this approach is Digital Frog, a company that describes itself as an organization whose corporate headquarters is "a converted barn surrounded by frogs, dogs and bogs in rural Ontario, Canada." The company has been producing computerized versions of the traditional frog dissection experiment familiar to many high school biology students since 1995. It claims that its Digital Frog is superior to the traditional wet-lab dissection because it allows a more completely integrated system of text, computerized laboratory work, and other elements to learning about frog and human anatomy. (See Digital Frog International at http://www.digitalfrog.com/index.html.)

Yet another approach to the development of alternatives to animal testing is the use of nonsentient organisms. The term *nonsentient* refers to organisms that are not capable of experiencing pain and suffering. The presumption has long been that it is morally acceptable to use such animals in research because they do not suffer the same unpleasant consequences of experimentation as do sentient organisms. The founder of the modern animal welfare movement, Peter Singer, for example, argues that nonsentient animals can legitimately be used in research because they do not suffer from the experience and, in fact, they are probably not even aware of the damage to which they are subjected ("Moral Status of Animals" 2012).

An interesting question that arises from this position, however, is what organisms can be said to be nonsentient and therefore legitimate candidates for research? One might feel safe using the simplest of all animals, such as the amoeba, paramecium, or hydra, because they lack a nervous system through which pain messages can be transmitted. For example, the hydra has already been used as a test organism in the detection and measurement of environmental pollutants. As simple as it is, it has a number of characteristics similar to those of humans, and the effects of substances such as pollutants on its body structure are easily measured. (See, for example, Ghaskadbi and Patwardhan 2012, 122–124.) It is not clear whether or not animal welfare proponents object to the use of hydra as an alternative to other animals in conducting such tests.

But where can one draw the line in limiting research to nonsentient animals? At one time, there was probably a consensus that "simple" animals such as fruit flies, anemones, and mosquitoes might be considered "fair game" as research subjects. But research reported over the last few decades challenges even this view, with increasing evidence that even these "simplest" of all animals may feel some type of pain and suffering. For example, the longtime view that fish can safely be used for most kinds of research has been challenged by the discovery that their bodies contain receptors for substance P, a chemical found in vertebrates (including humans) that acts as a carrier for pain messages (Chandroo, Duncan, and Moccia 2004; also see Mather 2011; Smith 1991).

The Ongoing Debate over Animal Experimentation

The story line of the debate between researchers and antivivisectionists told above ends in the 1990s. What has happened since that time? For the most part, this argument has become considerably more sophisticated than it was in the nineteenth and twentieth centuries, with many individuals and organizations on opposite sides of the debate often taking somewhat more modified views. For example, many pro- and antivivisectionists now accept the three Rs as an underlying given for all animal research. But to a considerable extent, the war goes on. What are the fundamental arguments in favor of and in opposition to the use of animals in research in the early twenty first century?

Arguments in Opposition to Animal Experimentation

The following are the primary arguments offered in opposition to animal experimentation. As has become clear in the above discussion, various individuals and organizations subscribe to each of these arguments to various degrees, and it is often difficult to say how widely any one argument would receive support from the antivivisectionist community.

- The life of any animal has intrinsic value that may be equal to that of a human but, in any case, is worthy of consideration. No animal should be subjected to procedures that cause extreme pain and suffering, that produce debilitating physical consequences, or that result in the animal's death. Some opponents of animal testing may accept exceptions to this general principle, agreeing, for example, that animal testing may be necessary in certain circumstances when no other options are available and the use of animals may result in profound benefits to human health or the health of other nonhuman animals.

- In any case, animal testing is never justified when the purpose of an experimentation is the development of cosmetics, household products, or other substances that do not contribute to the health and well-being of humans.

- The anatomy, physiology, and biochemistry of test animals are sufficiently different from those of humans that results obtained from animal testing may not be valid for humans. Extensive data exist to indicate that many substances found to be both efficacious and safe when used with laboratory animals do not pass the same tests with humans. The AAVS argues that 9 out of 10 drugs that appear to be promising as the result of animal trials fail when then subjected to similar trials with humans ("Problems with Animal Research" 2012). More troubling, perhaps, is the possibility that substances that *have* passed animal trials then go on to produce unanticipated side effects in humans. These side effects may pose life-threatening conditions that animal testing did not predict (Allen 2012; also see Croce 2012).

- The stress that animals experience when exposed to research procedures may further invalidate the results obtained from such experiments. Research indicates that many species of animals experience sufficient levels of stress to induce changes in their physiological responses to the environment, such as raising the concentration of stress hormones, diminishing the concentration of sex hormones, and producing changes in the animal's immune system. Such changes may, of course, produce research results that are not typical of the unstressed animal itself, let alone human responses to a tested substance. Indeed, regulatory agencies often provide very specific instructions about the care of animals to reduce to the extent possible the effect of stress on animal-testing results (Baldwin 2012; Reinhardt 2002, Introduction).

- Animal testing is a very expensive procedure. Housing, feeding, breeding, and maintaining animals, as well as their actual use in research, can be very high. Although authorities differ as to the actual costs of animal testing, at least one organization has set that number at about $16 billion per year in funding by the U.S. government of animal experimentation ("More than $16 Billion in Taxpayer Money Wasted Annually on Animal Testing" 2012).

Arguments in Favor of Animal Experimentation

The arguments in favor of animal testing have, again, been relatively well laid out above.

- The use of animals has produced huge benefits to human health in the past and is likely to do so in the future. Researchers typically cite a long list of diseases for which preventative or therapeutic procedures have been developed as the results of animal testing, including such major problems as cancer, HIV/AIDS, heart disease and stroke, diabetes, Parkinson's disease, hepatitis, birth defects, epilepsy, spinal cord injuries, cystic fibrosis, and a host of infectious diseases ("Animal Research Means Medical Progress" 2012).

- Virtually all researchers today subscribe to the three Rs principle as a guide to their use of animals in experimentation. However, they insist that there are still many circumstances in which the use of animals is essential in research, and that cell and tissue models, computer models, and other alternative forms of research cannot provide the data needed to answer biomedical questions.

- In contrast to the critics of animal testing, the anatomy, physiology, and biochemistry of nonhuman animals is often similar enough to that of humans so that the results of tests with nonhuman animals *can* be extrapolated to humans. Probably the best evidence for that position is the record of success in using nonhuman animals to produce new treatments for disease in the past.

- Animal testing is valuable not only for solving health and medical problems for humans but also for solving such problems for other species of animals, such as farm animals and pets.

- Researchers also hold a different moral view of the value of nonhuman life than do antivivisectionists. Although they may care deeply about animals, most researchers do not necessarily believe that their animal subjects are the moral equal of humans or that have "rights" of their own.

Bibliography

Abbott, Allison. "The Lowdown on Animal Testing for Cosmetics." *Nature*, March 11, 2009. http://www.nature.com/news/2009/090311/full/news.2009.147.html. Accessed August 2, 2009.

Allen, Arthur. "Of Mice and Men." June 1, 2006. *Slate*. http://www.slate.com/articles/health_and_science/medical_examiner/2006/06/of_mice_or_men.html. Accessed August 9, 2012.

"Altweb Resources." Center for Alternatives to Animal Testing. http://altweb.jhsph.edu/resources/. Accessed August 6, 2012.

"AMA Animal Research Plan." June 1989. http://issuu.com/conflictgypsy/docs/amaactionplan?mode=window&viewMode=doublePage. Accessed August 2, 2012.

Animal Care Annual Report of Activities. Fiscal Year 2007. September 2008. Washington, DC: U.S. Department of Agriculture, Animal and Plant Health Inspection Service. http://www.aphis.usda.gov/publications/animal_welfare/content/printable_version/2007_AC_Report.pdf. Accessed August 5, 2012.

"Animal Experiments: Overview." People for the Ethical Treatment of Animals. http://www.peta.org/issues/animals -used-for-experimentation/animal-experiments-overview .aspx. Accessed July 25, 2012.

"Animal Research Means Medical Progress." Americans for Medical Progress. http://www.amprogress.org/animal -research-benefits/. Accessed August 9, 2012.

"Animal Testing." 2002. U.S. Food and Drug Administration. http://www.fda.gov/Cosmetics/ProductandIngredient Safety/ProductTesting/ucm072268.htm. Accessed August 2, 2012.

"Animal Use Statistics." Canadian Council on Animal Care. http://www.ccac.ca/en_/publications/audf. Accessed August 6, 2012.

"Animal Welfare Act." U.S. Department of Agriculture. National Agricultural Library. http://awic.nal.usda.gov/ government-and-professional-resources/federal-laws/animal -welfare-act. Accessed July 25, 2012.

"Animal Welfare Act: Historical Perspectives and Future Directions." http://www.nal.usda.gov/awic/pubs/96symp/ awasymp.htm#Schwindaman. Accessed July 25, 2012.

"Animal Wrongs." http://www.animalwrongs.com/quotes/. Accessed July 29, 2012.

The Animals' Defender and Zoophilist. Vols. 16–17. 1896–1897. National Anti-Vivisection Society (Great Britain). http:// books.google.com/books?id=5FrJAAAAMAAJ. Accessed July 24, 2012.

Annual Report. 1895. Connecticut Humane Society. http:// books.google.com/books?id=DYwOAAAAIAAJ&oe=UTF-8. Accessed July 23, 2012.

"Avon, Mary Kay, Estée Lauder Paying for Tests on Animals." February 16, 2012. The PETA Files. http://www.peta.org/ b/thepetafiles/archive/2012/02/16/3-companies-booted-off -cruelty-free-list.aspx. Accessed August 2, 2012.

Baldwin, Ann. "The Stressful Life of Laboratory Animals." http://www.project-syndicate.org/commentary/the-stressful-life-of-laboratory-animals. Accessed August 9, 2012.

Bliss, Michael. *Banting: A Biography*. 2nd ed. Toronto: University of Toronto Press, 1993.

British Home Office. 2008. *Statistics of Scientific Procedures on Living Animals*. http://webarchive.nationalarchives.gov.uk/20110218135832/rds.homeoffice.gov.uk/rds/pdfs09/spanimals08tstabs.pdf. Accessed August 5, 2012.

"CAAT History." Johns Hopkins Bloomberg School of Public Health. http://caat.jhsph.edu/about/history.html. Accessed August 6, 2012.

Chandroo, K. P., I. J. H. Duncan, and R. D. Moccia. "Can Fish Suffer?: Perspectives on Sentience, Pain, Fear and Stress." *Applied Animal Behaviour Science* 86 (2004): 225–250.

"The Clarence Dennis Papers." Profiles in Science. The Library of Medicine. http://profiles.nlm.nih.gov/ps/retrieve/ResourceMetadata/BXBBLT. Accessed July 25, 2012.

Cohen, Carl, and Tom Regan. *The Animal Rights Debate*. Lanham, MD: Rowman & Littlefield, 2001.

Cohen, Henry. "The Animal Welfare Act." *Journal of Animal Law* 12 (2006). http://www.animallaw.info/articles/arus2journalanimallaw13.htm#_ftn7. Accessed August 5, 2012.

"Commission Staff Working Document." *Sixth Report on the Statistics of the Number of Animals Used for Experimental and Other Scientific Purposes in the Member States of the European Union*. Brussels: European Commission, December 8, 2010. http://ec.europa.eu/environment/chemicals/lab_animals/pdf/sec_2010_1107.pdf. Accessed August 5, 2012.

"Concentration Camp for Dogs." *Life*, February 4, 1966. http://books.google.ca/books/about/LIFE.html?id=JkwEAAAAMBAJ. Accessed July 25, 2012.

Congressional Serial Set. 54th Congress, 1st Session. Washington, DC: U.S. Government Printing Office, 1896. http://books.google.com/books?id=EyIaAAAAIAAJ. Accessed July 24, 2012.

Croce, Pietro. "Vivisection or Science: A Choice to Make." http://www.pnc.com.au/~cafmr/online/research/croce1 .html. Accessed August 9, 2012.

Daubert, G. Patrick. "Thallium Toxicity." Medscape Reference. http://emedicine.medscape.com/article/821465 -overview. Accessed on August 2, 2012.

"Death of Henry Bergh: Helpless Animals Losing their Protect-or." *New York Times*, March 13, 1888. http://query.nytimes .com/mem/archive-free/pdf?res=9F02E6D8173AE033A25 750C1A9659C94699FD7CF. Accessed July 24, 2012.

Derbyshire, Stuart. "A Timeline of Reaction." March 8, 2001. http://www.spiked-online.com/Articles/0000000054FF .htm. Accessed July 24, 2012.

Engber, Daniel. "Pepper Goes to Washington." June 3, 2009. *Slate.* http://www.slate.com/articles/health_and_science/ pepper/2009/06/pepper_goes_to_washington.html. Accessed July 25, 2012.

"Financial Review. 1 April 2010–31 March 2011." FRAME. http://www.frame.org.uk/dynamic_files/frame_annual _report_2010_2011.pdf. Accessed August 6, 2012.

"Food, Drug, and Cosmetic Act of 1938." eNotes. http://www .enotes.com/food-drug-cosmetic-act-1938-reference/federal -food-drug-cosmetic-act-1938. Accessed August 2, 2012.

Galvin, Shelley L., and Harold A. Herzog. "Attitudes and Dispositional Optimism of Animal Rights Demonstrators." *Society and Animals* 6, no. 1 (1998): 1–11.

Gensler, Harry. "Peter Singer—Moral Hero or Nazi?" October 8, 1999. *Times Higher Education*. http://www .timeshighereducation.co.uk/story.asp?

storyCode=157567&sectioncode=39. Accessed July 29, 2012.

Ghaskadbi, Surendra, and Vidya Patwardhan. "Invertebrate Alternatives for Toxicity Testing: Hydra Stakes Its Claim." January 3–7, 2012. http://www.isc2012.com/pdf/Plenary %20Session%20Abstracts%20of%20ISC-99.pdf. Accessed August 7, 2012.

H.R. 4805. CRS Summary. http://thomas.loc.gov/cgi-bin/ bdquery/D?d096:72:./temp/~bdxEpO:@@@D&summ2 =m&. Accessed August 3, 2012.

"History of the Animal Liberation Movement." North American Animal Liberation Press Office. http://www .animalliberationpressoffice.org/Background.htm. Accessed July 28, 2012.

"A History of Improving Animal Welfare." Universities Federation for Animal Welfare. http://www.ufaw.org.uk/ history.php. Accessed July 24, 2012.

Hume, Charles Wesley. *Man and Beast*. London: Universities Federation for Animal Welfare, 1962.

"The Impact of Crash Test Dummies in Automobile Safety." July 25, 2010. The Auto Insurance. http://www.theauto insurance.com/the-impact-of-crash-test-dummies-in -automobile-safety_2010-07-25/. Accessed August 2, 2012.

Jacquot, Jeremy Elton. "Episkin: Growing Skin in the Laboratory." July 8, 2007. http://www.treehugger.com/ clean-technology/episkin-growing-skin-in-the-lab.html. Accessed August 7, 2012.

"Jennifer Graham: The First Student to Legally Take on Dissection & Students' Rights." http://www.animalearn .org/img/pdf/graham.pdf. Accessed on August 2, 2012.

Lansbury, Coral. *The Old Brown Dog: Women, Workers, and Vivisection in Edwardian England*. Madison: University of Wisconsin Press, 1985.

"Lash Lure." Cosmetics and Skin. http://cosmeticsandskin.com/
    bcb/lash-lure.php. Accessed August 2, 2012.

"Laws on Product Testing." American Anti-Vivisection
    Society. http://www.aavs.org/site/c.bkLTKfOSLhK6E/b
    .6457863/k.72C6/Laws_on_Product_Testing.htm#
    .UBrvdk38u5J. Accessed August 2, 2012.

Leavitt, Emily Stewart. *Animals and Their Legal Rights: A
    Survey of American Laws from 1641 to 1990.* 4th ed.
    Washington, DC: Animal Welfare Institute, 1990.

"Legislative History of the Animal Welfare Act." U.S.
    Department of Agriculture. National Agricultural Library.
    http://www.nal.usda.gov/awic/pubs/AWA2007/intro.shtml.
    Accessed July 25, 2012.

Liddick, Don. *Eco-terrorism: Radical Environmental and Animal
    Liberation Movements.* Westport, CT: Praeger, 2006.

Loeb, Jerod M., et al. "Human vs Animal Rights. In Defense of
    Animal Research." *JAMA* 262, no. 19 (1989): 2716–2720.

Loftis, Rob. "Review—Refuting Peter Singer's Ethical
    Theory." 2002. (A review of *The Importance of Human
    Dignity*, by Susan Lufkin Kranz). Metapsychology Online
    Reviews. http://metapsychology.mentalhelp.net/poc/view
    _doc.php?type=book&id=1257. Accessed July 29, 2012.

Logan, Cheryl A. "Before There Were Standards: The Role of
    Test Animals in the Production of Empirical Generality in
    Physiology." *Journal of the History of Biology* 35, no. 2
    (2002): 329–363.

"The Lord Dowding Fund for Humane Research." http://
    www.ldf.org.uk/research/49/50/0/. Accessed August 6,
    2012.

"Mark Twain on Scientific Research." Animal Rights History.
    http://www.animalrightshistory.org/1837-1901-animal
    -rights/victorian-t/twa-mark-twain/1900-scientific-research
    .htm. Accessed July 23, 2012.

Mason, Peter. *The Brown Dog Affair: The Story of a Monument That Divided the Nation*. London: Two Stevens, 1997.

Mather, Jennifer. "Philosophical Background of Attitudes toward and Treatment of Invertebrates." *ILAR Journal* 52, no. 2 (2011): 205–221.

Merz, Beverly. "AMA: Speak Out about Need for Research on Animals." *American Medical News*, July 6, 1990. http://business.highbeam.com/137033/article-1G1-9238787/ama-speak-out-need-research-animals. Accessed August 3, 2012.

Metz, Herman A. "Solving Medical Mysteries by Help of Animals." *New York Times*, January 28, 1912. http://query.nytimes.com/mem/archive-free/pdf?res=9C00E2DD173CE633A2575BC2A9679C946396D6CF. Accessed July 23, 2012.

Michigan Society for Medical Research. "Mice, Rats, Birds Are Pawns in Radical Petition." National Animal Interest Alliance. http://www.mismr.org/index.html. Accessed August 4, 2012.

Molland, Noel. "Thirty Years of Direct Action." No Compromise. http://www.nocompromise.org/issues/18thirty_years.html. Accessed July 28, 2012.

Monamy, Vaughan. *Animal Experimentation: A Guide to the Issues*. 2nd ed. Cambridge: Cambridge University Press, 2009.

"Moral Status of Animals." Ethics Guide. http://www.bbc.co.uk/ethics/animals/rights/moralstatus_1.shtml. Accessed August 7, 2012.

"More than $16 Billion in Taxpayer Money Wasted Annually on Animal Testing." People for the Ethical Treatment of Animals. http://www.peta.org/features/more-than-16-billion-in-taxpayer-money-wasted-annually-on-animal-testing.aspx?c=weekly_enews. Accessed August 9, 2012.

"Mrs. Brown's Sad Story: A History of the Food, Drug, and Cosmetic Act." Research Animal Methods. http://www.uac .arizona.edu/vsc443/alternmethod/fdapap03.htm. Accessed August 2, 2012.

National Association of Biomedical Research. *25 Years of Advocating Sound Public Policy.* Washington, DC: National Association of Biomedical Research. http://www.nabr.org/ PB2Col.aspx?pageid=122. Accessed August 3, 2012.

"19,000 Animals Killed in Automotive Crash Tests." *New York Times,* September 28, 1991. http://www.nytimes.com/ 1991/09/28/us/19000-animals-killed-in-automotive-crash -tests.html. Accessed August 2, 2012.

Pacheco, Alex, and Anna Francione. "The Silver Spring Monkeys." In *In Defense of Animals.* Edited by Peter Singer, 135–147. New York: Basil Blackwell, 1985.

Paris, M., et al. "Phase I and II Results of a Validation Study to Evaluate In Vitro Cytotoxicity Assays for Estimating Rodent and Human Acute Systemic Toxicity." http://iccvam.niehs .nih.gov/meetings/SOT04/poster/04paris.pdf. Accessed August 7, 2012.

Park, William H. 1909. "Diphtheria and Its Cures: One Lasting Result from the Use of Vivisection." *New York Times,* February 28, 1909. http://query.nytimes.com/mem/ archive-free/pdf?res=FB0C10F83F5D12738DDDA10A 94DA405B898CF1D3. Accessed July 24, 2012.

Partridge, Ernest. "On the Rights of Animals and of Persons." 1999. *The Online Gadfly.* http://gadfly.igc.org/papers/ Animal.htm. Accessed July 29, 2012.

Perry, Nicole. "Pound Seizure: A Breach of Trust." *AV Magazine* 117, no. 2 (2009): 4–5.

Phelps, Norm. *The Longest Struggle: Animal Advocacy from Pythagoras to PETA.* New York: Lantern Books, 2007.

Phinizy, Coles. "The Lost Pets That Stray to the Labs: Science's Need for Experimental Animals Is Very Real but Is Often

Filled by Unscrupulous and Cruel Professional Dognappers." *Sports Illustrated*, November 29, 1965. http:// sportsillustrated.cnn.com/vault/article/magazine/MAG 1077956/index.htm. Accessed July 25, 2012.

"Physicians Committee for Responsible Medicine." Activist Cash.com. http://activistcash.com/organization_overview .cfm/o/23-physicians-committee-for-responsible-medicine. Accessed August 3, 2012.

"Problems with Animal Research." American Anti-Vivisection Society. http://www.aavs.org/site/c.bkLTKfOSLhK6E/b .6456997/k.3D74/Problems_with_Animal_Research.htm# .UCPr5Z38u5I. Accessed August 9, 2012.

Public Law 109-374. November 27, 2006. http://www.gpo .gov/fdsys/pkg/PLAW-109publ374/pdf/PLAW-109publ 374.pdf. Accessed July 28, 2012.

Regan, Tom. "The Case for Animal Rights." http://www .animal-rights-library.com/texts-m/regan03.pdf. Accessed July 29, 2012.

Reinhardt, Viktor and Annie. *Comfortable Quarters for Laboratory Animals*. 9th ed. Washington, DC: Animal Welfare Institute, 2002. http://labanimals.awionline.org/ pubs/cq02/cqindex.html. Accessed August 9, 2012.

Resolution 109. American Medical Association. http://www .consumerfreedom.com/downloads/reference/docs/050414 _PCRM_AMA2.pdf. Accessed August 3, 2012.

Resolutions. American Medical Association. House of Delegates. June 1990. http://ama.nmtvault.com/jsp/ viewer2.jsp?doc_id=House+of+Delegates+Proceedings% 2Fama_arch%2FHOD00001%2F00000130&view_width =640.0&rotation=0&query1=&collection_filter=House+of +Delegates+Proceedings&collection_name=House%252 52Bof%25252BDelegates%25252BProceedings&zoom _factor=current&page_name=03960392. Accessed August 3, 2012.

Rollin, B. E. "Animal Welfare, Animal Rights, and Agriculture." *Journal of Animal Science* 68, no. 10 (1990): 3456–3461. http://jas.fass.org/content/68/10/3456.full.pdf. Accessed July 30, 2012.

Rollin, Bernard E. *Animal Rights and Human Morality*. 2nd ed. New York: Prometheus Books, 1992.

Rowan, Andrew N. *Of Mice, Models, and Men: A Critical Evaluation of Animal Research*. Albany: State University of New York Press, 1984.

Russell, W. M. S., and R. L. Burch. *The Principles of Humane Experimental Technique*. London: Methuen, 1959. (The book is now available in its entirety at no charge on the Internet at a number of locations, including http://altweb .jhsph.edu/pubs/books/humane_exp/het-toc. Accessed August 4, 2012.)

"S. 3880 (109th): Animal Enterprise Terrorism Act." 2005–2006. GovTrack.US. http://www.govtrack.us/congress/bills/109/s3880/text. Accessed July 28, 2012.

Schneider, Howard A. "Animals! Who Needs Them?" *BioScience* 26, no. 4 (1976): 239.

Singer, Peter. "All Animals Are Equal." http://www.animal -rights-library.com/texts-m/singer02.pdf. Accessed July 29, 2012. (Reprinted from Tom Regan and Peter Singer, *Animal Rights and Human Obligations*, Englewood Cliffs, NJ: Prentice-Hall, 1989, 148–162.)

Singer, Peter. "Animal Liberation." April 5, 1973. *The New York Review of Books*. http://www.nybooks.com/articles/archives/1973/apr/05/animal-liberation/. Accessed July 29, 2012.

Singer, Peter. "Animal Liberation: A Personal View." Between the Species. 1986. http://digitalcommons.calpoly.edu/cgi/viewcontent.cgi?article=1603&context=bts. Accessed July 29, 2012.

Smith, Jane A. "A Question of Pain in Invertebrates." *ILAR Journal* 33, nos. 1–2 (1991): 25–31.

"State Sen. Chip Rogers and PCRM." April 6, 2010. Georgia Progress. http://www.gaprogress.com/en/2010/04/06/state -sen-chip-rogers-and-pcrm/. Accessed August 3, 2012.

Stephens, Martin L., Alan M. Goldberg, and Andrew N. Rowan. "The First Forty Years of the Alternatives Approach: Refining, Reducing, and Replacing the Use of Laboratory Animals." In *The State of the Animals 2001*. Edited by Deborah J. Salem and Andrew N. Rowan, 121–135. Washington, DC: Humane Society Press, 2001.

"A Teen Fights for Frog Rights and Bio May Never Be the Same." *People*, May 25, 1987. http://www.people.com/ people/archive/article/0,,20096365,00.html. Accessed August 2, 2012.

"Terror at UCLA." August 22, 2006. Critical Mass. http:// www.erinoconnor.org/archives/2006/08/terror_at_ucla .html. Accessed July 28, 2012.

Thompson, Harry V. "Animal Welfare and the Control of Vertebrates." March 6, 1990. DigitalCommons@University of Nebraska–Lincoln. http://digitalcommons.unl.edu/cgi/ viewcontent.cgi?article=1075&context=vpc14. Accessed July 24, 2012.

"25 Years of Saving Lives with the Animal Liberation Front." No Compromise. http://www.nocompromise.org/issues/ 24ALFstory.html. Accessed July 28, 2012.

U.S. Congress. Office of Technology Assessment. *Alternatives to Animal Use in Research, Testing, and Education.* Washington, DC: U.S. Government Printing Office, OTA -BA-273, February 1986. http://www.princeton.edu/~ota/ disk2/1986/8601/8601.PDF. Accessed August 6, 2012.

Wilhelmus, K. R. "The Draize Eye Test." *Survey of Ophthalmology* 45, no. 6 (2001): 493–515.

Wills, Quin, and Cathrine Mitchell. "Toxicogenomics in Drug Discovery and Development—Making an Impact." *ATLA* Supp. 1 (2009): 33–37.

"World Lab Animal Week 21–27 April." National Anti -Vivisection Society. http://www.navs.org.uk/take_action/ 41/0/1174/. Accessed August 1, 2012.

The issue of animal experimentation is as contentious today as it has been for well over a century. Well-informed, conscientious, good-hearted men and women on both sides of the issue believe strongly that animals are crucial in scientific and biomedical research, that animals should never be used under any circumstances in such research, or that circumstances determine whether and how animals should be used. This chapter provides an opportunity for individuals to outline the basis for their beliefs about animal experimentation. Dario Ringach is a neuroscientist who was subjected to harassment because of his use of animals in research; he explains here why he thinks animals are essential in that type of research. Tom Holder has been a spokesperson in support of animal testing in both the United Kingdom and the United States. Bella Williams and Michael Schaff present additional arguments in support of animal experimentation. Carol Frischmann discusses the role of companion animals in research, while Janette Fischer explains how animals can be used humanely in behavioral research. Doris Lin provides an overall summary of the reasons for oppose the use of animals in experimentation, while Michael Budkie reviews some of the most troublesome examples of that practice. Finally, Vilay Khandelwal outlines the history of his own struggles with the question of animal experimentation and the conclusion he eventually reached about it.

The Moral Dilemma of Animal Research

Dario Ringach

There are circumstances in which inaction is immoral. If we were to find a toddler drowning in a bathtub, we would feel morally obliged to act and to save her life, particularly because doing so would not require us to assume any significant risk to ourselves. Inaction sometimes requires a moral justification.

It is a fact that animal research has been able to alleviate much human and nonhuman suffering (Comroe and Dripps 1976). The work has contributed to the development of vaccines for polio, smallpox, diphtheria, tetanus, whooping cough, measles, rubella, mumps, hepatitis A/B, influenza, rotavirus, chickenpox, meningitis, and human papillomavirus, all of which combined saved billions of human lives ("The Effectiveness of Immunizations" 2012; "What Would Happen If We Stopped Vaccinations?" 2012). Animal research also played an important role in the development of antibiotics, blood transfusion, lung surfactants for neonatal care, insulin, antidepressants, antiretroviral therapy, and so on. The scientific consensus indicates that animal research is critical at the present time to advance medical research and human health ("Scientific Achievements Less Prominent than a Decade Ago: Public Praises Science; Scientists Fault Public, Media" 2009).

We are thus faced with an ethical dilemma. On one hand, opponents of animal research ask: *How can we possible justify harming other living beings in the course of scientific studies?* On the other, medical researchers respond with a question of their own: *How could we ignore the suffering of fellow humans and nonhuman animals when we know we have the ability to find cures and devise new therapies through scientific research? How could we justify our inaction?*

Animal rights activists justify their opposition with the belief that our moral consideration for the interests of all living beings must be equal. Given this premise, they conclude it would be morally wrong to experiment on a mouse to cure cancer for the same reasons it is wrong to experiment on a human being to do so—both have exactly the same basic rights to life and freedom.

Is the premise tenable? Must we give equal consideration to the life of a mouse than a human being? Although the premise has been asserted many times by animal philosophers, I do not think they have offered a solid argument for why this is so. In fact, prominent animal rights philosophers have stated some things are not at stake when we put the loss of human and non-human life on the balance. On this specific point, Peter Singer writes, "To take the life of a being who has been hoping, planning and working for some future goal is to deprive that being of the fulfillment of those efforts; to take the life of a being with a mental capacity below the level needed to grasp that one is a being with a future—much less make plans for the future— cannot involve this particular kind of loss" (Singer 2002, 46). Tom Regan concurs: "The harm that death is, is a function if the opportunities for satisfaction it forecloses, and no reasonable person would deny that the death of any . . . human would be a greater prima facie loss, and thus a greater prima facie harm, that would be true in the case [of] a dog" (Regan 2004, 324). I hardly need to add more, as this is exactly what makes animal research morally permissible.

Needless to say, the animal rights philosopher will come back with a complaint. They will point out that there are many humans who are cognitively impaired and may show interests in life comparable to those of nonhuman animals. Why not experiment on them? Or why is that we hold the life of these humans above those of animals of comparable abilities?

This so-called *marginal case argument* assumes that the intrinsic properties of an individual is all that should morally relevant. Once again, the premise is wrong and so are the conclusions that emerge from it. If intrinsic properties alone were all that mattered, then we should see no problem granting a rock, a dead cat, and human remains the same moral consideration since they are all inanimate objects with no interests of their own. And yet, while nobody will object to a child playfully kicking a rock, most will not feel comfortable with him kicking a dead cat for his or her amusement or using human remains in an art project for school. The suffering such acts will inflict on others must count as well. It would be wrong for someone to play with the remains of your dog because it will indirectly cause you harm and suffering.

In addition, the marginal-case scenario is typically posed by using an impaired human and a nonhuman animal as examples, rather than a normal human and a nonhuman animal with supernatural abilities. There is a clear difference between these two situations. Should an ape appear in front of us, such as in Kafka's *Report to the Academy*, speaking in fluent English, asking to be treated as a peer with equal rights, it seems difficult to think we could refuse on any grounds, even if this represents a single extraordinary instance. However, when human patients are impaired from their normal state, in most cases we have no absolute certainty the condition is permanent. A cure for Alzheimer's or autism may possibly be developed in the future and their mental capacities restored. On what grounds could we possible deny these patients and their families the hope of recovery even if the likelihood is minimal?

When one walks through the halls of a hospital, he or she is exposed to the myriad of patients and the suffering that they and their families experience. When we further recognize that we have the scientific ability to reduce and eliminate suffering from the world with our work, scientists feel a moral obligation to act. When asked to stop we have the right to ask the opposition to explain why it would be morally permissible to stop the work that has produced, and will continue to produce, immeasurable benefit to both animals and humans alike. They have failed to justify on moral grounds the inaction they promote. Animal research is a moral dilemma that must be confronted and not denied (Morrison 2002).

We agree all living beings deserve our moral consideration—but not equal consideration. When it comes to animal research, this moral principle is embedded in our regulations and guidelines. Experiments must be clearly justified and stand a reasonable chance of advancing important knowledge. Choice of species and animal numbers must be justified as well, and the work must be monitored by veterinary staff that care for the welfare of the animals. Careful, responsible, regulated, and lifesaving animal research must proceed. Inaction would be immoral.

Bibliography

Comroe, J. H., Jr., and R. D. Dripps. "Scientific Basis for the Support of Biomedical Science." *Science* 192, no. 4235 (1976): 105–111.

"The Effectiveness of Immunizations." HHS.GovArchive. http://archive.hhs.gov/nvpo/concepts/intro6.htm. Accessed July 31, 2012.

Morrison, A. R. "Perverting Medical History in the Service of 'Animal Rights.' " *Perspectives in Biology and Medicine* 45, no. 4 (2002): 606–619.

Regan, Tom. *The Case for Animal Rights*. 2nd ed. Berkeley: University of California Press, 2004.

"Scientific Achievements Less Prominent than a Decade Ago: Public Praises Science; Scientists Fault Public, Media." The Pew Research Center for the People & the Press. July 9, 2009. http://people-press.org/http:/people-press.org/files/legacy-pdf/528.pdf. Accessed July 31, 2012.

Singer, Peter. *Writings on an Ethical Life*. London: Fourth Estate, 2002.

"What Would Happen If We Stopped Vaccinations?" Centers for Disease Control and Prevention. http://www.cdc.gov/vaccines/vac-gen/whatifstop.htm. Accessed July 31, 2012.

Dario Ringach is a professor of neurobiology at the David Geffen School of Medicine at UCLA. Since attacks on his family by animal rights extremists in 2003, he has vocally defended the work and encouraged to a civil and open dialogue about the use of animals in research. He is one of the cofounders of Pro-Test for Science and a member of the Speaking of Research Committee. At UCLA he co-organized panel discussions on animal research and on the cognitive differences and similarities between humans and nonhuman primates. He has publicly debated animal rights philosophers and written on the ethics of animal research. For this work, he shared the AAAS Scientific Freedom and Responsibility Award in 2011. His scientific interests center around cortical function and the organization of the visual system.

What Has Animal Research Ever Done for Us?

Tom Holder

Take a group of 30 children—a typical school class size. One or two will be or become diabetic. Two or three will develop asthma. Many will need a blood transfusion at some point. Most will receive anesthetics during their lifetime (around 6 million general anesthetics are administered each year) (Aitken, Rerndt, and Cutler 2009). All are likely to be prescribed antibiotics at some time (around 40 million prescriptions are issued per year) (Laxminarayan and Malani 2007, 30). Almost all will be vaccinated against diphtheria, tetanus, polio, and meningitis C, but even a child whose parents refuse such vaccines will benefit from the immunity through the vaccination of other children.

Next time you go to the doctor, consider those numbers and spare a thought for the animals that made it possible for those 30 people to lead healthy lives. The history of scientific discoveries made possible by animal research is exemplary: insulin (dogs and rabbits), polio vaccine (monkeys), anesthetics (rabbits), blood transfusion (monkeys, dogs), antibiotics to cure tuberculosis (guinea pigs), asthma treatment (frogs and guinea pigs), meningitis vaccine (mice), deep brain stimulation for Parkinson's (monkeys), penicillin (mice) . . . the list goes on.

You might notice that many of the developments mentioned are decades old. So what has animal research done for us recently? Herceptin, originally developed in mice, has had a significant impact on the survival rates for breast cancers. As a mouse antibody (now humanized), it would not have come about without the use of animal research. Mice, far and away the most common animals used in scientific research, have also been used in conjunction with stem cell research to create a treatment for macular degeneration (one of the leading causes of blindness). Such research, pioneered in mice, has now been used successfully to treat humans.

Nonetheless, animals are an imperfect model for humans, but so are cell cultures, computer models, microdosing, and every other complementary method we care to name. Even results from one human will not necessarily apply to the next. We have an incredibly complex physiology, and it often requires a similarly complex physiology to understand what goes on in our bodies; this makes animal research invaluable.

And it is not just humans who benefit from animal testing; almost all human diseases have a similar or equivalent disease in another species. Ninety percent of veterinary medicines used to treat animals are the same or very similar to those developed to treat human patients. Surgical procedures, such as the removal of tumors and other intrusive procedures, are used in humans as well as animals and tend to be developed and refined in animals. Recently, studies on wild squirrels have discovered a virus that may be responsible for the decline in red squirrel populations in Europe. Hopefully, this may also lead to treatments being found.

Benefits or no, there are some who believe that animals have equal moral status to humans. I believe this view is indefensible, but let us explore it further. What would it mean?

Some conclusions are easy to draw—we must all stop wearing leather and become vegetarian. Yet this would not be enough to satisfy moral equivalence. You must not kill a mosquito; you must not cure your child's tapeworm; you must not accept the use of mice to eradicate polio from the face of the planet. In truth, few would agree with the demands and limits that moral equivalency would bring.

Scientists do not research using animals simply because they can. It is the human ability to empathize with others and to have the tools to confront disease by means of scientific research that calls for us to act in the face of so much suffering. It is a moral dilemma that must be confronted.

Humans are compassionate beings, and it is this very compassion that demands that we continue to do lifesaving animal research. Around two decades ago, AIDS was a death sentence. Today, developments in highly active antiretroviral treatments (HAARTs), created through the various animal models of HIV, mean sufferers can expect an ordinary life expectancy. It is compassion for our fellow human being that necessitates a continuation of animal research.

Researchers are not just guided by state and federal regulations and the Animal Welfare Act. Through the use of the three Rs, American research facilities continue to improve conditions for animals in labs. Refinement (better conditions for animals and better training for those using them), reduction (reducing the number of animals used), and replacement (using non-animal methods wherever possible) are the cornerstones of good science, ensuring that the best research can be done with the minimum suffering for animals. All research in U.S. labs must be approved by an Institutional Animal Care and Use Committee

(IACUC)—which includes a veterinarian and usually a lay member of the public—to ensure that animals are used only where there is no other option.

Given the high standards of care in laboratories across the United States, and the importance of animal research to the development of modern cures, it is essential that scientists are allowed to continue their research without harassment or intimidation from animal rights activists.

Sadly, animal research is frequently misrepresented. Pictures of monkeys in terrible conditions circulate the Internet. But they are often from decades past and fail to address a few simple facts, namely that:

- Approximately 98 percent of research is carried out using rodents, birds, and fish.
- The United States has stringent animal welfare regulations; all procedures must be approved by the IACUC; and laboratories are inspected at least once every six months by the USDA.
- Animal research is used only where there is no other suitable alternative.
- Animal research has contributed to nearly every medical breakthrough of the last century.

It is finally worth reminding ourselves that humans' moral status is what allows us to care for the suffering of other species. We have a responsibility to treat animals with respect. Scientists use as few animals as possible, use replacements if possible, and minimize suffering of animals (e.g., through anesthetics) wherever possible. Nonetheless, while animals remain a crucial part of our ability to fight cruel and debilitating diseases, it is important that we do not let others from preventing its continuation. Animal research is invaluable to human and animal health, and when carried out in a careful and regulated manner, remains an ethical tool for scientists.

Bibliography

Aitken, Murray, Ernst R. Rerndt, and David M. Cutler. "Prescription Drug Spending Trends in the United States: Looking beyond the Turning Point." *Health Affairs* 28, no. 1 (2009): w151–w160.

Laxminarayan, Ramanan, and Anup Malani. *Extending the Cure*. Washington, DC: Resources for the Future, 2007.

Tom Holder was a founding member of the Pro-Test movement in 2006, which led around 1,000 scientists and students through the streets of Oxford to defend the use of animals in biomedical research. In 2008 Holder moved to the United States and founded Speaking of Research, which aims to provide accurate information about the role of animals in research in the United States. He has also played a key role in building the Pro-Test for Science movement, which held several rallies at UCLA in defense of animal research.

The Importance of Biomedical Research

Matt Schaff

No other scientific discipline makes as intimate an impact on average people as does biomedical research. From flu vaccines at the pharmacy to checkups at the doctor's office, the effects of biomedical research percolate throughout everyday life. Why? Because it has produced a practice of medicine that actually works.

Modern medicine would not work, however, without the use of animals in biomedical research. Since the dawn of scientific medicine, animals have served as invaluable partners to researchers seeking to understand the nature of disease and develop prevention methods, treatments, and cures. Think of taking away animals from biomedical research as removing the wheels from a car mid-drive: medical progress would screech to a halt, leaving generations of patients neglected and, most importantly, sick.

Those who are serious about answering clinically relevant questions—such as "Will this drug have the desired benefit?"

or "How do people contract that illness?"—appreciate the need for animals in biomedical research. They, like medical societies around the world, understand that animal systems have a lot to teach us about the human system.

The human body entails enormously complex biological machinery with countless moving parts, many of which we do not yet understand. Given that animals are similar to us—they share much of our DNA and often contract the same diseases—we can use animals to model our bodies. Armed with such animal models, researchers can access a vital platform on which to test bold ideas and make life-changing discoveries. Thanks to research with animals, doctors can understand the causes of patients' problems and know the safest, most effective ways to solve them.

The promise of animal research has been known at least since 1796. That is when English physician Edward Jenner, studying how more time spent around diseased cows generally meant more resistance to the smallpox virus, injected the pus from "cowpox" blisters into an eight-year-old boy, effectively inoculating him against the smallpox scourge and inaugurating the world's first vaccine. Over the next century, Jenner's "Eureka" moment inspired others to develop early vaccines for anthrax, typhoid, and rabies, of course with the crucial help of sheep, rodents, rabbits, and dogs.

Fast-forward to the 1900s, and things start to get especially interesting: virtually every major medical advance of the last century owes credit to animal models. Not only has animal research taught researchers to rein in viruses better than Jenner could have imagined (think Jonas Salk's 1952 world-changing polio vaccine); it has also drastically minimized the issue of bacterial infection. As the modern age of antibiotics was born in the first half of the twentieth century, much has been made about the role of fungus *Penicillium rubens* in Alexander Fleming's petri dish. But without the mice at the University of Oxford that in 1940 proved penicillin can safely staunch bacterial infection in living systems, the ensuing explosion of antibiotic research (which has largely depended on animals) might never have happened.

Animal research made big strides for diabetes treatment, as well. Before the 1920s, doctors had no reliable way of controlling blood sugar in diabetic patients. But after extracting insulin from the pancreas of dogs in 1921, Canadian scientists learned to appreciate the role of insulin in checking blood sugar and pioneered the first successful tests of user-injected insulin. Now after testing autonomous insulin pumps in rodent models, patients are even closer to leading lives unencumbered by some of the strains of diabetes.

Twentieth-century research with animal models also gifted medicine with the ability to safely replace tissues and organs. Research with monkeys and rabbits in the 1940s led to the discovery of the "Rh factor," a determinant of blood type now fundamental in coordinating blood transfusions. The 1950s and '60s then brought the first surgical procedures for kidney transplants, heart transplants, and hip replacements, collectively spawned from research with dogs, sheep, and goats.

Over the last 60 years, the benefits of research with animal models even reached above the neck. Rodent research in the 1950s and '60s led to the first antidepressants and antipsychotics, the latter of which reduce the delusions and disorganization associated with schizophrenia. The mysteries of Parkinson's disease were also unmasked since the 1960s, thanks to the understanding of the brain's dopamine system gained from rat studies, and these insights continue to produce treatments for Parkinson's disease to this day.

Whereas animal studies have made huge progress with the big health issues, it did not miss the small ones. In fact, research using animal models has made possible the family medicine cabinet. If not for animal research to prove drugs safe and effective, average people would not be able to get out the acetaminophen to alleviate headaches, wear contact lenses to see more clearly, take allergy medication to breathe easier outdoors, or even apply first-aid antibiotics to their children's cuts and scrapes.

Despite the widely appreciated value of animal research to advance human health – a—animal health, since many of the treatments derived for humans are also helping pets, zoo animals, and endangered species—certain individuals and organizations resist. The opposition to animal research thinks that medical progress could proceed just as smoothly if animals were taken out of biomedical research. Enticing the public with emotional appeals, they elevate computer models as equivalent research subjects to living, animal systems.

But such an argument flies counter to the facts: computer models serve as a helpful adjunct, but so far, no model yet produced comes anywhere close to reproducing in electronics the bewildering complexity found in animal biology. That is why when new pharmaceuticals go up for review before clinical trials, computer simulations do not make the cut. Reflecting the stark limitations of computer models, U.S. and international law mandate that all treatments must first be tried in animals before reaching people.

No one is expecting a god-like supercomputer, capable of modeling every facet of the human body, to somehow burst onto the market. Therefore the guide of history suggests that research with animals will continue to make medicine work even better. Studies involving animals are under way to help us fix broken spinal cords with stem cells, understand and more effectively treat drug addiction, apply gene therapy to muscular dystrophy and cystic fibrosis treatment, and search for answers to the 200 different types of cancer—to name but a few examples. Although their prospects are as bright as ever, future biomedical research advances cannot be fully predicted. But one thing's for certain: when they arrive, we'll be sure to thank animals.

Matt Schaff is a senior at the University of Pittsburgh studying neuroscience and economics. Between attending class, reporting science stories for *The Pitt News*, and conducting neurobiology research, Matt contributes to the efforts of the Foundation for Biomedical Research. In 2012, he received the Goldwater Scholarship for excellence and promise in science.

Companion Animal and Human Patients Work Together

Carol Frischmann

Few of us believe animal testing is desirable until we, a parent, or a pet needs a "promising" treatment for cancer or disease of aging. Rather than Mom receiving the first dose of a new drug, most people prefer someone else tries the elixir, survives, and heals. In the shouting over whether animal testing should be allowed, more alternatives than the binary "yes-no" are possible. Well grounded in the traditional methods of treatment design and testing, I was surprised to learn, while gathering information for several freelance writing assignments earlier this year, about the growing number of veterinary and human medical researchers' close cooperation in studying disease process and delivering new types of treatments more rapidly than in the past. Because of improved technology and changing values, people and companion animals can now be treated "under the same roof."

An example of this cooperation is the Gerald P. Murphy Cancer Foundation comparative oncology program—focusing on the people and companion dogs. One group of studies at the foundation examines the relationship between aging and cancer. In this study, Rottweilers that reached the equivalent of 100 human years of age contributed tissue samples, and their people contributed pedigrees that went back generations. Because of the compressed life span of dogs, the foundation can study the aging process from middle age to exceptional longevity in 6 to 8 years rather than the 50 years required for human studies. The companion animals and people supported the study with periodic veterinary visits and, at death, a final gift of the pet's tissues.

Because of this concern by dog lovers about eradicating disease from both dogs and humans, scientists have two new research tools. The first is the Exceptional Longevity Database, a database of exceptionally old dogs, comparable to the international database of humans older than 110 years, which provides a resource for scientists interested in aging research. In addition, a Bio-repository At Murphy is the world's first collection of annotated bio-specimens (tissue samples including serum, blood cells, and DNA) from these longest-living dogs. One use of these tools is to develop "biomarkers," which allow physicians to know cancer process has begun before visible symptoms develop. Early detection allows treatment to give patients a longer life of better quality.

New technology and changing values foster such developments. Advances in understanding the canine and human genome allow a "personalized" approach to medicine. Similarly, the role of genetics and environment in disease is better understood. In addition, the Internet has allowed the connection of people with common interests and needs—such as Rottweiler centenarian owners, people with age-related cancers, and the Murphy Cancer Foundation. Twenty years ago, such collaborations would not have been possible. Now, given our ability to seek out others with shared interests and the increasingly common view that companion animals as family members deserve a comparable standard of treatment, the treatment of people and animals together—each benefiting the other—seems a natural evolution. In addition, the use of animals living in the environment, natural–progression (not introduced) disease processes, and the similarity of the environment and large stretches of genome allow a natural companionability of human and canine diagnosis and treatment.

One of the most devastating diseases in young people is osteosarcoma, usually resulting in the amputation of the affected limb. If the disease is not caught very early, the tumor spreads to the lungs. In canines, the disease is always fatal. Among the cooperative efforts between canine and human disease researchers is one on limb-sparing surgery and another is the development of a vaccine to prevent the spread of the cancer through the body. For young people, finding a way to stop the disease but spare the arm or leg would improve their lives. A researcher at the department of orthopedic surgery at the Texas A&M College of Veterinary Medicine and Biomedical Sciences and a researcher at A&M's Health Science Center are collaborating on work to heal the bone around implants, replacing the tumor and removing the surrounding destroyed bone. Adult progenitor cells (or stem cells) are being tested in canines who also suffer from this disease.

Meanwhile, another researcher at the School of Veterinary Medicine at the University of Pennsylvania works in her laboratory with a highly modified bacterium that carries a protein expressed by the bone cancer into the body. Acting a bit like the Trojan horse that discharges its "hidden" contents once inside, the vaccine stimulates a response from the body's own immune system, a principle that could be applied to any type of cancer. The day I interviewed the researcher, the first vaccine patient, Sasha, had a successful first-stage introduction of the vaccine. Sasha had been diagnosed with osteosarcoma a month earlier, and her family is thrilled that the treatment is helping her. They are also excited that Sasha is a part of the process to help find a way to make osteosarcoma less of a death sentence for people. Pediatric oncologists are watching the vaccine's success in the test group of nine companion canines brought to the center by owners who want the best treatment for their beloved pets.

Sometimes, in our quest to make things simple, we hang onto ways of seeing that are black and white. Decision making is easier when we allow the binary emotional level to be the arbitrator of right and wrong. No data need be gathered. No higher order thinking, no reasoning, and no data collection need to be done. We see a picture of a sick animal taking a treatment and those emotions push us to "know" what is right and what is wrong.

If we can set this photograph aside and take a fresh look at the "new conditions" of changed technology and values, which provide an opportunity to use all animals, including *Homo sapiens*, as laboratories for perfecting disease treatment, we might develop a more humane attitude to the entire community of companion animals and their people. Unless you believe that

Mom must be the first living being to receive a new treatment, consider the potential rightness of treating previously fatal companion animal diseases and using those results to benefit human partners.

Bibliography

Gerald P. Murphy Cancer Foundation. http://www.gpmcf.org/celsmainpg.html. Accessed September 18, 2012.

Science writer, adjunct professor, and author, **Carol Frischmann** earned her MFA from Northwest Institute of Literary Arts and BA in science education from Duke University. Author of seven books and more than 400 magazine and newspaper articles, Carol is a member of the National Association of Science Writers and the Society of Children's Book Writers and Illustrators. She resides in Portland, Oregon, with a grumpy African Grey parrot. Find Carol at http://thiswildlife.com and @thiswildlifecom.

The Use of Animals in Behavioral Research

Janette Fischer

Using animals in research for our own immediate needs and ends all too often results in animals being made "objects" instead of "subjects," and as objects they become expendable. There are a number of advantages to using whole, unviolated organisms in behavioral research. If the experiment is well designed and works, it is less likely to lead the researcher into the trap of preconceived expectation. However, in making animals "objects" rather than "subjects" anthropocentrism ensues, resulting in humans being viewed as distinct and isolated from, rather than part of, the animal world.

Animals are used as experimental subjects in fields ranging from biomedicine, where they stand in for humans in research intended to benefit mankind, to military applications, where in the extreme case they have been employed as kamakazis.

Researchers may justify the use of animals in terms of cost savings, of both money and human lives. Unfortunately, the study of whole, unviolated organisms, whether it be to understand their social systems, ecological niches, or unique behaviors, is not considered as immediately valuable as human health or national defense and therefore gets very little funding. Consequently, funding for research that involves animal experimentation is given preferentially to those projects with direct application to human health or military purposes.

Animal behavior in the laboratory is a bridge to the ecology of the animal, and thence to the ecosystem (because animals do not exist in isolation). The closer the laboratory subject is to its natural state, the more representative are its behaviors, and the better the bridge to the natural world. Whole-animal behavior bridges reductionist analytical experimental data (e.g., the molecular biology of gene expression) and the ecological context without which neither behavior nor genetics is intelligible. However, there are interesting challenges in behavior experiments. Because of the different levels of complexity involved in behavioral responses, a broader range of phenomena needs to be considered when formulating hypotheses or considering the results of experiments. Therefore scientists need a different set of intellectual skills to deal with behavior.

But how will such studies continue? Most students are no longer trained in long hours of observation. It takes years to build the observational skills necessary to tease out relationships between complex systems—more time than it would take to solve one black-and-white question about a biochemical interaction or physiological phenomenon. Therefore fewer and fewer students follow the longer, harder path, and within the sciences the skills required for successful noninvasive research into animal behavior are disappearing. Couple this with the meager funding for noninvasive behavioral research and we are left with animal experimentation that is intrusive and reductionist. Scientifically, we are losing sight of the bigger picture.

My own research employed noninvasive techniques to investigate animals' use of the Earth's magnetic field for navigation. I used the behavior of red-spotted newts during their migratory season to show that newts are exquisitely sensitive to minute changes in the Earth's magnetic field, and, in fact, use those changes to navigate back to their home ponds to mate. To show this I captured red-spotted newts from ponds, tested them once in specific magnetic field settings, then released them back into their home ponds (because their ability to survive was not impaired by my study and their release back to their homes did not threaten the health of the ponds' populations). I did not inject or implant any foreign substances into them, nor did I cut off any body parts to mark them for identification purposes. I did not harm the newts in any way. Thus the newts' responses to the subtly altered magnetic cues I provided them were unperturbed and reflected their natural migratory responses. The geomagnetic field is complex, comprised of locally variable components, and the newts' migratory behaviors are likewise complex: therefore teasing out the subtleties of the interaction between them required healthy newts capable of exhibiting normal migratory behavior (Fischer, Freake, Borland, and Phillips 2001).

It should be mentioned that skill in handling the newts played a crucial role in the success of the experiments. I developed those skills through devoted observation of the newts, leading to a solid understanding of their behaviors when in my care. Having an understanding of the animal—of what makes it comfortable or what frightens it, for example—does not impede the progress of science. Rather, the research progresses because the behavioral responses subsequently revealed are the natural responses the animal would exhibit in its native habitat.

Using animals as experimental subjects is a sensitive issue, even among ethologists. Even though there are global ethical standards governing the use of animal subjects, a researcher must calculate her own cost-benefit analysis, considering both costs and benefits for both animals and humans in the design of experiments. Despite being a member of a large department, I was alone in my commitment to using solely noninvasive research techniques. Other researchers of animal behavior sometimes expressed their disapproval of what they thought of as my "limiting" the scope of the research. At times some even seemed to feel threatened by the success of my noninvasive approach. Ultimately, though, my experimental results silenced my critics and hopefully opened their minds to the benefits of noninvasive studies of animal behavior.

Animals will continue to be used (and sometimes misused) in experiments. Until substitutions for animal subjects, such as computer modeling or tissue cultures, for instance, become more economical than using animals themselves, institutions will continue invasive experimentation on animals. However, there is no need for the lack of respect or empathy, nor for the lack of understanding that some researchers exhibit for their experimental subjects. Animals are not here for us to use and discard, like disposable gloves. Rather, we can learn from animals as they are, naturally. We learn about ourselves, about our own behavior, by observing and studying animals' behavior, whether it be psychological, instinctive, or learned. It is our relationship to other living things that puts humanity into humans.

Bibliography

Fischer, J. H., M. J. Freake, S. C. Borland, and J. B. Phillips. "Evidence for the Use of Magnetic Map Information by an Amphibian." *Animal Behaviour* 62, no. 1 (2001): 1–10.

Janette Fischer received her BA from St. John's College in Santa Fe, and a master's in education, specializing in science, from the University of New Mexico. She earned her PhD in zoology/animal behavior from a major university in the Midwest, where she focused on the use of geomagnetic cues in migratory behavior of red-spotted newts. Her geomagnetic work took her briefly to Australia, where she also studied migratory Tasmanian silvereyes, always using noninvasive techniques. She is a long-term admirer of the classic behavioral works of Tinbergen, Lorenz, and von Frisch, and the more humorous books of Gerald Durrell.

Objections to the Use of Animals in Research

Doris Lin

Animal advocates often object to the use of animals in research. Some find certain practices objectionable, while others oppose all uses of animals in research.

Views on animal experimentation (and all use of animals) generally fall into one of two categories. "Animal welfare" is the belief that using animals for our own purposes is morally acceptable if the animals are treated well and the use is not too frivolous. "Animal rights" is the belief that humans do not have the right to use animals for our own purposes, no matter how well the animals are treated or how noble the intentions.

While the animal rights view is absolute and accepts no exploitation of animals, the animal welfare view is more subjective. Drawing that line between acceptable animal research and unacceptable animal research will be different for each individual. For example, some animal welfare advocates might approve of experiments on rats but not on primates, while others might believe that experiments on primates are justified to advance human medicine.

Why Do Animal Rights Activists Object to Using Animals in Experiments?

Animal rights activists believe that animals have a right to live free of human use, abuse, and exploitation. Animal experimentation violates that right, which is based on the fact that animals are sentient (which means they are capable of suffering) and the belief that speciesism (treating beings differently based on their species) is wrong. Even breeding, buying, and selling the animals violate their rights because they are being controlled and confined against their will. Their mates are chosen for them, and families are ripped apart so that the individuals can be sold to laboratories.

Under the animal rights view, experiments on animals are not justified even if the research could lead to advances in human medicine. Just as we do not experiment on human beings against their will, no matter how many people might be saved, such experiments should not be performed on animals.

What Are the Animal Welfare Concerns about Animals in Research?

Scientists and institutions strive for the three Rs: reduce, refine, and replace. They seek to reduce the number of animals used, refine experiments to minimize the pain and suffering of the animals, and replace animals with nonanimal models. However, animal advocates question the effectiveness of the three Rs, especially considering that the people doing the reducing, refining, and replacing are the vivisectors themselves or their peers.

Some animal welfare advocates draw the line at certain types of research or practices that they find particularly objectionable, such as pound seizure, testing of cosmetics and household products, or the use of primates.

Pound Seizure

Pound seizure is the practice of animal shelters giving or selling unwanted, live animals to laboratories instead of killing the animals, and is illegal in some states. Some people find pound seizure particularly offensive because they believe that cats and dogs are special and because turning former pets over to vivisectors is a cruel betrayal of their trust in humans.

Testing of Cosmetics and Household Products

Many people also find that using animals to test cosmetics and household products is unacceptable because a new lipstick or a new detergent is not a good reason to harm and kill animals. In the United States, no law requires cosmetics or household products to be tested on animals unless they contain a new chemical. Companies often develop new chemicals so that they can patent their inventions and then have exclusive rights to sell that product. Some companies do not test on animals but instead use substances that are already known to be safe.

Primates

Some animal welfare advocates object to all uses of primates (such as chimpanzees, baboons, and rhesus monkeys) in experiments because primates are believed to be highly sensitive and intelligent. Humans are also primates but can be used for research only if they give voluntary, informed consent, which means they must fully understand and agree to the procedure and any possible risks.

The Animal Welfare Act

The Animal Welfare Act (AWA) is the U.S. law that governs animals in laboratories, but it offers little protection to the animals. The AWA requires laboratories to be licensed and registered and be subject to unannounced inspections. The AWA also establishes minimum care requirements relating to stimulation, food, shelter, and water. Institutions must also establish IACUCs to review and approve proposals for animal experiments. However, a major criticism of the AWA is that it does not cover mice, rats, or birds used in research. Also, many animal advocates believe that IACUCs do little to regulate the researchers because they are comprised of fellow researchers.

Can We Make Medical Advances without Animal Research?
Medical advances would continue without vivisection, using methods such as tissue cultures, cell cultures, epidemiological studies (observing trends in human populations to try to identify causes and risk factors for diseases), computer models, and consenting human subjects. In the past, the cause and cure for scurvy, the vaccine for smallpox, and penicillin were all discovered without animal research. Additionally, epidemiological studies have shown the connection between cholesterol and heart disease, as well as the connection between tobacco and cancer.

Doris Lin, Esq., is an animal rights attorney and the director of legal affairs for the Animal Protection League of New Jersey. She holds a BS in applied biological sciences from the Massachusetts Institute of Technology (where she opted out of dissection) and a JD from the University of Southern California.

Tolerance

Michael Budkie

According to the annual report filed with the USDA by the University of Kansas Medical Center (UKMED), this facility experiments on and/or holds captive about 130 primates per year (2009). The report that contains this statistic is a bland, one-page document that belies the cruel reality that it represents. (All data and quotations cited in this article are available at Facility Reports and Information, University of Kansas Medical Center, Kansas City, KS, 2012.)

The lives of these primates are represented by a stack of documents just over a foot tall. The existence of highly intelligent animals has been reduced to paper and ink, their identities reduced to numbers, their passing marked only by the word *euthanized*.

UKMED has become known for violating the Animal Welfare Act. Recent inspections for the period from September 2007 to June of 2009 catalog 58 pages of violations, many relevant to primates and their deaths. The USDA inspectors uncovered heinous acts of cruelty, which prolonged the pain these animals endured.

One monkey who died during 2008, #0A0, lost 22 percent of his body weight, which should have been sufficient to qualify for euthanasia. However, the suffering of this animal was allowed to continue. The USDA report states:

> He was sitting curled up on his perch while I was hosing his cage and would make a screeching sound. He is very feeble, he can't stand on his legs; he scoots. His hand-eye coordination is very bad; he has a pronounced tremble in his hands and has to try several times to grab things. He is doing a lot of grimacing and makes a horrible screeching/chirping noise. I know he is scheduled for tomorrow, but I am not sure he will make it that long.

It is hard to believe that after being cited for such a cruel death that this facility would not prevent further deaths of this nature from taking place. Apparently this is not the case. Two other primates suffered fates very similar to #0A0's one year later.

UKMED internal records reveal that a rhesus monkey, #3A5, endured terrible pain on August 4, 2009: "increased agitation and stress from morphine withdrawal." Other observations from the same day reveal continued agony:

> Patient is agitated and vocalizing more. Appears to be more aggressive and keeps moving from perch to floor and back. . . . Patient is screeching very loudly when moving and grimacing a lot. Muscle tremors noted along with lying down in cage. . . . P.M. (8:00): Severe muscle tremors noted to the point that animal could not control his right leg and started to bite it; no lacerations or punctures noted.

On the next day he is described as:

Similar to last night, severe muscle tremors when moving, a little ataxia with grimacing and screeching. . . . Noon: Patient is doing better, significant tremors still noted, but screeching has decreased, appetite and fluid consumption is good. Face is a little flushed as well as mildly swollen on the right side. Afternoon/evening: Patient is very aggressive. . . . Only about 20% of the Gatorade is gone from the a.m. Face is still flushed with possible hives.

On the following day, his torture continues unabated: "P.M. observation: Patient is having increased muscle tremors of legs and arms, will try and bite at feet if a large tremor occurs. No puncture wounds or lacerations noted on feet or legs."

His record for August 21, 2009, shows that the monkey's ordeal has continued for 17 days: "patient with vomit in cage yesterday afternoon and this a.m." On August 25, 2009, his record states: "Vomit all over cage and floor in front of cage. Food left in cage. . . . Right testicle is enlarged and left testicle is very small. Monkey is reserved today and will get up on perch only when approached." On the next day: "His testicles are swollen, enlarged and scrotum has purplish hue. His eyes are sunken area around eyes are puffy and his pupils are dilated. He appears to be in pain from swollen scrotum. He will only move off of floor of cage with a lot of stimulation. . . . PI is consulting . . . about options." By the 27th of August, he has deteriorated even further: "Monkey is very subdued and curled up on perch-will only move when stimulated a lot. Eyes are shrunken and dilated. Hair coat is spiked. Testicles are swollen, hard, and scrotum has purplish hue. Monkey did eat his biscuits, but it appeared that he vomited overnight." Monkey #3A5 was apparently killed that day because a necropsy was performed.

Unbelievably, the life of #3A5 was not unique. Another male rhesus monkey, #84Z, suffered in a very similar fate. On August 4, 2009, primate 84Z is:

Screeching a lot, grimacing noted as well. Patient is lying down in the bottom of the cage and will only move when stimulated. Muscle tremors noted. Appetite is decreased-no biscuits eaten, but has eaten fruit. Screeching is excessive and grimacing noted whenever moving; mild muscle tremors noted.

His misery continues the next day:

A.M. observations: patient is very reluctant to move on stimulation. Once he got up, he screeched once and then fell back over. Moderate muscle tremors noted. Appetite is severely decreased; a couple of biscuits eaten and some fruit. P.M. observation: Patient is sitting up on the floor, but reluctant to move . . . muscle tremors are present and significant.

On the third day, his nightmare ends:

A.M. Observation: Patient is sitting up this a.m., but still reluctant to move. Face is very red, but screeching was not noted this a.m. Noon: Patient is down in cage and not responding to stimulation. . . . Patient is down and only minimally responsive. 10:00 p.m.: Patient is euthanized per PI protocol.

The symptoms described in these animals are at least partially due to withdrawal from morphine. However, the issue here—the problem—is tolerance. During the process of addicting these animals to morphine, they develop a tolerance to the drug, just as humans do. And so when they have developed a physical addiction to the drug, when we have forced morphine to become one of the defining characteristics of their existence, we take it away from them, precipitating crash withdrawal.

The primates discussed here are not the only ones who suffered inside UKMED. The majority of these captives are described as losing hair, due to overgrooming. They also often exhibit other abnormal behavior such as circling, pacing, etc. Several animals are listed as dying of dehydration.

As I read these documents, I also reach a point of tolerance. I can only psychologically handle so much. Monkeys vomiting all over their cages, too weak to move off the floor onto their perches, suffering from such severe tremors that they can respond only by attacking their own limbs.

It all becomes too much to bear, and I have to walk away. But the real question is, why do we, as a society, tolerate this? Even if we put aside the idea of how difficult it is to generalize from highly stressed psychologically abnormal macaque monkeys to human beings, even if there was some wonder cure to be found, do we not reach a point, is there not a level at which it is just plain wrong? How much suffering are we willing to inflict on other animals, in the quest for a drug, vaccine, or treatment that might work? How utterly self-important are we?

Is there not a point where the potential benefits become irrelevant? Can we not agree that some things are just too wrong, too painful, too difficult even to read—let alone experience—that they should never ever be allowed to happen? The question is, how can we, as a supposedly enlightened society, tolerate this?

If we will not say that some things—no matter what they might bring—are wrong, then we should be honest with ourselves and abolish all laws governing the way that animals are treated in labs. If anything goes, then we should remove the restrictions that we have put in place solely to give our consciences ground upon which to stand. Rip away the curtain. Take a good hard look at what we are willing to do. These are the facts and we had better be able to live with ourselves.

But, and I sincerely hope this is true, if we as a species are willing to say that there are limits that should never ever be crossed, then we must go down a different road. If we actually believe that some things are simply wrong and can *never* be right, then we must make radical changes about the way animals are treated in laboratories.

Some things simply should not be tolerated. Human beings should not perform them, animals should not endure them, and people who care deeply about animals should not have to read them.

Bibliography

"Facility Reports and Information. University of Kansas Medical Center, Kansas City, KS." Stop Animal Exploitation NOW! http://www.all-creatures.org/saen/ks/res-fr-ks-ukmc.html. Accessed September 15, 2012.

Michael Budkie, AHT, is the cofounder and executive director of Stop Animal Exploitation NOW! (SAEN). After witnessing the atrocities of animal experimentation during his education, he successfully ended a head injury experiment on cats at the University of Cincinnati. In the mid-1990s, Michael cofounded SAEN, which works to terminate research projects and force the USDA to take legal action against laboratories. He has been published and travels extensively, appearing on TV and radio programs to expose the truth about animal experimentation.

Animals and Research: 150 Years of Medical Advance

Bella Williams

All of us have benefited, in one way or another, from animal research. Most of us do not even think about it. We take our health for granted and cannot imagine a world without pain-killers, vaccines, and antibiotics. Even blood transfusions, organ transplants, and treatments for cancers have become routine medical practice. These breakthroughs were possible only because of the research carried out by pioneering scientists, and the animals they worked with, and anyone who has suffered from serious disease, stayed in hospital, or needed blood, owes a life debt to these animals.

Medical research has brought society a long way in a comparatively short time. In 1800, London was in the grip of a cholera epidemic, people lived in squalid conditions, and human life expectancy worldwide was less than 30 years. Little was understood either about human physiology or about how disease was spread. Comparing this with modern health care, our understanding of how to prevent disease, and a life expectancy of 80 years in developed countries and an average of 63 years worldwide, it is evident that our better understanding of how the body functions in health and disease has brought enormous benefits for human health.

The nineteenth century saw a rapid advancement of scientific knowledge, and this process transformed health care. Improvements to sanitation and hygiene took place alongside an approach to medicine based on evidence and scientific rationale. In the first half of the nineteenth century, Edward Jenner's experiments produced the first vaccine, eventually leading to the elimination of smallpox. By the end of the nineteenth century, Louis Pasteur had demonstrated the germ theory of disease, a concept essential to treatment of infection. Although Pasteur was not the first to propose that disease was caused by microorganisms, the new scientific approach demanded evidence, and he was the first to demonstrate that microorganisms could be infectious agents, through his experiments on yeast, silk worms, and sheep.

Over the past 150 years, there have been great advances in science-based medicine, and there is still an enormous amount of work to be done. All of the Nobel Prizes given for medicine or physiology either have been based directly on animal experiments or have relied on data from animal studies to support their ideas. Much of this work has led to medical advances that are relevant to humans, while the rest has built the scientific understanding that underpins modern medicine.

Looking at just a single disease shows the impact of this approach. Asthma is a very common condition that causes narrowing of the airways of the lungs. It is made worse by allergens and eased by medication. Attacks can be triggered by any one of 200 allergens, causing the airways to become inflamed and causing coughing, wheezing, breathlessness, and chest tightness. The symptoms are reversed by treatment, but they can be severe and are sometimes fatal.

All current asthma medications were developed using animals. Therapy for asthma relies on inhaled medicines that suppress the underlying inflammation and relieve airway constriction. Much of this research was carried out in guinea pigs, a species that are particularly sensitive to allergens. Many studies were carried out on animals, from the 1970s to the present day, to find effective asthma medication that would not stimulate the heart, as was the case with early drugs. Work still continues to develop better medications that are effective in preventing severe attacks before they occur.

Research methods are constantly changing, and in some cases animals can now be replaced altogether. Magnetic resonance imaging, computer models, and new ways of growing cells in tissue cultures all contribute to building understanding of the body and its functions. But some questions can be answered only by studying a whole, living organism. We simply do not understand enough about how the body works to build a computerized simulation of a mammal, and the body (human or animal) is much more than the sum of its parts.

An example is the clearest way to show why it is not always possible to simply replace animals with other methodologies. When cancer causes disease, one of the most difficult and deadly problems is that tumors metastasize. This is the process by which they break off and spread to other parts of the body, and is studied by researchers around the world who hope to find ways to prevent this spread. Clearly, it is not possible to study this process in a dish or a test tube, nor, since we do not fully understand what is happening, can it be studied on a computer. Human volunteers are not suitable for studying this process, as cancer needs to be examined in its very early stages, and giving human volunteers cancer so that we can follow this process is not an option. We can, however, look at mutant mice, which are genetically predisposed to develop particular cancers. Using imaging, their tumors can be studied at early stages, and data can be collected long before the cancer causes the mice to become sick. The mice are killed before the cancer causes them to suffer. This type of experiment is teaching researchers more and more about how cancers develop and spread, leading to the development of new methods to detect and treat cancers.

It is not only humans that benefit from animal research. When dogs are taken to the vet for a vaccine or cats need a special diet to control disease, these too have been developed using animals. In 2010, the eradication of rinderpest was announced, after many years of research and an intensive vaccination and testing program. This lethal disease of cattle once spread rapidly, devastating livestock and causing poverty and starvation in affected areas. Rinderpest is only the second virus to have been completely eliminated (the other being smallpox), representing a massive breakthrough for world health that relied on animal studies.

All scientists strive for the day when animal research will be a thing of the past and constantly develop new techniques that will lead to fewer animals being used. But for now, animals remain an essential part of the research process, as we endeavor to learn more about how our bodies function, stop human suffering, and ensure that research animals are used with care, consideration, and to the greatest benefit of people and animals around the world.

Bella Williams has a background in pharmacology, but moved from the lab to work in science communication and medical ethics. She is editor of the AnimalResearch.Info website, and has spoken around the world on the role of animals in research. Bella is currently head of Engagement at Understanding Animal Research, a nonprofit organization based in the UK, which aims to secure understanding and acceptance of the humane use of animals for scientific research.

Reasoning with Myself

Vilay Khandelwal

I work in clinical research. My job entails testing new therapies on human beings, some meant to rid people of their cancers, others to slow disease progression or alleviate cancer symptoms and improve overall quality of life. What image does this description evoke?

Now, here is a little bit more about me. For the past five years of my life, I have being conducting basic science research. I have worked exclusively with animals (no pun intended toward my coworkers)—both vertebrates and invertebrates—to understand how the normal brain functions. Has my mental image changed?

Some of you are seeing me as an awkward guy in a white lab coat with unkempt hair, maliciously deriving pleasure performing heinous experiments on animals in the name of science. Others might be seeing the same guy in a white lab coat, completely engrossed in developing the latest of technologies and working to save lives with a big calming smile on my face. While many might side with the latter image, why is the former not completely unheard of? Should I be blaming the brilliance of the Hollywood machine or the bad PR skills of the scientific community?

When I was growing up, I wanted to be an astronaut, movie star, or even a bartender. Never in my wildest imagination did I want to embark on the crazy path that resulted in Frankenstein or Edward Scissorhands. But somehow I landed in the vicinity.

As a kid, I loved physics. After all, it explained so many of my experiences—the jerk I felt when Dad hit the brakes hard, the fact that I could estimate the trajectory of a tennis ball, and why floaties were helpful while learning to swim. But it was a biology class that led to real fireworks. Staring down at millions of similar hexagonal cells making up the onion skin blew my mind. The world became too big and too small at the same time. We are composed of hundreds of millions of tiny cells, each with the same DNA. Mind-blowing!

My 12-year-old self knew of smallpox eradication. Every January I saw the Polio Foundation dispense oral vaccines in their door-to-door campaign. I remember feeling the sting of a tetanus shot after I cut my leg on a rusted nail. Or the seven pills of different colors I saw my grandmother take each day. Doctors said medicines were needed to protect us. No questions needed to be asked. Who made them; where did they come from; how were they discovered? It was irrelevant.

Soon, however, I learned how the antibiotics were discovered. How the drugs were tested. It made sense. After all, I belong to the most superior race to walk this planet. On some divine level, the "lower" organisms existed for our convenience and consumption. The use of animals in research was moot.

But grad school changed everything. I was no longer an eager undergrad trying to examine the medicinal properties of plant extracts. I had moved up the ladder and into the animal kingdom with both vertebrates and invertebrates serving as my subjects.

My first day in lab, I was told not to refer to research animals as cute. Not to play with them. They were nothing but investigational tools. Weird, I thought. But as I saw the animal, whose fur coat streaks I had been appreciating, put to sleep, something changed. I was uncomfortable. I wondered how the moral superiority I so clung to gave way to sadness and even guilt.

I struggled with this for some time, defining my sense of morality. After 22 years in hibernation, my Hindu identity exerted itself and reasoned that research animals are bred for experimentation, the purpose for their existence. Denying this would be cruel to their spirits. But this circumlocution of the logic did not stand long. My rational self roared its head. If life is life, then why is that that I do not find animal research deplorable, when the thought of some of the same experiments on human beings is downright unacceptable?

Then it came to me. The answer was so simple. No matter how civilized humans get, we are still animals. We will still stand by member of our tribe, ever ready to sacrifice others to ensure our well-being and survival.

Our higher cognitive abilities enable us to humanize other species and extend them the same rights as we claim. No wonder one has to jump through so many hoops before conducting animal research. Not only do scientists have to justify the use of animals; they also must show that this is their last resort—that the research they propose is necessary and cannot be accomplished with computer simulations or experiments on microorganisms or even single cells, that numbers of animals to be used are strictly controlled and the experimental strategies tightly monitored.

No scientist I know loves working with animals. But as humanity continues its onslaught on diseases, what choice do they have? Even the most sophisticated of computer simulations are not able to capture all interactions between molecules. Cell lines and microorganisms might help us to understand behavior on a single-cell level. But what is good for the heart can be toxic for the liver. How can methods to alleviate pain be studied without pain? Are we to test the safety of neonatal drugs in newborns? Even today, for every 5,000 drugs that are being tested in animals, only 50 are making it to human testing and only 1 of these is actually approved for human use.

Scientists walk on eggshells when talking about their research. While extolling the virtues of their scientific discoveries, neither they nor the media highlight the use of animals. At the same time, some self-described animal rights activists have taken extreme positions. Sending threat letters to someone's house, or bombing someone's front porch while their kids are sleeping is not airing out your views. It is exactly how the federal government describes it—an act of domestic terrorism.

My position on animal research has evolved from apathy and ignorance to conflict and finally support. I believe in the good that it has and will contribute to. So I defend it.

Vilay Khandelwal currently works as a data manager at Stanford University Medical Center performing clinical research. He is an engineer with an MS in neuroscience from the University of Southern California.

Introduction

The debate over the use of animals in experimental research goes on among individuals and organizations, most of whom have strong feelings about one side or the other of the debate. This chapter contains brief sketches of some of the individuals and organizations who are important in understanding the arguments as to why and how animals should be an essential part of biomedical and other forms of scientific research. The list provided here is, of course, incomplete. A number of the organizations listed themselves have links on their web pages to other organizations with similar viewpoints.

American Anti-Vivisection Society

801 Old York Rd., Suite 204
Jenkintown, PA 19046-1611
Phone: (215) 887-0816
(800) SAY-AAVS (729-2287)
E-mail: aavs@aavs.org
URL: http://www.aavs.org/

Frances Powers Cobbe, the force behind the British Union to Abolish Vivisection (BUAV), an organization formed in 1898 that is still active today. (Hulton-Deutsch Collection/CORBIS)

The American Anti-Vivisection Society (AAVS) is the oldest nonprofit organization in the United States devoted exclusively to the elimination of animal testing in scientific and biomedical research. The organization was formed in response to the growing use of animal-based research in the United Kingdom and the United States in the late nineteenth century. It took as its model the young National Anti-Vivisection Society founded in England in 1875. Although based on the English model, the roots of AAVS actually preceded the groundbreaking Cruelty to Animals Act of 1876 in Great Britain by a decade. In 1866, Philadelphia businessman Colonel M. Richards Mucklé announced his intention to establish a law enforcement society aimed at protecting animals from the worst abuses to which they were then exposed, a society that became the Philadelphia Society to Prevent Cruelty to Animals. Shortly thereafter, the wives of two members of that early group, Caroline Earle White and Mary Frances Lovell, decided to form a women's auxiliary, the Women's Branch of the PSPCA (WBPSPCA), which survives today as the Women's Humane Society of Pennsylvania (WHSP). As White and Lovell began to hear of the growing popularity of animal experimentation in the United States at the end of the century, they decided to form yet another group with the very specific objective of "preventing torture in the labs" of research scientists. That decision led to the creation of the American Anti-Vivisection Society in 1883.

AAVS was not slow in addressing its agenda among legislators. In 1885 it submitted its first bill before the U.S. Congress, the Bill to Restrict Vivisection. The bill was defeated, as were virtually all of the organization's legislative efforts over the next half century. The one success it points to during this period was blockage of an attempt to overturn the so-called 28-hour rule, which provided for the humane care of animals in transit across state lines. On its website, AAVS admits that these early legislative efforts were "not always successful," but the organization was successful in other ways, primarily by making the general public aware of the moral and ethical problems posed by the growing use of animals in scientific and biomedical research. In fact, it was not until passage of the Animal Welfare Act in 1966 that the AAVS began to experience concrete legislative accomplishments in realization of its mission to reduce or eliminate the use of animals in research and testing.

Today, AAVS campaigns continue to focus on animal experimentation and animal testing, although they have expanded to include a number of other related topics. The End Animal Cloning project, for example, is an attempt to convince federal agencies to end and prohibit the cloning of animals for food production and other purposes, arguing that such practices not only pose a threat to public health, but also represent a health risk to cloned animals themselves. Similarly, the Stop Animal Patents campaign is an effort to get governmental agencies from approving patents for the development of certain types of altered animal species, such as rabbits whose eyes have been intentionally damaged for product-testing purposes. The association points out that more than 650 patents have already been granted for animals that have been altered in one way or another to make them more useful for research projects.

Most AAVS campaigns continue to focus on animal experimentation and animal-testing issues. For example, its Ban Pound Seizure campaign aims to completely eliminate the practice of requiring or allowing public shelters to release unclaimed animals to researchers for experimentation. Only two states, Ohio and Oklahoma, still have laws that require shelters to release animals, and the AAVS admits that the problem is a "small, but troubling" part of the antivivisection challenge. Still, it has its goal the total elimination of such laws in all their forms and the complete protection of all animals who find their way into shelters. Similarly, the Animal Welfare Act campaign is an ongoing effort to get the USDA to include rats, mice, and birds in the list of species protected by the Animal Welfare Act of 1966. AAVS and other animal welfare groups have had some success in this campaign, but it has continually been counteracted by greater success of research groups, such as the NABR.

The AAVS website is a rich source of information on a variety of animal welfare topics, including basic information about the use of animals in research and the moral and ethical issues involved in such practices; alternatives to the use of animals in research; the role of animal experimentation and testing in educational programs and options available to students who do not wish to participate in such exercises; the use of animals in product testing; and laws relating to animal experimentation on a federal and state level. AAVS's primary publication for the general public is its quarterly magazine, *AV Magazine*, which can be downloaded from its website at http://www.aavs.org/site/c.bkLTKfOSLhK 6E/b.8127027/k.921F/AV_Magazine.htm#.UC-_5d38u5J. The organization also publishes in print and electronic form a number of reports on topics such as "Primates by the Numbers," on the importation and use of nonhuman primates for research in the United States; "Dying to Learn," the report of a study on the use of dead and live animals by U.S. colleges and universities for classroom instruction; and "Genetic Engineering and Animal Welfare," which outlines the risks posed by genetic engineering for both human consumers and the animals produced by such research.

Americans for Medical Progress

526 King Street, Suite # 201
Alexandria, VA 22314
Phone: (703) 836-9595 ext. 100
E-mail: amp@amprogress.org
URL: http://www.amprogress.org/content/home

Americans for Medical Progress (AMP) is a 501(c)3 nonprofit organization founded in 1991 "to develop responsive, media-savvy and effective strategies to mitigate the animal rights threat to biomedical research." The organization's guiding principle is that animal research is an essential component of the research needed to find treatments and cures for a host of human diseases. While it recognizes this critical role of animal experimentation in research, it also acknowledges the need for sensitive and humane treatment of those animals in experimentation. The organization is supported primarily by donations from private donations.

AMP makes use of a number of activities in carrying out its goal for the support of using animals in biological and medical research:

- It works to increase public knowledge about and support of animal-based research through its website and its print publications.
- It publicizes the stories of individuals who have benefited from research as a way of illustrating the essential character of animal-based research.
- It provides a host of publications aimed at improving the public image of animal-based research.
- It provides guest columns, letters to the editor, news interviews, and journal articles to promote fair and accurate media coverage of scientists' responsible use of animals in research.
- It works with biomedical researchers to learn more about the activities of animal rights proponents and to develop strategies for providing alternative views for the publicity provided by these individuals and organizations.
- It suggests tactics for preventing the actions of animal rights groups that would result in the delay or termination of research involving the use of animal experimentation.
- It works with state, national, and international research organizations in order to sustain and improve the efficiency of biomedical research.

One of the organization's most important campaigns is called "Raising Voices, Saving Lives." The goal of the campaign is for individual supporters of animal research to speak out about their own experiences with animal research, whether as a researcher or as someone who has benefited from animal-based biomedical research. The three elements of the campaign are listed as (1) know the issues, (2) know your audience, and (3) know your opposition. Some of the ways in which AMP supporters can make their position known is through casual conversations with friends and neighbors; public presentations at local seminars, conferences, conventions, and other types of meetings; media outreach, such as writing letters to the editors of local newspapers and responding to radio and television programs in which animal research is mentioned; becoming involved with local animal research committees and activities, such as volunteering to serve on local IACUCs; and involving others, by attempting to recruit friends, coworkers, and others who may have common interests with those of the AMP program.

AMP has an extensive publications program, perhaps the most important element of which is its weekly electronic newsletter, *AMP News Service Digest*, which is available to interested readers at no cost. The organization also publishes a series of posters that feature key points about the use of animals in research, including posters on the role of the nude mouse, the laboratory rat, and the genetically engineered "fat rat" in biomedical research. It also produces two videos supporting the philosophy of the AMP, "Veterinarians Speaking for Research" and "Physicians Speaking for Research." Another useful publication is a pocket-size guide to talking points about animal research, "Facts about Research." Most of these materials are also available in Spanish, French, and Portuguese.

AMP also sponsors the Michael D. Hayre Fellowship in Public Outreach, a program established in 2008 to promote peer education about animal research among students and young adults aged 18 to 30. The program attempts to locate college students and young adults in the United States who are "frustrated by the domination of animal rights rhetoric against biomedical research and who are committed to making a case for the necessary and humane use of laboratory animals in the pursuit of treatments and cures." The fellowship provides a stipend of $5,000 and an additional grant of up to $2,000 to pay for educational programs developed by Hayre fellows.

The four programs supported by Hayre fellowships thus far are:

- Speaking of Research, a program developed by Tom Holder, a graduate of Oxford University, to provide university students and faculty with better information about animal experimentation

- Pro-Test for Science, one of whose activities was the distribution of a petition in support of the continued use of animals for biomedical research (see the petition at http://www .amprogress.org/sites/default/files/Signatories_Pro-Test%20 Petition%20149.pdf)

- Thank a Mouse, a program in which veterinarians are recruited to provide accurate information about the importance of using animals in biomedical research

- Speaking Honestly—Animal Research Education, whose goal it is to provide the general public with more accurate information about the use of animals in research to counteract "the often sensationalized campaigns and false claims prevalent in today's media."

The organization's website also offers a number of links to research advocacy groups, student sites, professional and scientific resources, and alternatives to animal testing.

Animal Defenders International. *See* National Anti-Vivisection Society (UK)

Association for Assessment and Accreditation of Laboratory Animal Care

5283 Corporate Drive, Suite 203
Frederick, MD 21703-2879

Phone: (301) 696-9626
Fax: (301) 696-9627
E-mail: accredit@aaalac.org
URL: http://www.aaalac.org/

The Association for Assessment and Accreditation of Laboratory Animal Care (AAALAC) is a private, nonprofit organization that assesses and accredits programs that use animals in scientific and biomedical research. It consists of more than 850 companies, universities, hospitals, government agencies, and other research institutions in 36 countries who participate voluntarily in the program. Participation is often motivated by an institutions interest in and need for meeting federal, state, local, or other laws and regulations dealing with the use of animals in experiments.

During the late 1940s, a group of veterinarians in the Chicago area began to meet to discuss issues related to the use of animals in scientific and biomedical research. Those meetings eventually led to the formation of a national organization in 1950 called the Animal Care Panel (ACP). One of the organization's earliest and most important accomplishments was the publication of *Standards for the Care of the Dog Used in Medical Research*, a set of guidelines for use by research institutions. More than a decade later, in 1963, the ACP published a more extended version of the *Care of the Dog* publication called *The Guide for Laboratory Animals Facilities and Care*. That publication was later taken over by the Institute for Laboratory Animal Research of the National Academy of Sciences, and is currently available in its eighth edition.

Publication of the *Guide* represented a long process by which the ACP attempted to develop standards for the proper care and treatment of experimental animals, and then to develop a program by which institutions could be inspected and approved within light of these standards. By 1965, all of the elements of an acceptable assessment and accreditation program were in place, and the ACP reorganized and changed its name to the American Association for Accreditation of

Laboratory Animal Care (AAALAC). The first meeting of the organization was attended by representatives from 14 professional organizations such as the American Association of Dental Schools, American College of Physicians, American Heart Association, American Hospital Association, American Medical Association, American Veterinary Medical Association, National Association of State Universities and Land Grant Colleges, Federation of American Societies for Experimental Biology, National Society of Medical Research, the Pharmaceutical Manufacturer's Association. During its first year of operation, the AAALAC conducted investigations of 30 institutions that had applied for accreditation from the organization.

In 1996, the AAALAC changed its name once more (but kept its acronym) to the Association for the Assessment and Accreditation of Laboratory Animal Care International. This change in names reflected the fact that the organization had extended its reach far beyond the borders of the United States to more than two dozen other countries. Today, the AAALAC has overseas offices in Pamplona, Spain (for Europe), and Samutprakarn, Thailand (for Southeast Asia), as well as a Pacific Rim office in Frederick, Maryland.

In addition to its primary mission of assessment and accreditation, AAALAC provides a number of other services to research institutions and organizations, as well as to the general public. For example, it provides a searchable database on its website to all organizations that have been accredited by state and country (with the exception of a few institutions and companies that have asked not to be listed). The organization also has a number of publications for sale dealing with issues of research animal care and maintenance. Some examples include *Administration of Substances and Removal of Blood, Animal Surgery, DNA Research, Humane Endpoints, Neoplasia, Neuroscience and Behavioral Research, Amphibians and Reptiles, Dogs, Nonhuman Primates, Rodents and Lagomorphs, Wild Animals, Biosafety in Microbiological and Biomedical Laboratories, Euthanasia of Experimental Animals, Guidelines for Construction and Equipment of Hospital and Medical Facilities*, and *FELASA Guidelines for Education of Specialists in Laboratory Animal Science.*

The AAALAC educational program takes three forms:

- On-site courses, in which AAALAC instructors visit institutions and organizations to provide instruction on general or specific issues
- Online instruction, in which courses are available through the Internet
- Webinars, which deal with topics such as animal care and use; environment, housing and management ; veterinary care; and physical plant

Regular publications from AAALAC include the online newsletter, *Connections*; *AAALAC Update*, intended specially for international members; and *AAALAC Ag Update*, designed for agricultural animal professionals. Publications intended specifically for institutions and organizations interested in applying for accreditation are available on the AAALAC website. They deal with topics such as the benefits of accreditation, the process for applying for assessment and accreditation, and the procedures involved in program status evaluation, a kind of pre-assessment procedure. Many of these materials are also available in Chinese, French, German, Japanese, Korean, Spanish, and Thai, in addition to English.

Francis Balkwill (1952–)

Balkwill is professor of cancer biology at Barts Cancer Institute of the University of London, center lead for the Centre for Cancer and Inflammation, director of the Centre of the Cell, and chair of Understanding Animal Research (UAR), an English organization that supports the use of animals in biomedical and scientific research. Her position on animal testing, like that of the UAR itself, is that every effort should be made to reduce the use of animals in research, but that there may be times when there are no alternatives to animal experimentation. In a 2012 interview with cancer survivor David Taylor, for example, she pointed out that, at this time in history, a commitment to the three Rs of animal research (replacement, reduction, and refinement) is now "part of our DNA" for researchers. Nonetheless, she feels that, even when every available alternative is considered, there are still occasions when animal testing must be included in a research program. It is, she says, just "one part of the jigsaw puzzle" involved in solving a medical problem, such as finding a way of dealing with cancer.

Francis Rosemary Balkwill was born in southwest London in 1952. She is commonly known by the name of Fran Balkwill. At the age of 11, Balkwill was awarded a scholarship to Surbiton High School at Kingston upon Thames, Surrey. She then matriculated at Bristol University in 1969, where she earned her bachelor of science degree (with honors) in cellular pathology. She continued her graduate studies in the Faculty of Medicine at the University of London, from which she received her PhD in 1976. Her major field of study at London was cell biology of leukemia. Her work in this field was carried out at the Medical Oncology Department of St. Bartholomew's Hospital in London.

Upon completion of her doctoral studies, Balkwill took a postdoctoral position in the laboratory of Joyce Taylor-Papadimitriou for the Imperial Cancer Research Fund (ICRF) at Lincoln's Inn Fields (now the Cancer Research UK London Research Institute). Her primary field of interest was the use of interferons for the treatment of cancer. In an interview with Fiona Watt in 2005 for the *Journal of Cell Science*, Balkwill noted that working with Taylor-Papadimitriou was not only a valuable professional experience but also an opportunity to learn how married women can balance a professional career in science with a married life that includes the care of two children.

After a brief two-year hiatus from Lincoln's Inn Fields at her own laboratory, Balkwill returned to ICRF, where she remained for the next two decades. At ICRF, she held the title of principal scientist and head of the biological therapy laboratory. Her primary research interest during this time has been the role of cytokines in the development of cancers. Cytokines are a group of proteins the regulate the action of the immune system. In recent years, she has focused in particular on the relationship between cancer and inflammation, most especially in regards to the character and development of ovarian cancer.

In 2000, Balkwill left ICRF to accept an appointment as professor of cancer biology and center lead of the Centre for Cancer and Inflammation at Barts Cancer Institute of Queen Mary University of London, posts that she continues to hold today. In 2001, she was also instrumental in the formation of a new program of science education for young people, the Centre of the Cell. The goal of the program has been to bring children and young adults directly into the milieu of scientific research. It has worked toward this goal first of all by locating the center directly within the confines of St. Barts and the Queen Mary School of Medicine, where visitors can observe and interact with researchers in the field. In 2007, the center opened its website for the first time, providing visitors with a wide-ranging introduction to all aspects of cells, medical research, ethical issues, patient histories, and other background information. In 2009, the center also opened the Centre of the Cell visitor center in London, a £4 million ($6.2 million) project aimed at young people age 9 to 19, families, and community groups. The major feature of the center is a large pod suspended over the main floor of the center, representing a 16-cell stage embryo.

In addition to her research program, Balkwill has written 13 books for children about science, inspired in part she has said by the desire to find ways of explaining to her own children the kind of research in which she and her colleagues are involved. In 2004 she received the EMBO Award for Communication in Life Sciences from the European Molecular Biology Organization for her children's books. She has also received the

Michael Faraday Medal of the Royal Society (2005) and was awarded an OBE (Order of the British Empire) by Queen Elizabeth II in 2008. In 2006, Balkwill was elected to the Academy of Medical Sciences, and in 2009 was given an honorary fellowship in the British Science Association. As of mid-2012, she had authored or coauthored more than 230 peer-reviewed publications and given more than four dozen lectures on topics in scientific research and communication.

Jeremy Bentham (1748–1832)

Bentham was a jurist, political theorist, and philosopher, some-times known as the Father of Utilitarianism. Utilitarianism is an ethical principle claiming that the proper course of action in any situation is one that brings the greatest amount of pleasure to the greatest number of individuals. He was a prolific writer and profound thinker interested in a wide range of topics, only one of which was the moral status of animals. Prior to the eighteenth century, animals were regarded largely as "items" or "things" with no emotions or even any sense of pain or feeling. Their only role in the world was to be of service to humans, a view supported by both pagan and religious teachings. Bentham took a very different view, based on his utilitarian philosophy. He argued that animals deserved to be thought of in the same way as humans, and that they had the same rights as humans, not because they might not feel or have useful lives of their own, but because they deserved to be happy in the same way that humans need to be happy. His most famous comment in this regard was a line in his 1823 work, *Introduction to the Principles of Moral and Legislation*. "The question," he said, "is not Can they *reason*? Can they *talk*? but, Can they *suffer*?" And, since the answer to that question seemed to Bentham to clearly be "yes, they can suffer," animals must then be accorded the same moral rights as are available to humans.

Jeremy Bentham was born in London on February 15, 1748, into a prosperous and socially respected family. He is said to have been a child prodigy who entertained himself as a child by reading works such as a four-volume history of Great Britain. He was fluent in Latin, Greek, and French by the age of 10, and was sometimes referred to by other members of his family as "the philosopher." Bentham completed his secondary education at the Westminster School in 1760 and matriculated at Queen's College, Oxford, where he took his bachelor's degree in 1763 at the age of 15. He then continued his education at Lincoln's Inn, from which he received his master's degree in 1766. Bentham was then called to the bar, but declined to pursue a career in the law because of the disdain he had developed for the English legal system. Indeed, he spent much of his adult life outlining ways in which that system could be improved to function more effectively.

With his father's death in 1792, Bentham became sufficiently wealthy not to have to think about gainful employment for the rest of his life. Instead, he purchased an elegant home in London, which soon become the center of intellectual and social life for many of his friends and colleagues. He developed an interest in a wide range of social, political, legal, and economic topics and wrote voraciously about all of them. He is reputed to have written in a somewhat haphazard way, moving from topic to topic without necessarily finishing any one subject before moving on to another. Among the subjects he discussed were the revolutions then taking place in the United States and France. He wrote a short essay in 1776 about the absurdity of the new political system being proposed in the United States and called the French "Declaration of the Rights of Man" "nonsense on stilts."

The principle of utilitarianism was hardly original with Bentham. But he probably expressed that principle more clearly and more powerfully than did most (or any) of his predecessors. He argued that the fundamental fact of life was that God had created life with the ability to experience either pain or pleasure. The only proper way to judge the morality of any particular action by a person or an institution, then, was to decide the extent to which it maximized one of those emotions—pleasure—and diminished the other—pain. He said that abstract concepts such as "the good," "the right," or "the moral" were worthless measures against which to judge the quality of an action.

Bentham died in London on June 6, 1832. One of his final acts was the donation of a large sum of money to the recently established University College in London, one of the few academic institutions to welcome nontraditional students, that is, Catholics, Jews, and nonconformists. In a reflection of Bentham's somewhat unconventional character, his dead body was dissected, embalmed, fully dressed, and placed in a chair in the main corridor of University College, where it remains today.

Henry Bergh (1813–1888)

Bergh spent much of the first part of his life as a wealthy world traveler, with no specific occupation or professional responsibilities. Around the age of 50, however, he became interested in issues of animal and child welfare, and devoted the last part of his life to working on these issues. He was largely responsible for the founding of the ASPCA in 1866 and the formation of the MSPCA in 1874. Probably his most important contribution was the advancement of the principle that animals and children were individuals of value in and of themselves, and not to be regarded simply as the property or chattels of others. His actions in the last third of his life were all predicated on this general principle, which was to become the guiding light of much of the animal welfare movement that has survived to the present day.

Henry Bergh was born in New York City on August 28, 1813. His father, Christian Bergh, was a very successful ship builder who had supplied vessels for the United States in the War of 1812 against Great Britain. In addition to becoming very wealthy in this enterprise, Christian Bergh also developed a reputation for honesty and fairness in his dealings with others and, in particular, with his employees. He is said to have been one of the few industrialists to offer employed to freed black slaves and to pay them on the same wage scale used with white workers. Henry's mother, Elizabeth Ivers Bergh, was apparently instrumental also in developing his character. His biographer, Stephen Zawistowski, says that Elizabeth "softened his edges" and "influenced his sense of honesty and integrity."

Bergh matriculated at Columbia College (now Columbia University) in 1834, but did not complete his degree. Instead, he joined his father and brother, Edwin, in the shipbuilding business. Within a matter of years, Christian Bergh retired from the business, leaving his two sons in charge. Shortly thereafter, the business was sold, leaving Henry and Edwin with a considerable fortune, at least enough money to live for the rest of their lives in comfort without having to consider future employment. Henry took his share of the shipyard profits and traveled throughout Europe for five years from 1831 to 1836, having some vague notions of becoming a writer. Those plans came to naught, however, and after his father's death in 1843, he used his inheritance to move permanently to Europe. In 1863, he took on one of his few regular positions, accepting an appointment as legation secretary to the court of Czar Alexander II in St. Petersburg.

During his time in St. Petersburg, Bergh experienced one of those moments of enlightenment, according to Stephen Zawistowski, in which he became starkly conscious of the abuse humans heaped upon animals. He is said to have stopped a peasant in the street from beating his horse and, in a flash, recognized that what he had been witnessing was one of the great injustices in the modern world. Shortly after the incident, Bergh returned to the United States by way of London, where he met with the Earl of Harrowby, then president of the RSPCA. Bergh arrived in the United States with the emotional mind-set and a specific strategy to attack the problem of animal abuse in the United States.

The official website of the ASPCA notes that the seminal event in Bergh's program was a meeting held at Clinton Hall in New York City on February 8, 1866, at which he described to his audience the horrors of bullfighting he had witnessed in Spain and the more local problem of the inhumane and regular beating of horses, dogs, and other animals on the streets of New York. He found enough interest and enthusiasm to establish a new organization to deal with these problems (the ASPCA) only three months later, on April 10, 1866. In the run-up to this act, a group of animal welfare enthusiasts had been lobbying the state legislature in New York to adopt new animal protection laws, legislation that was finally adopted only three days before the founding of the ASPCA itself. By the middle of April, then, Bergh was already on the streets of New York, carrying with him a copy of the legislation and confronting cab drivers, trolley operators, butchers, and anyone else dealing with animals as to their treatment of animals. Shortly thereafter, he was on the lecture trail that took him to cities across the country, where his passion and strategy led to the foundation of many new local chapters of the ASPCA.

By the early 1870s, Bergh's work had become widely known and, to a large extent, highly respected throughout the United States. (A number of detractors did object to his work, however, and gave him the title "King of Meddlers.") One individual to whom this reputation had special meaning was a Massachusetts social worker by the name of Etta Wheeler. Wheeler came to Bergh with the story of a young girl, Mary Ellen, who was being constantly and brutally beaten by her foster parents in Massachusetts. Wheeler asked Bergh if he could apply to young children the same spirit of justice he had obtained for animals. Through his lawyer, Elbridge Gerry, Bergh was able to have Mary Ellen removed from her foster home and, encouraged by the success of that endeavor, worked for the foundation of the MSPCA in 1874. A year later, he and Gerry also founded the American Society for the Prevention of Cruelty to Children in New York City.

Bergh's activities on behalf of animals and children had sapped his strength, and he was in ill health for most of the last decade of his life. He finally died in New York City on March 12, 1888.

British Union to Abolish Vivisection

16a Crane Grove
London, England
N7 8NN
Phone: +44 (0) 20 7700 4888
Fax: +44 (0) 20 7700 0252
Email: info@buav.org
URL: http://www.buav.org/

The British Union to Abolish Vivisection (BUAV) was established on June 14, 1898, at a meeting held in Bristol, England, under the auspices of Frances Powers Cobbe. Cobbe was a prominent suffragette, women's advocate, Unitarian proponent, and advocate for animal rights in the second half of the nineteenth century. She had founded an earlier antivivisectionist organization, the NAVS, more than two decades earlier, in 1875. Between those two events, however, the NAVS had grown somewhat more accepting of the necessity of at least some forms of vivisection under at least some circumstances. Cobbe was unwilling to yield her original position that the goal of her efforts should be directed toward *abolishing* vivisection, not finding suitable means under which it could be conducted. For this reason, she decided that a new organization was needed, which led to the 1898 founding of the BUAV.

During its first years, the BUAV was a decentralized, but very successful organization. After only a year in existence, it had eight regional offices and had begun publication of a regular newsletter, *The Abolitionist*. By 1903, the organization had grown to 20 regional offices and a central Parliamentary Association that lobbied for legislation prohibiting vivisection. In 1904, Cobbe finally achieved her dream for the BUAV with the opening of a national headquarters in London.

Interest in the BUAV continued to grow throughout the first half of the twentieth century, with the organization reaching its maximum size of 154 branches (including six in Australia and one in New Zealand) in 1940. After that point, a number of efforts were made to consolidate the efforts of different animal welfare and antivivisectionist organizations. One such joint association was the British Federation of Animal Welfare Societies, of which BUAV was a founding member in 1952. Such efforts, including an attempt to consolidate the BUAV and NAVS into a single organization in the mid-1960s, eventually failed, and the BUAV returned to its dedicated efforts to eliminate vivisection entirely from all research programs.

Today, the BUAV points to a number of accomplishments, some of which it alone is responsible for, and others of which it was a cooperating resource. These accomplishments include:

- A ban by the British government in 1995 on the imported of wild animals for use in scientific research
- A ban by the British government in 1997 on the use of animals for the testing of cosmetics
- A ban by the British government in 2001 on so-called LD50 toxicity tests in which animals are killed to determine the toxicity of chemicals
- Adoption by the EU in 2006 of a REACH (registration, evaluation, authorization, and restriction of chemical substances) policy promoted by the BUAV, among other groups
- A legal victory in 2007 against the British government for withholding information about suffering experienced by animals being used in licensed research at Cambridge University
- A reduction in the use of animals in 2011 by the European Medicines Agency
- Rejection of the British government in 2012 of an application to breed beagles for scientific and medical research in the country

Much of the society's work is carried out through a variety of campaigns with specific goals. Some examples of those campaigns are the following:

- Cargo Cruelty: A program to get international air carriers to stop carrying animals into Great Britain for use as subjects of research. As of 2012, almost 80 international airlines had signed on to this campaign. Some of the major holdouts include Air Canada, Air China, Air France, and Philippine Airlines.

- No Cruel Cosmetics: Loopholes in the 2009 EU ban on the use of cosmetics that have been tested on animals allows the marketing of such products under special conditions that could permit the practice to continue for another decade. This campaign is designed to eliminate the sale of such products as soon as possible.

- Clean Up Cruelty: This campaign aims to expand prohibitions on the animal testing of cosmetics to other household products.

- Freedom of Information: Existing freedom of information (FOI) laws in Great Britain contain exceptions that allow information about research procedures to be withheld under certain specified conditions. The goal of this campaign is to eliminate those exceptions so that anyone can learn more about the way animals are used in research in the UK.

- 12 Million Reasons: This campaign is aimed at tightening and expanding Directive 86/609/EEC on the protection of animals used in experiments, amended most recently in 2010. The BUAV argues that provisions that allow the use of animals in testing are still so weak that as many as 12 million research animals may die each year under the present terms of the directive.

In addition to these public campaigns, the BUAV also conducts a number of undercover investigations. As the name suggests, these investigations are carried out by individuals who seek employment with companies known to or suspected of using or supplying animals for scientific or medical research experiments. BUAV conducted the first such undercover investigation in 1989 at the Huntingdon Research Centre (now Huntingdon Life Sciences Ltd.), in Cambridgeshire, England, on the use of beagles for toxicity testing. Since that time, the organization has expanded its investigations to a number of sites worldwide, including botox testing of mice at Wickham Research Laboratory, the breeding of beagles at the Harlan-Hillcrest company, the collection of dogs from a number of shelters throughout Europe for research in England, and the farming and trapping of primates for research in a number of Asian countries including Cambodia, Indonesia, Laos, Malaysia, and Vietnam.

Francis Power Cobbe (1822–1904)

Cobbe was an ambitious woman of wide-ranging interests and accomplishments. She has been described in the *Dictionary of Unitarian and Universalist Biography* (*DUUB*) as "one of the most influential figures in the British Unitarian movement of her day." She was also very active in the suffragette movement in Great Britain and, in middle age, became interested and active in the antivivisectionist movement. In 1875, she founded the Society for the Protection of Animals Liable to Vivisection (SPALV), also known at the time as the Victoria Street Society. In 1897, the SPALV changed its name to the NAVS, an organization that remains active in the United Kingdom today. Cobbe also founded a second antivivisectionist organization in 1898, the BUAV, an organization that also remains active in the twenty-first century.

She found the need to create this second organization when the NAVS decided in the late 1890s to alter its focus from the complete abolition of vivisection to the promotion of procedures that would allow vivisection under more humane conditions for animals involved in experimentation. In her autobiography, Cobbe wrote about the "pain and mortification" she felt in having to leave the organization she founded more than two decades earlier for the protection of animals. But she said she felt she had no choice other than to remain faithful to the founding principles of the NAVS "whereby our party renounces all compromise with the 'abominable sin,' and refuses to be again cheated by the hocus-pocus of Vivisectors and their deceptive anesthetics." She worried at the time that she would not have the strength to carry on her work for animals at this late stage in her life, but that is precisely what she did in the few years remaining to her.

Francis Power Cobbe was born on December 4, 1822, at Newbridge House, Donabate County, Dublin, Ireland, into a family with a long and prestigious religious tradition that included five archbishops. She was the youngest of five children; the others were all boys. Her father and mother, Charles and Frances (Conway) Cobbe, raised their children in a religion of strict evangelical Christianity. Like all girls of the time, Cobbe was educated at home until the age of 14, when she was enrolled, according to the *DUUB*, at a "fashionable girls' boarding school for two years" with the hope of turning her into "a socially acceptable young lady."

Those plans did not conform to her own expectations, however, and she returned to Newbridge House, where she became the housekeeper for nearly two decades, from 1838 to 1857. During that period of time, she taught herself a variety of academic subjects that included astronomy, geometry, history, literature, philosophy, and writing. She also experienced a transformative religious experience at the age of 20 when she realized that she could no longer accept the strong religious beliefs with which she had been raised. She declared herself at first an agnostic, and then accepted the principles of Unitarianism, a faith with which she associated herself for the rest of her life. The crisis through which Cobbe went so outraged her father that he banished her to her brother's farmstead, a banishment that lasted only a short time before her father called her back to Newbridge House.

In 1857 Charles Cobbe died, leaving his daughter with a small inheritance that allowed her to travel and to live on her own. During her first trip to Europe she met the English sculptor Mary Lloyd, with whom she was to form a domestic partnership that lasted for the rest of her life. In her autobiography, she wrote that "God has given me two priceless benedictions in life;—in my youth, a perfect Mother; in my later years, a perfect Friend [Mary Lloyd]."

After her return to England from her 11-month trip to Europe, Cobbe accepted an opportunity to work with social reformer Mary Carpenter, who had established the Red Lodge school for abandoned and delinquent girls in Bristol. Although excited by the opportunity to put her commitment to social reform into practice, Cobbe was able to remain at the school for only a year. She found the day-to-day chores of the school too demanding for a woman of her girth. (She had a lifelong problem of obesity, noting in her autobiography that she could "always entertain myself with my knife and fork!") After leaving Red Lodge, she focused her energies on speaking and writing about a number of social causes, including the rights of women and Unitarian causes. For many years, she wrote a series of articles for the London newspaper *Echo*, which received widespread interest and support, at least partly because they were unsigned and thus unattributable to "only" a woman's viewpoint. She also spoke before the National Association for the Promotion of Social Science Congress on the topic of women's education; was a member of the Kensington Discussion Group, which dealt with women's issues; was a member of the Married Women's Property Committee; and served on the executive committee of the London National Society for Women's Suffrage. The *DUUB* quotes her as saying that the greatest satisfaction she received in looking back over this period of work was her efforts to "obtain protection for unhappy wives, beaten, mangled, mutilated or trampled on by brutal husbands."

For the last two decades of her life, her greatest passion was her work for the protection of animals, represented by her founding of and work with the NAVS and BUAV. In 1884, Cobbe and Lloyd left London to retire to the latter's family estate at Hengwrit, Wales. There she continued to write and work for the causes that had meant so much to her throughout her life, especially her battle against vivisection. Lloyd died in 1896, leaving Cobbe lonely and distraught. She followed her life partner eight years later, also dying at Hengwrit, on April 5, 1904, where she was buried next to Lloyd.

In Defense of Animals

3010 Kerner Blvd
San Rafael, CA 94901
Phone: (415) 448-0048
Fax: (415) 454-1031
idainfo@idausa.org
URL: http://www.idausa.org/

In Defense of Animals (IDA) was founded in 1983 by veterinarian Elliot Katz in response to concerns expressed by two researchers at the University of California at Berkeley, Dr. Bruce Feldman and Dr. Maxwell Redfearn, about the treatment of animals being used in experiments on campus. When Katz investigated these complaints, he found that conditions were far worse than anyone had realized. The problem was confounded by the fact that the university refused to abide by even the most basic requirements of the Animal Welfare Act of 1966 (AWA) and refused to forward to the U.S. Department of Agriculture Animal and Plant Health Inspection Service (APHIS) required documents about animal care at the university. Katz organized a group of concerned citizens under the title of Californians for Responsible Research (CRR), an organization that soon changed its name to In Defense of Animals. CRR brought suit against the USDA, which in turn investigated the university. When the USDA found the university guilty of violating the AWA, it assessed a fine of $12,000. As of 2012, Katz is still president of the organization, which now claims about 60,000 members with an operating budget of about $650,000.

Over the past three decades, IDA has greatly expanded the animal welfare topics in which it is interested and the geographical scope of its programs. Currently, it supports programs on animal abuse in Korea, focusing on that nation's huge program in providing dogs and cats for human foods; animals in entertainment, which includes campaigns against cockfighting, the use of elephants in zoos, circus animals, greyhound racing, bull fighting, and rodeo sports; protection of Canada geese; the use of dissection as an instructional tool in schools and colleges; the exotic-bird hobby; the Stop Force Feeding campaign to eliminate the force feeding of ducks on foie gras farms; the Fur Kills campaign against the inhumane raising of animals for the collection of their pelts; the wild-horses and -burros program aimed for the protection of these animals in the wild; and the campaign to monitor, regulate, and/or eliminate puppy mills. Details about all of these programs and others sponsored by the IDA are available at the organization's website at http://www.idausa.org/#campaigns.

In addition to these wider campaigns, the IDA promotes a number of very specific actions to which its members and supporters are invited to contribute on its website. These actions include programs such as an effort to get the California legislature to ban hound hunting of bears and bobcats; a petition to ask the governor of New Mexico to exclude the Ringling Brothers circus from the state; a petition to ask New York senator Kirsten Gillibrand to oppose geese killing in a New York State refuge; a request for the mayor of New York City to ban the use of horses in carriage rides in the city; a program to provide protection and improved living conditions for aged elephants in Thailand; an educational effort about commercial egg production programs; and a campaign to stop organized stampedes in the Nevada desert by the U.S. Bureau of Land Management.

The IDA website also had a very useful online resource center, which provides information on a number of topics related to individual and group activism. Some of the topics covered in that section are student projects, starting your own group, planning campaigns, effective picketing, effective outreach tips, rallies and marches, conducting a vigil, high school organizing, how to make the news, personalized stationery, creating your media list, writing a press release, sending out your release, promoting your event, dealing with the media, how to be interviewed by the media, making a media kit, following up an event, tips on writing effective letters to the editor, tips for writing an effective opinion editorial, and meeting with editorial boards.

In 2009, IDA released a special publication, *Celebrating 25 Years*, that summarized some of the achievements of which it was most proud in its history. Included in that list were:

- The first organized nonviolent civil disobedience for animals action at the University of California at Davis Primate Center (1985)

- The first World Week for Animals in Laboratories, an annual week of nonviolent civil disobedience, protests, marches, and educational events (1987);

- Cosponsorship of the first March for the Animals in Washington, D.C., in which an estimated 25,000 people took part (1990)

- Creating Project Hope in Mississippi to provide a shelter and a home for neglected and abandoned animals (1993)

- In cooperation with Sangre de Cristo Animal Protection halting a buffalo hunt at the Fort Wingate Military Depot in New Mexico (1996)

- Opening the Sanaga-Yong Sanctuary in Cameroon as a sanctuary for chimpanzee victims of the bush meat trade (1999)

- Initiating the termination of inhumane brain cancer experiments on beagles in Arizona and finding homes for dogs that have survived the research (2001)

- Initiating its campaign to provide more natural and comfortable lodging for zoo elephants (2003)

- IDA India becoming a reality, allowing the expansion of ambulance service and veterinary care for the street animals of Mumbai, India (2005)

- Largely as the result of IDA actions, the closing of the 112-year-old Schumacher Fur Salon, in Portland, Oregon(2007)

- The McClatchy newspaper chain publishing the most in-depth series of articles ever reported on the abuse of chimpanzees in research, based to a large extent on thousands of pages of medical records, information, and analysis collected by IDA and provided to McClatchy (2011)

(For a complete list of the organization's claimed achievements, see http://www.idausa.org/pdfs/Victories&Highlights 2008-spread.pdf.)

The Johns Hopkins Center for Alternatives to Animal Testing

Bloomberg School of Public Health
Department of Environmental Health Sciences
615 N. Wolfe St., W7032
Baltimore, MD 21205
Phone: (410) 614-4990
Fax: (410) 614-2871
E-mail: caat@jhsph.edu
URL: http://caat.jhsph.edu/

The Center for Alternatives to Animal Testing (CAAT) was founded in 1981 at the Johns Hopkins University, in Baltimore, Maryland, with a three-year, $1 million grant from the Cosmetic, Toiletry, and Fragrance Association. The purpose of the grant was to conduct research on alternatives to the use of using whole animals in the testing of new products designed for both cosmetic and therapeutic purposes. A strong motivating factor for the formation of CAAT was growing criticism from animal rights activists, the general public, and research scientists themselves about the improper and inhumane use of laboratory animals in research. The list of CAAT sponsors has expanded considerably since 1981, with that list currently consisting of major players in the field such as Abbott Laboratories, BASF, F. Hoffman-LaRoche Ltd., Johnson & Johnson, L'Oréal, Pepsi Company, Procter & Gamble, Pfizer Inc., Shell Oil Company, and Unilever. CAAT claims that its work has already had notable success, with an overall decrease in the number of laboratory animals used in research falling by as much as 90 percent in some cases, and by about 87 percent for some types of cosmetics research.

CAAT's mission statement consists of three major parts, the first of which is support for research on in vitro and other types of alternative technologies to replace whole-body animal research. The second focus is the provision of a forum for diverse groups to exchange information and ideas on this problem. The third focus is the education and training of individuals in new alternative technologies. The organization attempts to achieve these objectives in a variety of ways, one of which is the promotion and sponsorship of a number of symposia, workshops, and other meetings for the exchange of information on new developments in the field. Examples of such workshops include those on Acute Toxicity Testing: Alternative Approaches; *In Vitro* Toxicology: New Direction; *In Vitro* Approaches to Contact Dermatitis; 3-D Models in Cell Culture; Testicular Toxicity Workshop; BASF Workshop on Metabolomics; and Dried Blood Workshop.

A second feature of the CAAT program is an opportunity to earn a Human Sciences and Toxicology Policy Certificate. The certificate is designed for Johns Hopkins students who are enrolled in a graduate program and who have a degree in public health of biomedical sciences. It requires completion of six courses on topics such as Animals in Research: Law, Policy and Humane Sciences, Alternative Methods in Animal Testing, and Research Ethics and Integrity: US and International Issues. The center also offers an online course, Enhancing Human Science—Improving Animal Research, that consists of 12 audio lectures accompanied by slides, resource lists, and study questions. In 2007, an anonymous donor gave $1.5 million for use by the center in developing a public policy program designed to help policy makers and legislators understand the need for developing alternatives to traditional methods of using animals in research and to provide guidance in the formulation of such policies and practices.

One of CAAT's newest offerings is a postdoctoral program in translational toxicology, training in the transfer of new basic information on animal-testing alternatives into everyday practice. The CAAT Scholars program will fund postdoctoral students for a three-year program of research that aims to prepare industry and governmental agencies to put into practice fundamental new discoveries about animal research technology. CAAT also has a program of grants and awards for individual researchers and research teams working on new in vitro techniques. The 2012–2013 grants tended to focus on the use of somatic or stem cells in place of whole-body animals for testing the toxicity and allergic reactions of organisms to various chemical substances and cosmetic components.

One of the most powerful tools provided by CAAT is its own dedicated website, @LT WEB (http://altweb.jhsph.edu/index .html). Among the resources available on the website are a frequently asked question section on fundamental information about alternatives to animals; an extensive list of resources for scientists, researchers, and technicians; a similar list for teachers and students; a global listing of organizations interested in alternative forms of testing; links to alternatives information; and a comprehensive, A-to-Z listing of currently available information on all aspects of alternatives. The web page also provides access to the online journal *Altex*, the official journal of CAAT and a number of other alternative-testing organizations.

In 2009, CAAT concluded an agreement with the University of Konstantz, Germany, for the establishment of a European branch of the center. The primary function of the new branch is to create a European program on alternative forms of testing similar to the one that exists at CAAT. A second function is the development of a new program, the Transatlantic Think-Tank for Toxicology (t^4), designed to implement the recommendations of the National Academy of Sciences 2007 report titled *Toxicity Testing and Assessment in the Twenty-first Century: A Vision and a Strategy*. That report called for "sweeping and transformative changes in regulatory toxicity testing," a goal toward which CAAT itself had been working for nearly three decades.

An extensive list of books, articles, technical reports, and other print materials is also available from CAAT. This list includes items such as "Animal-free Toxicology: Sometimes, In Vitro Is Better" (*Science* magazine, March 2012); "Food for Thought . . . on Validation. A Puzzle or a Mystery: An Approach Founded on New Science (*Altex*, vol. 28, no. 2); "Developmental Neurotoxicity Testing: Recommendations for Developing Alternative Methods for the Screening and Prioritization of Chemicals (*Altex*, vol. 28, no. 2); "To 3R Is Humane" (*Environmental Forum*, July/August 2004); "The Three R's: The Way Forward" (*Environmental Health Perspectives*, August 1996); "The Three R's and Biomedical Research" (*Science* magazine, June 1996); and "Yes, Dad, There Are Alternatives" (*AV* magazine, Spring 2005).

Martin, Richard (1754–1834)

Martin was an Irish politician who served in both the Irish and British Parliaments. He is best known today for his lifelong campaign to reduce or eliminate cruelty to animals through activities such as bullbaiting, cockfighting, and the misuse of domestic animals, such as horses and cows. In 1821 he introduced a bill into the British Parliament called the Treatment of Horses Act, designed to prohibit the misuse of horses in hauling domestic passengers and cargo. That bill was laughed off the floor of the Parliament by Martin's colleagues, who thought the concept of protection for domestic animals totally out of touch with British culture at the time. Martin introduced a similar bill a year later, the so-called Ill Treatment of Cattle Act, intended to eliminate the painful and debilitating conditions under which many farm animals in Great Britain, including horses, goats, sheep, and other farm animals, were kept. This time the bill passed, to become the first animal welfare act of any consequence adopted by the British Parliament. Reflecting his role in passing the act, it has since been referred to more commonly as Martin's Act.

In addition to his legislative efforts, Martin was also widely known for his activities in everyday life to protect animals from misuse. On a number of occasions, he intervened himself (or, in some cases, hired others to carry out the same actions) to stop men from beating or overworking their horses. In recognition of these activities, the Prince Regent at the time (later to become King George IV) dubbed Martin "Humanity Dick," a name with which Martin has been associated ever since. (The Prince Regent was only one of a number of notable individuals whom Martin listed as friends at the time, including the Irish statesmen Henry Flood and Henry Grattan; Daniel O'Connell, known as the Liberator of Ireland; twice prime minister and chancellor of the exchequer William Pitt; and the wife of George II, Queen Caroline.)

Richard Martin was born on January 15, 1754, at Ballynahinch Castle, County Galway, Ireland. His father was Robert Martin Fitz Anthony, a member of one of the Tribes of Galway, and his mother was the Honorable Bridget Barnewall, a daughter of Robert Barnewall, 12th Baron Trimlestown. The Tribes of Galway was an informal group of 14 families who had dominated Galway politics for more than three centuries. The estate on which Martin grew up, Dangan House, was said to cover more than 200,000 acres, with more than 100 miles of coastline, making it the largest estate in Ireland at the time. Although both his parents were Catholic, Martin was sent to England to be educated in a Protestant environment. That decision is easy to understand given that Catholics at the time stood virtually no chance of gaining advancement in the political system of the British Isles. After completing his education at Harrow Public School and Trinity College, Cambridge, he returned to Ireland, where he was elected to the Irish House of Commons in 1776 from the constituency of Jamestown. He held that seat until 1783 when he left to become High Sheriff of County Galway. When the Act of Union (which joined Ireland and Great Britain) was passed in 1800, Martin became a member of the British Parliament, where he served until 1812 and then a second time from 1818 to 1826. In addition to his work on behalf of animals in the Parliament, he was also an active supporter of and spokesperson for Catholic Emancipation, a movement to remove many of the restrictions in Great Britain against those of the Roman Catholic faith.

Martin lost his seat in Parliament in 1826 and almost immediately left for Europe. In spite of his illustrious heritage, he had been in debt for much of his adult life, and the loss of his parliamentary protection meant that his creditors were finally able to pursue him for the money he owed them. He remained in France for the rest of his life, dying in Boulogne on January 6, 1834.

Martin was a forthright and pugnacious man who is said to have fought over a hundred duels. Yet he maintained a charming manner and was also well known for being able to bring the Parliament down in gales of laughter. Although he held intense views regarding the welfare of animals of all sorts, he also had compassion for those who ran afoul of Martin's Act and similar legislation, sometimes paying the fines such individuals were assessed for their violations. Shortly after Martin's Act was adopted by the Parliament, he attended a meeting at Old Slaughter's Café in London at which the Society for the Prevention of Cruelty to Animals was formed.

National Anti-Vivisection Society (U.S.)

53 West Jackson Blvd., Suite 1552
Chicago, IL 60604
Phone: (800) 888-NAVS or (312) 427-6065
Fax: (312) 427-6524
E-mail: feedback@navs.org
URL: http://www.navs.org/page.aspx?pid=375

The National Anti-Vivisection Society (NAVS) was founded in Illinois in 1929 for the purpose of educating researchers and the general public about the need to eliminate the use of animals in product testing, education, and biomedical research. The association's mission statement calls for "greater compassion, respect and justice for animals through educational programs based on respected ethical and scientific theory and supported by extensive documentation of the cruelty and waste of vivisection." In 2010, the organization had a paid staff of 12 members and a budget of about $3 million.

NAVS provides information to professional scientists, educators, legislators, and the general public about a number of issues related to vivisection. Its website divides this information into four general categories, dealing with animals in science, animals in education, legal issues, and cruelty-free living. The first of these sections deals with topics such as the way in which animals are used in scientific research, the truth about animal research claims, ways in which animal models are not accurate in the extrapolation of research to human applications, the ways in which animals are used in product testing, possible alternatives to the use of animals in research, and current issues and challenges in the use of vivisection in research. The section also outlines a number of ways in which members and interested individuals can contribute to the causes for which NAVS was formed and for which it works. For example, the organization is a primary source of financial resource for the International Foundation for Ethical Research, which provides grants to researchers who develop scientifically valid alternatives to the use of animals in experiments. The association also produces a weekly newsletter, *Science First*, which provides information on current issues and activities of the NAVS.

The Animals in Education portion of the NAVS website also provides information on a variety of topics, such as the use of dissection as an instructional tool in the classroom, alternatives to that practice, student choice laws that permit students to opt out of dissection exercises in their classrooms, the role of dissection and its alternatives in science fairs, and the BioLEAP Lending Program. The Biology Education Advancement Program (BioLEAP) was created in 1993 to provide teachers and students with alternatives to traditional and conventional uses of vivisection in the classroom. The program consists of a wide variety of three-dimensional plastic models, computer software programs, color transparencies, DVDs, and other materials designed for the teaching of biological concepts without sacrificing animals for that purpose. As a part of the BioLEAP program, NAVS operates the NAVS Dissection Hotline, which provides information for parents, students, teachers, and other individuals who object to the use of live or dead animals in classroom instruction.

The Legal Arena section of the NAVS website is a resource of information on current state, regional, local, and national laws on vivisection, as well as legislation currently under consideration at all levels of government. The association's legislative staff has a number of responsibilities, ranging from the monitoring of existing laws and regulations to recommendations for new legislation to lawmakers to lecturing at law schools and other meetings on animal welfare issues. The association also issues to all interested individuals its free e-mail alert on legislative issues, *Take Action Thursday*, as well as its regular weekly newsletter *Science First*. NAVS also maintains a website, AnimalLaw.com, which provides information free of charge on topics such as current laws and legislation, model laws, case law summaries, animals in the news, and a bibliography of animal law resources.

Finally, the Cruelty Free section of the website makes it possible for someone to enter information about any commercial product and its producer to see to what extent it follows guidelines for the use of animals in testing its products.

NAVS makes available a limited number of print and electronic publications, including especially its magazine, *A New Perspective*, which provides an excellent outline for the case against the use of animals in research. Other publications consist of a number of *Animal Action Reports* dating to 2005. Four brochures are also available on topics such as the BioLEAP program, the association's sanctuary fund, and the organization's Project Reach Out for Animals program.

National Association for Biomedical Research

818 Connecticut Ave., NW, Suite 900
Washington, D.C. 20006
Phone: (202) 857-0540
Fax: (202) 659-1902
E-mail: info@nabr.org
URL: http://www.nabr.org

The 1960s and 1970s saw a rapid growth in concerns about the welfare of animals used in laboratory research in the United States and other parts of the world. As the chronology for this book (chapter 7) shows, the period witnessed the formation of a number of animal welfare and animal rights groups, as well as passage of the first comprehensive federal legislation dealing with animal welfare, the Animal Welfare Act of 1966, followed by a number of amendments to that act. In some ways, the peak event during the period was introduction to the U.S. Congress in 1981 of the Research Modernization Act (H.R. 556), which made drastic changes in the regulation of animal testing in the United States. A key feature of that act was the requirement that no less than 30 percent of federal funding for research in which animals were to be used was to be spent on the search for alternatives for the use of animals in experiments.

That act was never passed in anything near its original form, but the threat it posed to traditional methods of animal experimentation prompted a number of researchers to band together to form a new lobbying group, the Research Animal Alliance (RAA). The purpose of that group, according to the National Association of Biomedical Research (NABR) website, was "to protect the scientific community's ability to conduct biomedical research." Two years later, RAA changed its name to the Association for Biomedical Research (ABR), and continued and expanded its lobbying for the continued use of animals in biomedical research. Finally, in 1985, the ABR merged with the much older (founded in 1945) National Society for Medical Research (NSMR) to become the present-day National Association for Biomedical Research. Today, the NABR is a consortium of 325 institutions that includes, according to the organization's website "every major pharmaceutical company, 80% of medical schools, nearly every veterinary medical school, and nearly every research university."

The NABR mission is to lobby for the development of an "ethical and essential" animal research policy, which includes an emphasis on the critical role that animals play in biomedical research along with an understanding of the necessity for considering the health and welfare of those animals. The association generally accepts the need for the implementation of the 3 R's (reduction, refinement, replacement), with the understanding that there remain situations in which no substitute for animals are available in some research activities.

The three events to which NABR points as its most important accomplishments are (1) modifications of the 1985 amendments to the Animal Welfare Act that retained the much of the traditional role of animals in biomedical research, (2) passage of the 1992 Animal Enterprise Protection Act, and (3) adoption of the 2006 Animal Enterprise Terrorism Act. In the last two of these acts, the U.S. Congress took a very strong stand against the use of violent action by animal rights activists against individuals and institutions who use animals in their biomedical research programs.

An important aspect of NABR's work is to clarify for the general public and policymakers the necessity of using animals in some forms of research. A major section of the organization's website deals with a discussion of medical advances that have been made with the use of animals, the proper treatment of research animals, careers in biomedical research, and oversight provided by governmental and research organizations in the use of animals in experimentation. The website also discusses at some length the meaning of animal welfare and animal rights activities and how these two differ from each other. It also reviews the ways in which NABR is involved with and acts to support animal welfare activities, while, at the same time, opposing and working against the more violent activities sometimes associated with the animal rights movement.

NABR is also very much concerned with issues of the growing field of animal laws, which it views in general as "potentially disruptive." Its website contains information on existing federal and state laws, animal law courses, sections and committees within bar associations devoted to animal law issues, international laws dealing with animal welfare, and existing laws and regulations that protect the rights of researchers in their use of animals in experiments. A legal topic of some concern to NABR is the modern-day "personhood" movement among some scholars, an effort to have animals defined as "persons" so that they can benefit from the same legal rights as do humans.

The association also provides regular webinars on topics of interest to its members. Some recent topics include "Animal Rights: What to Do When Your Institution Is Targeted" "Examining USDA's 'Age of Enforcement,'" "Surviving the Age of Enforcement," "Planning Your Institutional Response to Animal Rights Activists," "A Guided Tour of USDA's Inspection Guide," and "Managing the USDA Inspections

Process." The NABR website also has a valuable list of links to governmental agencies dealing with animal welfare issues; associations, foundations, and other organizations; and international organizations with interests in animal experimentation. The Members Only section of the association's website contains useful information for research institutions. An example is the "Crisis Management Guide," which provides information to institutions on how to "prevent, prepare for, and respond to animal rights extremist campaigns against researchers and research institutions."

New England Anti-Vivisection Society

333 Washington St., Ste. 850
Boston, MA 02108-5100
Phone: (617) 523-6020
Fax: (617) 523-7925
E-mail: info@neavs.org
URL: http://www.neavs.org/

The New England Anti-Vivisection Society (NEAVS) is one of the oldest associations in the United States (after the NAVS) working for the abolition of animals as subject of scientific and medical research. The association was formed in 1895 at a meeting held in Boston called by Joseph Greene. Greene had earlier won a prize of $250 for writing an essay, "Why I Am against Vivisection," and had decided that the essay was not sufficient to bring about real change in the use of animals for medical and scientific research. The antivivisectionist movement in New England itself had begun more than two decades earlier when researchers at Harvard University had decided to adopt the "new approach" to anatomical and physiological studies then popular in Europe, which made extensive use of animals as subjects. Opposition to the Harvard decision was widespread in the New England area, but achieved concrete organizational results only with the convening of the 1895 meeting. Within a month of its formation, the new society had more than 200 members, many from the highest levels of Boston society.

NEAVS's stated goal was "to expose and oppose secret or painful experiments upon living animals, lunatics, paupers or criminals." Members felt that all they really had to do was to inform the general public of the horrors of animal experimentation, and the practice would be brought to a conclusion in the region. They very soon found out, of course, that such a hope was naive and that far more aggressive actions were needed to bring out abolition of animal testing, and even then, their efforts produced only modest results. In discouragement, the association floundered for a number of years and by 1905 had only a hundred dollars in its treasury. The NEAVS historical records report that a prominent physician of the time, one S. A. Knopf, gloated that "the New England Anti-Vivisection Society appears to be drawing its last useless breaths, and that without the use of any anesthetic, strange as it may seem. . . . The soul of the antivivisection movement is probably dead, killed by facts and common sense." Knopf's prediction was premature, however, and the organization soon sprang back with a flood of new members and generous donations. It has remained an active and successful association ever since.

The association's current agenda consists of five major foci: legislative and policy changes, scientific research, public outreach, education and medical training, and rescue and sanctuary. The first of these goals involves the lobbying and petitioning of government organizations with responsibility for the use of animals in experimentation. For example, NEAVS has worked aggressively in support of the Great Ape Protection and Cost Savings Act of 2012, which aims to abolish the use of such animals in research in the United States. The second goal focuses on the search for alternative to the use of animals in research. The third goal consists of a number of elements, one of which is promotion of the Leaping Bunny cruelty-free shopping campaign in which consumers are encouraged to purchase only products certified free from animal testing. The fourth goal also has a number of elements, the most important of which involve the elimination of dissections by students at all level, offers of awards for humane science projects, and provides scholarship support for doctoral students who decide to pursue careers in animal-free research. The fifth goal aims to find and relocate animals who have survived research projects, providing them with a safe and comfortable environment in which to live out their lives.

The NEAVS has taken credit for participating in a number of steps forward in the war against animal experimentation, such as:

- A reprieve in 2011 for 186 chimpanzees at the Alamogordo Primate Facility, scheduled to be used in research
- Cancellation in 2010 by NASA of plans to expose monkeys to radiation as a test for space travel
- The termination of the use of dogs for surgery training at the Michigan State University College of Veterinary Medicine in 2010
- Elimination in 2010 by the state of Utah and the District of Columbia of regulations requiring the release of shelter animals to scientists for research
- The replacement in 2009 of rats and frogs for neuroscience courses with computer-simulated experiments
- The creation in 2007 by the FDA of a committee to explore possible alternatives for the use of animals in scientific and medical research

The association has an extensive collection of resources on the topic of animal experimentation intended for researchers in the field, legislative and policy experts, and the general public. For the first of these groups, NEAVS makes available a number of scientific papers that report on technical aspects of the use of animals in research, such as, for example, "The Bioethics of Great Ape Well-Being: Psychiatric Injury and Duty of Care." For the general public, the organization also provides an irregular newsletter called *UPDATE*, which is available at no cost online at http://www.neavs.org/resources/outreach-materials. The NEAVS library also contains more than 600 books and videos, as well as over 300 nonanimal dissection alternatives, such as anatomical models, charts, manuals, dissection videos, and computer software programs. These materials are available to researchers and the general public by appointment. The association's website also provides a useful section on current news in the field of antivivisection activities, links to like-minded organizations, a suggested reading list, and action alerts to the association's current activities and events.

Ingrid Newkirk (1949–)

Newkirk is one of the founders of the organization PETA, and probably one of the most controversial individuals in the antivivisection movement in the world. She has been president and primary spokesperson for PETA for over three decades, since its founding in 1980. Newkirk's philosophy about her work is that she has an obligation to keep issues of animal experimentation constantly in the forefront of public opinion, devising ever more striking and even bizarre activities to achieve this goal. One such activity is the annual Running of the Nudes event, held in Pamplona, Spain, in concert with that city's famous Running of the Bulls event. Such events have often raised eyebrows among both her critics (one of whom has called Newkirk "the worst person in the world") and her allies in the animal welfare movement, who may feel that somewhat more nuanced approaches might produce better results for their cause. Perhaps her most famous expression of her views about animals is her statement that "animals are not ours to eat, wear, experiment on, or use for entertainment." After so many years in the animal welfare movement, it seems unlikely that Newkirk is likely to moderate either her views or her activities at this stage in her life.

Ingrid E. Newkirk was born in Surrey, England, on June 11, 1949. She grew up in Ware, Hertfordshire, and the Orkney Islands, before moving with her family to India at the age of seven. The family settled in New Delhi, where Newkirk's father worked as a navigational engineer, and her mother volunteered to work with Mother Theresa in serving lepers of the region. Newkirk has probably best described the first two decades of her life in an op-ed written for PETA in 2009: "I was conceived in Denmark," she wrote, "grew up on the wild, rugged Cornish coast of England and was sent to school in the Orkney Islands, crossing the sea in a light plane. Next stop, France, where we children wore clogs to school, then eight years among the bears in the everlasting snows near Shimla, India, followed by a marriage in Spain during the frightening days of martial law under General Franco."

Newkirk explains that she developed an empathy for animals early in her life. For example, she was horrified in India to see a man beating his packhorse who was so tired that he could not stand. The episode that actually changed her life, however, may have occurred in 1972, when she was studying to become a stockbroker in Maryland. She collected a litter of abandoned kittens from a neighbor's house, and brought them to the local animal shelter, expecting that they would be put up for adoption. She learned a few days later that the kittens had all been euthanized immediately. She decided that such actions were inexcusable and gave up her stockbroker ambitions to devote her life full-time to the protection of animals.

At first, Newkirk decided to try working primarily within the system to deal with the animal abuse she perceived. After the kitten episode, she volunteered to work at the local animal shelter to see firsthand how animals were cared for and treated at the facility. She was horrified by what she saw and reported the shelter to local officials. To do what she could in such situations, she took a job as an animal protection officer, first in Montgomery County, Maryland, and later in the District of Columbia. She was eventually appointed the first pound master in the District and, in 1976, was appointed head of animal disease control in the District Commission on Public Health.

Only a few years later, Newkirk became involved in one of the most widely publicized animal abuse cases in modern American history, the Silver Spring Monkeys case. The case developed when a researcher performed aggressive neurological surgery on a group of 17 macaque monkeys in an attempt to develop a treatment for neurological damage to the human body. That case dragged on through a series of courts for more than a decade, by which time all but 2 of the original monkeys had either died or been euthanized. In the meantime, Newkirk and her newfound companion in the battle for animal rights, Alex Pacheco, decided to establish an organization through which they could carry out their program for the defense of animals, PETA. PETA has since grown to one of the largest animal welfare organizations in the world with more than 2 million members, over 300 employees, and an annual budget of more than $34 million.

For all her critics, Newkirk has become a widely popular speaker on animal rights and a prolific writer on the topic. Among her many books are *The PETA Practical Guide to Animal Rights—Simple Acts of Kindness to Help Animals in Trouble, One Can Make a Difference: Original Stories by the Dalai Lama, Paul McCartney, Willie Nelson, Dennis Kucinich, Russell Simmons, Bridgitte Bardot* (with Jane Ratcliffe), *Let's Have a Dog Party!: 20 Tail-Wagging Celebrations to Share with Your Best Friend, 50 Awesome Ways Kids Can Help Animals, Making Kind Choices: Everyday Ways to Enhance Your Life through Earth- and Animal-Friendly Living, PETA 2005 Shopping Guide for Caring Consumers: A Guide to Products That Are Not Tested on Animals, Free the Animals: The Story of the Animal Liberation Front,* and *You Can Save the Animals: 251 Simple Ways to Stop Thoughtless Cruelty.*

Sir William Paton (1917–1993)

William Paton was an experimental pharmacologist who became very much involved in the debate over animal experimentation during his professional career. He was especially concerned about the most violent actions of antivivisectionists, such as ALF, who sought to bring a complete end to the use of all animals in research. He referred to the members of such groups as "animal hooligans." But he also felt strongly that more moderate antivivisectionists, who claimed to oppose the violent actions of groups like ALF, were equally to blame for interfering for the very valuable role that animals can play in scientific and biomedical research. Paton also found fault with the media who, he suggested, did not work hard enough to inform the general public about the benefits of using animals in research and therefore, unwittingly, contributed to the actions and campaigns of antivivisectionists.

Paton is perhaps best known outside the professional community for a book he wrote in 1984 entitled *Man and Mouse: Animals in Medical Research,* in which he attempted to lay out the history of animal research along with the enormous benefits that he believed had result from that research. The book was widely praised by his research colleagues for its clear and convincing presentation of the case for animal testing, and widely criticized by antivivisectionists for his effort to excuse a practice they found to be deplorable and unacceptable. The book appeared in a second edition shortly before Paton's death in 1993. In the first edition of his book, Paton attempted to put the issue of animal testing into perspective (as he saw it). After providing data on the number of laboratory animals used at the time, he said, "The current figures represent one mouse per head of population every 15 years. Is that big or small in relation to the hundreds of millions of animals used for food each year? Or the hundreds of thousands of cats and dogs killed annually as unwanted? Or indeed, the 100 million smaller animals killed by our cats each year?"

William Drummond Macdonald Paton was born in Hendon, Middlesex, England, on May 5, 191,7 to the Reverend William Paton and his wife, Grace MacKenzie Paton. He received his primary and secondary education at Winchester House, Brackley, and the Repton School, Derby, before matriculating at New College, Oxford, where he majored in animal physiology. He was graduated from New College with first-class honors in 1938, and then continued his studies in medicine at University College Hospital (UCH) in London. He received his MD and was certified as a physician in 1942. His work at UCH was recognized by the Goldsmid award in 1939 and the Gold Medal in clinical medicine in 1941.

After graduation from UCH, Paton accepted a position in pathology at the King Edward VII Sanatorium in Midhurst, where he remained for two years. He was then offered a post as a researcher with the National Institute for Medical Research (NIMR) in Hampstead. His time at NIMR has been described by biographer Walter Perry as "eight of his most productive research years." The first topic to which he turned his attention at NIMR was respiratory problems associated with diving, an issue that arose because of its association with military issues arising during the early years of World War II. After the war, Paton became more interested in pharmacological questions, studying the methonium drugs, histamine liberators, neuromuscular blocking compounds, and ganglion blockers.

In 1952, Paton left NIMR to become reader in applied pharmacology at UCH. Two years later, he was appointed to the post of Vandervell Chair of Pharmacology at the Royal College of Surgeons (RSC) in London, where he remained until 1959. It was at RSC that Paton developed an important technique using laboratory animals for the testing of pharmacological preparations and, in the process, made his department one of the leading research institutions in the world. In 1959, Paton assumed yet another new post, that of professor of pharmacology at the University of Oxford and fellow at Balliol College, titles that he retained until his retirement in 1984.

Paton was not only an active an influential researcher but also a concerned public citizen. He is said at one point in his life to have been a member of 72 different committees, many of which he chaired. For example, he served on the Medical Research Council (MRC) Committee on Non-Explosive Anaesthetic Agents, MRC Working Party on Biochemical and Physiological Aspects of Drug Dependence, Institute of Animal Technicians, Central Advisory Council for Science and Technology, Committee on the Scheme for the Suppression of Doping in Horse-Racing, Research Defence Society, and Independent Scientific Committee on Smoking and Health.

Paton was awarded the Gold Medal of Apothecaries in 1979, the Baly Medal of the Royal College of Physicians in 1983, and the British Pharmacological Society's Wellcome Gold Medal in 1991. He shared the 1956 Cameron Prize and the 1959 Gardiner Foundation Award with Eleanor Zaimis for their work on methonium compounds. Paton was made a fellow of the Royal Society in 1956, commander of the British Empire in 1968, fellow of the Royal College of Physicians in 1969, fellow of the Faculty of Anaesthetists of the Royal College of Surgeons in 1975, and knight bachelor in 1979.

Although he suffered from poor health throughout his life, Paton was a dedicated and diligent researchers with a commitment not only to scientific research but also to a consideration of the social impact of research on the everyday lives of ordinary women and men. One of his biographers described Paton as "a deeply inspiring and yet approachable colleague who gave sympathetic advice, often with a delightful sense of humour." He died in Oxford on October 17, 1993.

Tom Regan (1938–)

Regan has been called in an exhibition of his work at North Carolina State University "the philosophical leader of the animal rights movement in the United States." His 1983 book *The Case for Animal Rights* is widely regarded as one of the basic documents in the antivivisectionist movement because of the sound philosophical basis on which he places his argument for the treatment of animals. In that book, he lays out his fundamental premise about the rights of animals:

> We are each of us the experiencing subject of a life, a conscious creature having an individual welfare that has importance to us whatever our usefulness to others.... As the same is true of those animals that concern us (the ones that are eaten and trapped, for example), they too must be viewed as the experiencing subjects of a life, with inherent value of their own.

For more than half a century, Regan has thought, written, and spoken about the issue of animal rights. His published books on the topic include *All That Dwell Therein: Animal Rights and Environmental Ethics* (1982), *Animal Rights, Human Wrongs: An Introduction to Moral Philosophy* (2003), *Defending Animal Rights* (2006), *Empty Cages: Facing the Challenge of Animal Rights* (2003), and *The Struggle for Animal Rights* (1987). Regan has long been a popular speaker on the topic of animal rights, having given talks at well over 200 institutions ranging from the University of Kansas, the University of South Dakota, and Drexel University to the Harvard, Yale, and Vanderbilt divinity schools to the universities of Melbourne (Australia), Auckland (New Zealand), and Stockholm and the University of Milan Law School.

Tom Regan was born in Pittsburgh, Pennsylvania, on November 28, 1938, to Thomas and Marie Regan. As a high school student, he was interested in writing and literature, although he later said that he "wrote horrible fiction and worse poetry." He also participated in football, golf, and track, while earning money on the side by playing in "big band" groups. He matriculated at Thiel College, in Greenville, Pennsylvania, from which he earned his bachelor's degree in 1960. He then continued his education at the University of Virginia, from which he earned his master's degree and PhD in 1962 and 1966, respectively.

Regan's first academic job was as assistant professor of philosophy at Sweet Briar College, in Sweet Briar, Virginia, while he was working for his doctorate at the University of Virginia. After completing his degree, he accepted an appointment as assistant professor of philosophy at North Carolina State University in 1967, where he remained throughout his academic career. He was promoted to associate professor in 1972 and to full professor in 1978. He retired from his post at North Carolina State in 2000 and now holds the title of professor emeritus. In addition to his regular appointment, Regan has also served at a number of other institutions, including Oxford University (summer 1973), University of Calgary (spring 1977), Brooklyn College (fall 1982), University of Essex (summer 1988), Eastern Michigan University (fall 1996), and Massey University, New Zealand (fall 1997).

Regan's teaching career at North Carolina State began much as has that of most other beginning professors: offering courses that are broadly similar to ones that they themselves took during their college years. In Regan's case, those courses were in moral philosophy. However, he has written in his autobiography, *The Bird in a Cage: A Glimpse of My Life*, that this relatively satisfying approach to teaching soon ran head on into the reality of everyday life in the United States in the late 1960s, namely, the war in Vietnam. Having to watch news from the field almost every night, Regan began to ask how his potentially remote field of philosophy was related to the good and bad, right and wrong decisions that people had to make every day, both about the war and about any number of other events in their daily lives. He decided to use his academic training to see how the principles of moral philosophy might apply to making such decisions. As a result, a number of his books other than those on animal rights have dealt with real-life issues, such as the difficult decisions that people face when confronted with environmental problems. Thus, although his contributions in the field of animal welfare will probably always be the accomplishment for which he is best known, his influence in the application of philosophy to a person's life has also been significant.

Regan has received a host of honors and awards for his research, writing, and teaching, including a Phillip Francis duPont fellowship from the University of Virginia, an Outstanding Teacher Award from North Carolina State University, the Gandhi Award for Outstanding Contributions to the Animal Rights Movement, Outstanding Alumni Award of Thiel College, the Joseph Wood Krutch Medal of the Humane Society of the United States, Leys Lecturership of the University of Southern Illinois at Carbondale, the Ryle Lectureship of Trent University (Canada), the Dunbar Lectureship of Millsaps College, and the William Quarles Holliday Medal of the Board of Trustees of North Carolina State. In addition to his book, Regan has published more than 150 peer-reviewed papers and book chapters, some of which have been translated into Chinese, Finnish, German, Italian, Portuguese, and Spanish.

Bernard Rollin (1943–)

Rollin is generally regarded as the founder and father of the field of veterinary medical ethics. He developed and taught the first course anywhere in the world on that topic in 1978 and has a dozen books on the subject. He is in wide demand as a speaker on veterinary medical ethics and has given over a thousand lectures on the topic in virtually every part of the world. He was the principal architect of the 1985 Improved Standards for Laboratory Animals Act, one of the most important amendments to the 1966 Animal Welfare Act. He has also served as a consultant to other national governments, including Australia, Canada, the Netherlands, New Zealand, and South Africa, on similar animal welfare legislation. He also serves regularly as a consultant to the National Institute of Health, the Department of Agriculture, the World Health Organization, and other governmental agencies on the humane care of research animals.

Bernard Elliot Rollin was born in Brooklyn, New York, in 1943. In an autobiographical sketch he has written entitled "How I Put the Horse before Descartes," he mentions that one of his earliest memories had to do with the way "humane" organizations and animal "shelters" seemed to spend most of their time "putting animals to sleep." He has struggled most of his adult life in trying to understand this conflict of principles. Rollin attended the City College of New York, from which he received his bachelor of arts degree in philosophy in 1964. He then spent a year as a Fulbright Scholar at the University of Edinburgh from 1964 to 1965 before returning to Columbia University for his graduate studies. He received his PhD in philosophy from Columbia in 1968. At the time, Rollin's fields of interest included the philosophy of language, theory of meaning, and history of philosophy, topics about as far from his present-day interests as one might imagine.

In 1969, Rollin accepted his first academic appointment in the department of philosophy at Colorado State University (CSU) in Fort Collins. For the next decade, he continued to study and teach in mainstream areas of philosophy. His only excursion outside that field, he wrote in his autobiography, came in 1969 when he decided to follow up on his childhood interests in animal welfare by writing to a number of publishers with the suggestion for a book on human obligations to other animals. When those letters of inquiry went nowhere, Rollin returned to his regular work in philosophy.

By the 1970s, Rollin had found a new field in which he was interested: ethical and philosophical issues in medicine. When he first offered a course in that field, it was generally thought to be the first course of its kind in the United States. In 1975, a colleague in the CSU School of Veterinary Medicine asked Rollin if he could develop a similar course for veterinary students. It was not long before he realized that the course would be "right down his alley," helping him to deal with issues that had floated around in his mind for at least three decades. The course was a great success and, since 1978, it has been a required part of the veterinary curriculum at CSU.

In fact, news of Rollin's success soon spread across the country and around the world. He notes in his autobiography that, by 1984, had lectured on animal welfare ethics at more than three-quarters of the veterinary schools and colleges in the United States and Canada. At that point, he had also become active in working for the adoption of legislation promoting the humane use of laboratory animals, a topic that only a few years later had been regarded largely as anathema by most federal government officials. In 1983, in recognition of his contribution to the CSU veterinary program, Rollin was awarded the Veterinary Service Award of the Colorado Veterinary Medical Association.

He is currently only one of 12 individuals to hold an appointment as university distinguished professor at CSU. He is also a member of National Western Stock Show Association and of the Stock Show Animal Care and Use Committee. Among his books are *Animal Rights and Human Morality* (Prometheus Books, 1981); *The Teaching of Responsibility* (Universities Federation for Animal Welfare, 1983); *The Experimental Animal in Biomedical Research: A Survey of Scientific and Ethical Issues for Investigators* (with M. Lynne Kesel, editors, CRC Press, 1989); *Farm Animal Welfare: School, Bioethical, and Research Issues* (Iowa State Press, 1995); *The Frankenstein Syndrome: Ethical and Social Issues in the Genetic Engineering of Animals* (Cambridge University Press, 1995); *Complementary and Alternative Veterinary Medicine Considered* (Wiley-Blackwell, 2003); *An Introduction to Veterinary Medical Ethics: Theory And Cases*, 2nd ed. (Wiley-Blackwell, 2006); and *Putting the Horse before Descartes: My Life's Work on Behalf of Animals* (Temple University Press, 2011).

W. M. S. Russell (1925–2005) and Rex L. Burch (1926–1996)

Russell and Burch were coauthors of one of the most famous books in the history of animal testing, *The Principles of Humane Experimental Technique*, published in 1959. The idea behind the book originated in a proposal developed five years earlier by Charles Hume, founder of the UFAW. Hume felt that it would be useful if the UFAW could develop recommendations and guidelines for the use of animals in scientific and biomedical research. The two individuals selected to guide this project were W. M. S. Russell, a polymath intellectual with a background in zoology, psychology, music, philosophy, and the classics, and his assistant, Rex L. Burch, a microbiologist. After extensive study of the issue of maintaining animal welfare in scientific experiments, Russell and Burch produced a book the most significant portion of which dealt with the so-called three Rs of animal experimentation: replacement (the use of entities other than live animals wherever possible), reduction (cutting back on the number of animals used and the tests to which they are exposed wherever possible), and refinement (the use of procedures that reduce as much as possible the pain and suffering experienced by animals in an experiment). Today, the three Rs are taken as an essential requirement of animal experimentation not only by antivivisectionists but also by virtually all researchers in the field.

William Moy Stratten Russell was born in Plymouth, England, on March 26, 1925. His father was Sir Frederick Stratten Russell, director of the Plymouth Marine Laboratory, and the former Gweneth Moy Evans, who had given up an opportunity to study at Oxford to participate in the war effort. (The story is told that the only impediment to their marriage was that Gweneth had vowed never to marry a man named Frederick, and so called her husband "Jim" throughout their 55-year marriage.) The only child of this apparently very happy marriage, William attended Marlborough College for his secondary education before receiving a scholarship to study classics at New College, Oxford, in 1942. His acceptance of that scholarship was delayed for a period because of the war, during which he served as a rifleman in the King's Royal Rifle Corps. At the war's conclusion, he took up his seat at New College, where he soon changed his major from classics to zoology, a subject in which he graduated with first-class honors in 1948. He then continued his graduated studies in zoology, earning his DPhil degree in animal behavior in 1952.

While studying for his doctoral degree, Russell also worked as a junior agricultural research fellow at Oxford, a position he retained until 1954. He then joined the staff at the UFAW as a zoologist, where he was chosen to lead Hume's project on the humane treatment of laboratory animals. Interestingly enough, the book drew relatively little attention when it was first published, and became widely known only in the 1970s and 1980s. The book was finally reprinted in 1992.

By the time *Principles* first appeared in print, Russell had drifted off into a new career. In effort at self-improvement, he had undergone a program of psychoanalysis in the early 1950s, eventually marrying his therapist, Clair Hillel. The two then began working together on a wide variety of topics associated with animal—both human and nonhuman—behavior. For a period of five years, Russell himself worked as a psychotherapist on a freelance basis. Then in 1964, he joined the Commonwealth Bureau of Pastures and Field Crops as a scientific information officer. In his new position, he decided to learn Japanese so that he could translate agriculture books from that language into English. Two years later, his career took yet another turn, this time accepting an appointment in the new Department of Sociology at Reading University. He served at Reading for the next 25 years as lecturer (1966), reader (1976), professor (1986), and, after retirement, emeritus professor (1990).

Space does not permit an adequate review of Russell's array of talents. For example, he is known among science fiction aficionados for his 1995 book *The Barber of Alvervran*, and among former students for his tendency to include rhyming couplets in his lectures, sung in his respectable bass-baritone voice. In addition to their many research papers, he and his wife also published two books, *Population Crisis and Population Cycles* and *The Myths of Greece and Rome*. Russell died in Reading on July 27, 2006, after almost a decade of ill health associated with kidney problems that required regular dialysis treatments. His biographers have noted that this debilitating experienced appears to have little or no effect on his consistent good humor and high spirits.

Rex Leonard Burch was perhaps the less well-known half of the illustrious three Rs writing team. He first became involved in the issue of the humane treatment of laboratory animals during World War II when he was employed at the North Riding Laboratory of Pathology and Public Health at Scarborough. There, as part of his research, he was required to kill guinea pigs on a regular basis and first began to think about the problem of humane euthanasia for experimental animals. After the war, his plans to study medicine were aborted because he had to find work to support his parents, who had suffered serious financial setbacks during the war. He was able to find work at the Boots Pure Drug Company, where he developed the research skills that were to sustain his future career. After leaving Boots, he established his own research and breeding facility in Huntingdonshire, where he remained until he received word of a research opening at UFAW working with Russell.

After completion of the research that led to *Principles*, Burch and Russell went their separate ways and, as he said in his autobiographical sketch for the journal *ATLA*, "were sporadically in touch" with each other and with the UFAW. "Absorbed in our own occupations," Burch wrote, "we had no idea of the remarkable advances that were occurring in the 1980s, and assumed that, as was indeed still true in 1978, there had been little progress in the field since our own book appeared." In fact, it was not until 1990 when they both received letters from the Humane Society of the United States (HSUS) asking permission for use of their names for a new Russell and Burch Award for contributions to the three Rs and laboratory animal welfare that they realized the changes that had occurred in the field.

Burch's career after *Principles* consisted of work as an independent consulting microbiologist for environmental health services and other industries both in Great Britain and around the world. He called that work "demanding, but never lacking in variety."

In 1995, Burch and Russell were awarded the first HSUS Russell and Burch Award, although Burch was too ill to travel to Washington to receive the award. To compensate for that circumstance, the HSUS decided to hold a workshop on the three Rs in Sheringham, England, on May 30–June 3, 1995, at which both Russell and Burch were present. It was Burch's last major public event, however, as he died in Norwich, Norfolk, England, less than a year later on March 9, 1996.

Peter Singer (1946–)

Singer is an Australian-born moral philosopher whose special interest is practical ethics. The field of practical ethics deals with the application of theoretical ethics to practical situations, such as business practices, environmental issues, and biological and medical questions. He is best known for his 1975 book, *Animal Liberation*, one of the most famous texts on animal welfare and animal rights issues ever written. In this book, Singer argues that the fundamental question in animal experimentation was not so much as to whether animals have rights or moral standing. Instead, he argued that since they experienced pain and suffering during animal testing, they could not morally be used for such purposes. His philosophical approach in the book is based in the field of utilitarianism, that is, "the greatest good for the greatest number of individuals," a principle originated by the English philosopher Jeremy Bentham in the late eighteenth century. (Bentham also spoke and wrote against the practice of using

Ethicist Peter Singer, whose 1975 book *Animal Liberation* became the iconic text of the modern animal welfare movement. (AP Photo/Brian Branch-Price)

animals for scientific and biomedical research.) *Animal Liberation* has now been translated into more than two dozen languages and sold more than a half million copies.

Peter Albert David Singer was born in Melbourne, Australia, on July 6, 1946. His parents left Vienna in 1938 after Germany had annexed Austria, and the Nazi Party had begun arresting Jews and sending them to concentration camps. His paternal grandparents and maternal grandfather eventually died in such camps, although he and his parents were able to escape before being arrested. After settling in Melbourne, Peter's mother continued her practice of medicine, and his father opened a cof-fee- and tea-importing business. Peter attended primary school at the Margaret Lyttle Memorial School (better known as Preshil) and secondary school at Scotch College, an indepen-dent school outside of Melbourne.

Singer matriculated at the University of Melbourne in 1963 planning to become a lawyer. At the suggestion of a friend, he decided to major in the arts also, with a specialty in philosophy. As he approached graduation, he decided that his interest in philoso-phy was much greater than that in law, and upon receiving his BA in 1967, he continued his studies in philosophy. He received his MA in that field in 1969 and was awarded a scholarship to the University of Oxford, from which he received his BPhil in 1971. After graduation, Singer remained at Oxford, where he served as Radcliffe lecturer at University College for two years. He then taught in the Department of Philosophy at New York University for one year, from 1973 to 1974. In 1975, Singer returned to Australia to take a position as senior lecturer in the Department of Philosophy at La Trobe University, in Melbourne. A year later, he joined the Department of Philosophy at Monash University, also in Melbourne, as professor of philosophy. He remained at Monash for the next two decades, serving as associate dean of the Faculty of Arts, director of the Centre for Human Bioethics, and codirector of the Institute for Ethics and Public Policy.

In 1999, Singer accepted an appointment as Ira W. De Camp professor of bioethics at Princeton University, a post he held until 2004. He then continued in that position part-time while also serving as laureate professor at the Centre for Applied Philosophy and Public Ethics at the University of Melbourne. In addition to his regular appointments, he has also served as guest scholar at the Institute for Society, Ethics & the Life Sciences, Hastings-on-Hudson, New York; fellow at the Woodrow Wilson International Center for Scholars of the Smithsonian Institution in Washington, D.C.; Cecil Green visiting professor at the University of British Columbia, Vancouver; visiting distinguished humanist at the University of Colorado, Boulder; distinguished visiting professor at the University of California, Irvine; Italian National Research Council visiting scholar at the University of Rome "La Sapienza"; Erskine fellow at the University of Canterbury, Christchurch, New Zealand; and Ferrater Mora chair of contemporary thought at the University of Girona, Spain.

In addition to *Animal Liberation*, Singer is the author of more than 40 books on a wide variety of topics. His other animal-related books include *Animal Rights and Human Obligations: An Anthology* (with Thomas Regan), *Animal Factories* (with James Mason) *In Defence of Animals* (editor), *Save the Animals!* (Barbara Dover and Ingrid Newkirk), *The Great Ape Project: Equality beyond Humanity* (coedited with Paola Cavalieri), and *The Way We Eat: Why Our Food Choices Matter/the Ethics of What We Eat* (with Jim Mason). He has also written on a host of other topics, including *Test-Tube Babies: A Guide to Moral Questions, Present Techniques, and Future Possibilities* (coedited with William Walters), *Should the Baby Live?: The Problem of Handicapped Infants* (with Helga Kuhse), *Ethical and Legal Issues in Guardianship Options for Intellectually Disadvantaged People* (with Terry Carney), *Embryo Experimentation* (coedited with Helga Kuhse, Stephen Buckle, Karen Dawson, and Pascal Kasimba), *Individuals, Humans and Persons: Questions of Life and Death* (with Helga Kuhse), and *Rethinking Life and Death: The Collapse of Our Traditional Ethics*. Most of these books have been translated into a wide variety of languages ranging from Swedish, Spanish, and Croatian to Chinese, Japanese, and Brazilian.

In addition to having been selected for a number of prestigious guest lectureships, Singer has received the World Technology Network Ethics Award, Australian Humanist of the Year, Humanist Laureate of the International Academy of Humanism, Emperor Has No Clothes Award of the Freedom from Religion Foundation, listing in the "Time 100" *Time* magazine's list of the world's most influential people for 2005, Scott Nearing Award for Courageous Scholarship of the

University of Pennsylvania, 50th Anniversary Research Award of Monash University, and Ethics Prize of the Giordano Bruni Stiftung (with Paola Cavalieri). In 2012, Singer was appointed as a Companion of the Order of Australia.

Ernest Starling (1866–1927)

Starling was an English physiologist who made important contributions in a number of fields. He also became very much embroiled in the debate over vivisection in the early years of the twentieth century, perhaps none so well known as the famous Brown Dog affair. That incident involved the use of a "brown dog" that had been picked up wandering the streets of London as a stray. He was taken to the Department of Physiology at University College London, where he was used in a demonstration of the secretion of hormones by the pancreas gland by Starling and his brother-in-law and equally famous physiologist William Bayliss. A number of female antivivisectionists from Sweden were present at the demonstration and proceeded to produce an uproar over the fate of the dog. Although Bayliss was the main focus of this attack, Starling decided to respond aggressively to the antivivisectionist complaints and spoke widely and loudly about the many benefits produced for humans by the use of animals, such as the brown dog, by animal experimentation. A 1906 edition of the antivivisectionist newsletter *The Zoophilist and Animals' Defender* described in detail an occasion on which Starling appeared uninvited at a meeting of the Hampstead Branch of the NAVS and made a passionate appeal for the use of animals in research, pointing out how the practice had been responsible for significant advances in the conquest of plaque, malaria, yellow fever, and other diseases. To no one's surprise, the report concludes Starling "could not succeed in getting any sympathy from the audience."

Ernest Henry Starling was born in London on April 17, 1866. His father served at the time as clerk to the Crown in

Bombay, while his mother raised Ernest and his six siblings in London. He attended King's College School in London and then matriculated at the University of London in 1882 at the age of 16. He originally to pursue a career in medicine, and studied the subject at Guy's Hospital along with his studies at London. One of his biographers has called him "a brilliant student" who collected two-thirds of the academic prizes that were available to him during his college years. His goal to practice medicine was diverted to some extent by having come into contact with two physiological researchers at Guys, who opened to him the possibilities of a career in medical research. His interest in research was furthered in 1886 when he took a year's leave of absence from London and Guys to study in Germany, where he worked with the eminent German physiologist Wilhelm Friedrich Kühne. He returned to London with an even greater interest in research and eventually was granted his master's degree in physiology from London in 1889 and his MD from Guys a year later.

After graduation, Starling was offered a post as demonstrator in physiology at Guys. The post paid poorly, but he parlayed additional grants and awards to a point that he was able to leave London for a period of time to continue his studies in Germany. After his return to London, he began to build Guys into one of the most important research institutes in physiology in England. It was there that he met William Bayliss and began a lifelong partnership in physiological research that was only made stronger when Bayliss married Starling's sister Gertrude Ellen in 1893.

One of the first joint projects conducted by Starling and Bayliss dealt with the electrical activity of the heart and, in the early 1890s, they produced only the second electroencephalogram ever made of the heart. Starling also studied the circulatory system, with special attention to the relationship between blood and lymph. Between 1912 and 1914, he published a series of papers that showed that the osmotic pressure of plasma is equal to the hydrostatic pressure within a capillary, a finding that is now known as the Starling principle (or, more accurately, the Frank-Starling principle for its cofounder). In the series of experiments associated with the brown-dog affair, Starling and Bayliss also discovered the first hormone, which they named secretin. Starling suggested the term *hormone* for the substance they discovered from the Greek expression "I excite/arouse," because of the compound's ability to initiate a biological action at some distance from the point at which it is produced.

Starling's research was interrupted by the outbreak of World War I. After his induction into the army, he was originally assigned to work on systems for protection against poison gas attacks. Eventually, however, he was transferred to a British post in Thessalonika, Greece, because his superiors found him somewhat difficult to work with. The war also eliminated the possibility of a Nobel Prize for himself and Bayliss for their discovery of secretin, since no prizes were given out during the war. Starling never returned to his prewar productivity, although one of his biographers has noted that in 1919 he gave "the most significant lecture of his career" on the control of the circulatory system. That lecture has, according to the biographer, never been given the full credit it deserves in the history of physiology. With the exception of the Foulerton Research Professorship of the Royal Society, Starling received relatively few awards and honors during his lifetime. He died on May 2, 1927, on a Caribbean cruise, and was buried in Kingston, Jamaica.

Understanding Animal Research

Charles Darwin House
London
WC1N 2JU
Phone: 020 7685 2670
Fax: 020 7685 2684
E-mail: info@uar.org.uk
URL: http://www.understandinganimalresearch.org.uk/

Understanding Animal Research (UAR) was formed in 2008 through the merger of two existing organizations, the Research Defence Society and the Coalition for Medical Progress. The former organization was originally established in January 1908 "to make known the facts as to experiments on animals in this country; the immense importance to the welfare of mankind of such experiments; and the great saving of human life and health directly attributable to them," according to a letter published in English papers of the time. The Coalition for Medical Progress (CMP) was a much younger organization, having been created in 2003 to, according to its head at the time, Philip Connolly, to provide a single voice to speak on behalf of all those individuals engaged in medical research in the United Kingdom. The CMP consisted of academic funding agencies, companies involved in medical research, trade unions, medical research charities, and trade associations.

In its 2011–2015 Strategic Plan, UAR lists three "top-level goals": to maintain and shape public opinion toward a more positive attitude about the use of animals in research; to build support for animal research in the future by engaging teachers and students in such activities now; and to lobby for favorable legislation on topics such as licensing for those individuals and organizations engaged in animal experimentation. The primary objective of the organization is to counteract what it regards as extremism among animal rights and animal welfare proponents with the objective of obtaining a more balanced view about the use of animals in biomedical and scientific research.

ARM currently claims more than 100 institutional members including the Academy of Royal Medical Colleges, Bioindustry Association, British Horseracing Authority, Charles River Laboratories, GlaxoSmithKline, Kings College London Pharmaceutical Research Division and Department of Pharmacology and Therapeutics, Nutrition Society, Procter & Gamble, Southampton General Hospital, Wellcome Trust, and William Harvey Research Foundation. The organization is run by a council of 13 members who operate as a board of directors for the association. Its annual budget as of 2009 was about £767,000 ($1,200,000), which was provided by grants from member organizations.

UAR divides its activities into four major categories, aimed at scientists, journalists, schools, and policy makers. The first category includes a whole range of information about the use of animals in research, including the website AnimalResearch.org, which the association calls "the global resource for scientific evidence in animal research." Other topics covered in this division include a discussion of methods and procedures used in animal research, a review of the five main areas in which animal research is used, a discussion of the three Rs of animal research (reduction, refinement, and replacement), and statistics on the types and kinds of animals used in research in the United Kingdom. This category also provides updates on latest accomplishments in research that can be traced to the use of animals.

The journalist category of UAR's work focuses on providing the kind of information that science writers need to discuss issues of animal testing intelligently and in an unbiased way. These include a broad summary about animal health, the contributions that animal research has made to human health, and print, electronic, and visual resources. The education category of the UAR mission is similar to that of the journalist section, although it includes additional materials that are designed for use specifically for teachers and students at the schools level. This includes lesson plans and notes for teachers, as well as a list of speakers available to visit school classrooms.

The policy maker portion of UAR's mission also provides basic information on the use of animals and research with additional material specifically of interest to those responsible for making and carrying out directives about animal testing. An important part of this section is a review of the 2010 European Directive, which sets continent-wide policy on the conditions under which animals are to be used in biomedical and scientific research. This section also provides a detailed section on myths and facts about animal research and information on provisions of the UK Freedom of Information act, especially as it applies to animal research.

The News section of the UAR website is an excellent source of breakthroughs achieved in recent research in which animals were used as subjects. Some recent advances mentioned here include identification of the gene responsible for one form of cancer in children, advances in our understanding of liver disease based on research with opossums, treatment of Huntington's disease using stem cells, and discovery of a hormone with promise in the treatment of type 2 diabetes. The News section also includes articles about the controversy between pro- and antivivisectionists.

UAR's document library has a number of useful publications available for download at no cost. Those publications cover topics such as the process by which new medicines are discovered, statistics on the use of research animals, the benefits of animal research, the meaning and implication of 3R research, and the regulation of animal research.

The UAR website also provides its own viewpoint on the programs of antivivisection groups, such as NAVS and PETA. It acknowledges that individuals and organizations may have different views on the use of animals, but it argues against the extreme method used by some groups to make their position known about animal experimentation. (See http://www.understanding animalresearch.org.uk/policy/animal-rights-extremism.)

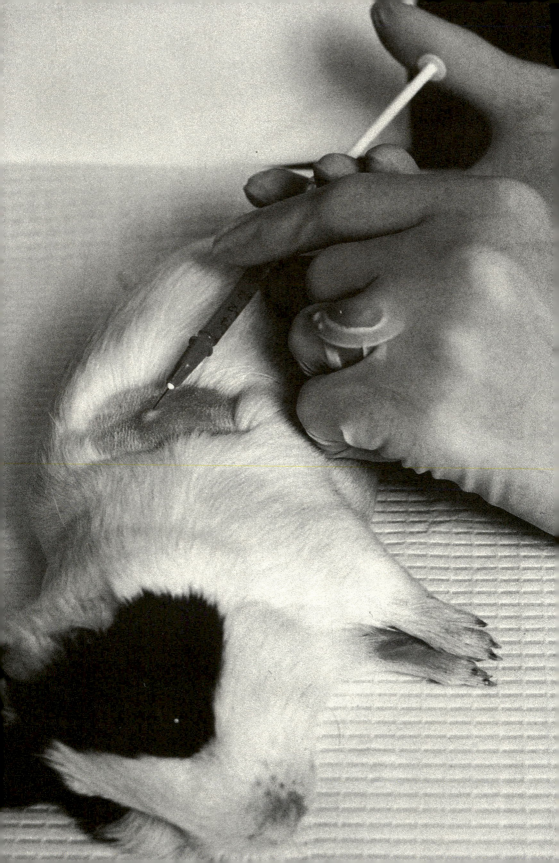

This chapter provides some relevant data and documents dealing with issues associated with animal experimentation. Data provide information on the number and types of animals used in scientific and biomedical research in the United States over various periods of time. Documents include statements in support of or opposed to vivisection, laws dealing with the use of animals in research, and court cases that have arisen out of animal testing.

Data

Table 5.1: Animals Used in Research in the United States, 2010

The Animal and Plant Health Inspection Service of the USDA is required by the Animal Welfare Act of 1966 to conduct a survey of animals being used in research projects in the United States. Table 5.1 summarizes these statistics for the latest year available, 2010.

A guinea pig is injected as part of a tumor study at the National Cancer Institute. According to USDA statistics, in 2010, other than rats and mice, guinea pigs and rabbits topped the list of animals most used as research subjects. (National Cancer Institute)

Table 5.1   Animals Used in Research in the United States, 2010

Animal	Total Used in Research	Pain with Drugs	Pain without Drugs	No Pain, No Drugs	Not Yet Used
Cats	21,578	8,595	153	12,830	2,136
Dogs	64,930	24,710	697	39,523	9,368
Guinea pigs	213,029	63,889	33,652	115,488	8,489
Hamsters	145,895	34,204	48,015	63,676	11,416
Marine mammals	126	10	0	116	0
Nonhuman primates	71,317	29,413	1,395	40,509	54,435
Pigs	53,260	40,911	770	11,579	7,634
Rabbits	210,172	81,303	5,996	122,873	17,219
Sheep	13,271	8,223	65	4,983	2,027
Other farm animals	38,008	12,884	187	24,937	8,064
All other species	303,107	35,627	6,193	261,287	29,221
Total	1,134,693	339,769	97,123	697,801	150,009

Source: "Annual Report Animal Usage by Fiscal Year," U.S. Department of Agriculture, Animal and Plant Health Inspection Service, 2010, available online at http://www.aphis.usda.gov/animal_welfare/efoia/downloads/2010_Animals _Used_In_Research.pdf (accessed July 1, 2012).

Table 5.2: Scientific Procedures by Species of Animal and Primary Purpose of the Procedure

Like the United States, the United Kingdom collects data annually about the number of animals used in scientific research. The UK data go somewhat further than the U.S. data, however. For example, as shown in this table, the UK data show the purposes for which animals have been used in research.

Table 5.3: Research Animal Cases Examined by APHIS, 2007–2009

Each year, APHIS of the USDA visits research facilities throughout the United States to make sure that they are operating in accord with the Animal Welfare Act of 1966 and its

Table 5.2 Scientific Procedures by Species of Animal and Primary Purpose of the Procedure

Species	Primary Purpose of Procedure								
Mammal	1	2	3	4	5	6	7	8	Total
Mouse	832,801	322,304	12,515	21,340	953	–	4,10	1,476,051	2,670,067
Rat	90,530	165,822	101	33,810	654	677	6	13,539	305,139
Guinea pig	1,336	10,736	1,263	39	96	–	190	–	13,660
Hamster	853	2,751	478	61	–	–	–	–	4,143
Gerbil	560	–	–	–	–	–	–	–	560
Other rodent	909	5	64	566	–	–	–	–	1,544
Rabbit	1,310	8,463	2,239	1,191	12	–	1,574	44	14,833
Cat	13	–	174	–	–	–	–	–	187
Dog	285	5,235	168	94	–	–	–	–	5,782
Ferret	317	454	2	–	13	–	6	–	792
Other carnivore	374	–	75	322	–	–	–	–	771
Horse and other equids	130	2	151	32	–	–	8,009	–	8,324
Pig	923	1,168	1,075	9	–	–	–	–	3,175
Goat	1	2	4	10	–	–	10	–	27
Sheep	4,548	794	1,431	24	–	–	30,862	136	37,795
Cattle	2,433	45	974	121	6	–	6	–	3,585
Deer	59	–	–	3	–	–	–	–	62
Camelid	13	20	–	–	–	–	–	–	33

(continued)

Table 5.2 (*continued*)

Species Mammal	Primary Purpose of Procedure								Total
	1	2	3	4	5	6	7	8	
Other ungulate	-	-	-	11	-	-	-	-	11
Marmoset and tamarin	289	814	-	-	-	-	-	-	1,103
Macaque	270	2,894	4	417	-	-	-	-	3,585
Other mammal	812	-	-	402	-	-	-	-	1,216
Domestic fowl	7,022	884	119,570	198	66	-	1,290	890	129,920
Turkey	448	191	1,696	25	-	-	186	-	2,546
Quail	426	-	-	359	-	-	-	-	785
Other bird	7,756	-	-	562	-	-	465	-	8,783
Reptile	860	-	29	-	-	-	-	-	829
Amphibian	12,516	-	-	513	-	-	-	1,438	14,467
Fish	326,709	804	18,469	15,688	360	677	-	128,914	490,944
Total	1,294,503	523,388	160,482	75,797	2,160	677	46,707	1,621,012	3,724,726

1 = Fundamental biological research
2 = Applied studies in human medicine or dentistry
3 = Applied studies in veterinary medicine
4 = Protection of man, animals, or the environment
5 = Education
6 = Training
7 = Direct diagnosis
8 = Breeding of genetically modified animals

Source: Statistics of Scientific Procedures on Living Animals Great Britain 2010 (London: Her Majesty's Stationery Office, 2011), Table 1, 20–21, also available online at http://www.homeoffice.gov.uk/publications/science-research-statistics/research-statistics/other-science-research/spanimals10/spanimals10?view=Binary (accessed July 1, 2012).

Table 5.3   Research Animal Cases Examined by APHIS, 2007–2009

Fiscal Year	2007	2008	2009
Licensed research facilities	1,088	1,296	1,257
Cases	482	480	575
IES review	302	249	391
Warnings	83	283	219
Stipulations	191	95	87
Submitted to Office of General Counsel	73	80	76
Administration law judge decision	78	96	82
No violations	67	53	208
Submitted to external review/ penalty	82	24	11
Stipulations paid	$262,200	$263,596	$160,184
Civil penalty	$614,132	$644,220	$946,184

Source: *Animal Care Annual Report of Activities*, U.S. Department of Agriculture, Animal and Plant Health Inspection Service, Fiscal Year 2007, Table 9, page 15, http://www.aphis.usda.gov/publications/animal_welfare/content/printable_version/2007_AC_Report.pdf (accessed July 4, 2012); "Animal Welfare," U.S. Department of Agriculture, Animal and Plant Health Inspection Service, http://www.aphis.usda.gov/animal_welfare/inspections_type.shtml (accessed July 4, 2012).

amendments. When violations of the act are discovered, they may be handled in a variety of ways, as outlined in this table.

Table 5.4: Number of Animals Used in Research, Historic Trends, 1973–2004

APHIS of the USDA is charged by the Animal Welfare Act of 1966 with conducting an annual census of the number of animals used in research programs in the United States. Trends in those censuses over the three-decade period from 1973 to 2004 are shown here.

Table 5.4   Number of Animals Used in Research, Historic Trends, 1973–2004

Year	Dogs	Cats	Primates	Guinea Pigs	Hamsters
1973	195,157	66,165	42,298	408,970	454,986
1974	199,204	74,259	51,253	430,439	430,766
1975	154,489	51,439	36,202	436,446	456,031
1976	210,330	70,468	50,115	486,310	503,590
1977	176,430	62,31	53,116	348,741	393,533
1978	197,010	65,929	57,009	419,341	414,394
1979	211,104	69,103	59,359	457,134	419,504
1980	188,783	68,482	56,024	422,390	405,826
1981	188,649	58,090	57,515	432,632	397,522
1982	161,396	49,923	46,388	459,246	337,790
1983	174,542	53,344	54,926	485,048	337,023
1984	201,936	56,910	55,338	561,184	437,123
1985	194,905	59,211	57,271	598,903	414,460
1986	176,141	54,125	48,540	462,699	370,655
1987	180,169	50,145	61,392	538,998	416,002
1988	140,471	42,27	51,641	431,457	331,945
1989	156,443	50,812	51,688	481,712	389,042
1990	109,992	33,700	47,177	352,627	311,068
1991	107,908	34,613	42,620	378,582	304,207
1992	124,161	38,592	55,105	375,063	396,585
1993	106,191	33,991	49,561	392,138	318,268
1994	101,090	32,610	55,113	360,184	298,934
1995	89,420	29,569	50,206	333,379	248,402
1996	82,420	26,035	52,327	299,011	246,415
1997	75,429	26,091	56,381	272,797	217,079
1998	76,071	24,712	57,377	261,305	206,243
1999	70,541	23,238	54,927	266,129	201,593
2000	69,516	25,560	57,518	266,873	174,146
2001	70,082	22,755	49,382	256,193	167,231
2002	68,253	24,222	52,279	245,576	180,000
2003	67,875	25,997	53,586	260,809	177,991
2004	64,932	23,640	54,998	244,104	175,721

Year	Rabbits	Farm Animals	Other Covered Animals	Total
1973	447,570	Not reported	38,169	1,653,345
1974	425,585	Not reported	81,021	1,692,527
1975	448,530	Not reported	42,523	1,625,660

(continued)

Table 5.4   (*continued*)

Year	Rabbits	Farm Animals	Other Covered Animals	Total
1976	527,551	Not reported	73,736	1,922,100
1977	439,003	Not reported	46,535	1,519,669
1978	475,162	Not reported	58,356	1,687,201
1979	539,594	Not reported	76,247	1,832,045
1980	471,297	Not reported	49,102	1,661,904
1981	473,922	Not reported	50,111	1,658,441
1982	453,506	Not reported	69,043	1,577,292
1983	466,810	Not reported	108,549	1,680 242
1984	529,101	Not reported	232,541	2,074,133
1985	544,621	Not reported	284,416	2,153,787
1986	521,773	Not reported	144,470	1,778,403
1987	554,385	Not reported	168,032	1,969,123
1988	459,254	Not reported	178,249	1,635,288
1989	471,037	Not reported	153,722	1,754,456
1990	399,264	66,702	257,569	1,578,099
1991	396,046	214,759	363,685	1,842,420
1992	431,432	210,936	529,308	2,134,182
1993	426,501	165,416	212,309	1,704,505
1994	393,751	180,667	202,300	1,624,649
1995	354,076	163,985	126,426	1,395,463
1996	338,574	154,344	146,579	1,345,739
1997	309,322	159,742	150,987	1,267,828
1998	287,523	157,620	142,963	1,213,814
1999	280,222	155,409	165,939	1,217,998
2000	258,754	159,711	166,429	1,286,412
2001	267,351	161,658	242,251	1,236,903
2002	243,838	143,061	180,351	1,137,580
2003	236,250	166,135	199,826	1,188,469
2004	261,573	105,678	171,312	1,101,958

Source: *Animal Care Annual Report of Activities*, U.S. Department of Agriculture, Animal and Plant Health Inspection Service, Fiscal Year 2007, Appendix 5, page 45, http://www.aphis.usda.gov/publications/animal_welfare/content/printable_version/2007_AC_Report.pdf (accessed July 4, 2012).

Documents

On Medicine (about 50 CE; 1756)

Aulus Cornelius Celsus was a Roman encyclopedist who lived between about 25 BCE and 50 CE. He is best known for his very long work, *On Medicine*, which reviews the medical work of the ancient Greeks and the early Romans. In this passage, he describes vivisection conducted by the Greek physicians Herophilus and Erasistratus in the third century BCE and explains why such procedures were not regarded negatively by people of the time:

> Besides, as pains, and various other disorders, attack the internal parts, they [Greek scholars] believe no person can apply proper remedies to those parts, which he is ignorant of—, and therefore, that it is necessary to dissect dead bodies, and examine their viscera and intestines and that Herophilus and Erasistratus had taken by far the best method *for attaining that knowledge* who procured criminals out of prison, by royal permission, and dissecting them alive, contemplated, while they were even breathing, the parts, which nature had before concealed; considering their position, colour, figure, size, order, hardness, softness, smoothness, and asperity; also the processes and depressions of each, or what is inserted into, or received by another part ; for, *say they*, when there happens any inward pain, a person cannot discover the seat of that pain, if he have not learned where every viscus or intestine is situated; nor can the part, which suffers, be cured by one, who does not know what part it is; and that when the viscera happen to be exposed by a wound, if one is ignorant of the natural colour of each part, he cannot know what is found and what corrupted; and for that reason is not qualified to cure the corrupted parts; besides they maintain, that external remedies are applied with much more judgment, when we are acquainted with the situation, figure, and size of the internal parts—, and that the same reasoning holds

in all the other instances above mentioned. And that it is by no means cruel, as most people represent it, by the tortures of a few guilty, to search after remedies for the whole innocent race of mankind in all ages.

Source: Celsus, A. Cornelius. *Of Medicine*. In 8 books. London: D. Wilson and T. Durham, 1756. http://ia700801 .us.archive.org/7/items/acorneliuscelsus00cels/acorneliuscelsus 00cels.pdf. Accessed July 3, 2012.

Thomas Aquinas on the Role of Animals (1265–1274)

The attitude of the Christian Church during the Middle Ages toward vivisection was shaped to a large extent by Biblical teachings about the place of animals in the world. That teaching was framed perhaps most famously in the writings of St. Thomas Aquinas in his mammoth work, *Summa Theologica*. In that work, he points out that humans are granted dominion over the animals by God, and that they are to use animals for their own purposes as they wish:

Reply to Objection 8. Affection in man is twofold: it may be an affection of reason, or it may be an affection of passion. If a man's affection be one of reason, it matters not how man behaves to animals, because God has subjected all things to man's power, according to Ps. viii. 8: *Thou hast subjected all things under his feet*: and it is in this sense that the Apostle says that *God has no care for oxen*; because God does not ask of man what he does with oxen or other animals. (italics in original)

Source: Aquinas, Thomas. *Summa Theologica*. First Part of the Second Part. London: R. and T. Washbourne, 1915, 221. http://ia600609.us.archive.org/20/items/summatheologi08thom/ summatheologi08thom.pdf. Accessed July 3, 2012.

A Father's Instructions (1789)

Thomas Percival was an English physician who drew up the first code of medical ethics in 1794. He is known as the father of that field of ethics. In the same year, he wrote a pamphlet in which he discussed the morality of using animals as the subjects of experiments. He tells as the subject of this pamphlet a tale of the research of Joseph Priestley on a new element he had just discovered, oxygen. In that research, Priestley introduces fish to water saturated with oxygen. After swimming with unusual speed for a few minutes, the fish fall dead to the bottom of the tank. When the young boy observing the experiment expresses amazement and joy at the results of the experiments, Priestley adds the following warning:

> The Philosopher, who has in contemplation the establishment of some important truth; or the discovery of what will tend to the advancement of *real science*, and to the good and happiness of making; may perhaps be justified, if he sacrifice to his pursuits the life or enjoyment of an inferior animal. But the emotions of humanity should never be stifled in his breast; his trials should be made with tenderness, repeated with reluctance, and carried no further than the object in view unavoidably requires. Wanton experiments on living creatures, and even those which are merely subservient to the gratification of curiosity, merit the severest censure. They degrade the man of letters into a brute; and are fit amusements only for the Cannibals of New Zealand. I condemn myself for the indulgence which I just shewed you. But I knew your fishes would endure less pain from an instant, than from a lingering death which awaited them.

Source: Percival, Thomas. *A Father's Instructions*. [n.p.]. [1789]. http://books.google.com/books?id=SQcGAAAAQA AJ&oe=UTF-8. Accessed July 5, 2012.

An Act to Amend the Law Relating to Cruelty to Animals (1876)

The British Parliament passed a number of "cruelty to animals" bills in the first three-quarters of the nineteenth century, most of them applying to domestic animals such as cattle and horses and to domestic pets, such as dogs. In 1876, the Parliament for the first time considered a comparable bill for the protection of animals used in laboratory experiments, the first of its kind in the world. The main part of the act reads as follows:

> Whereas it is expedient to amend the law relating to cruelty to animals by extending it to the cases of animals which for medical, physiological or other scientific purposes are subjected when alive to experiments calculated to inflict pain:
>
> Be it enacted by the Queen's most Excellent Majesty, by and with the advice and consent of the Lords Spiritual and Temporal and Commons in this present Parliament assembled and by the authority of the same, as follows:
>
> This Act may be cited for all purposes as "The Cruelty to Animals Act, 1876."
>
> A person shall not perform on a living animal any experiment calculated to give pain, except subject to the restrictions imposed by this Act. Any person performing or taking part in performing any experiment calculated to give pain, in contravention of this Act, shall be guilty of an offence against this Act, and shall, if it be the first offence, be liable to a penalty not exceeding fifty pounds, and if it be the second or any subsequent offence, be liable, at the discretion of the court by which he is tried, to a penalty not exceeding one hundred pounds or to imprisonment for a period not exceeding three months.
>
> The following restrictions are imposed by this Act with respect to the performance on any living animal of an experiment calculated to give pain; that is to say,

(1) The experiment must be performed with a view to the advancement by new discovery of physiological knowledge or of knowledge which will be useful for saving or prolonging life or alleviating suffering; and

(2) The experiment must be performed by a person holding such license from one of Her Majesty's Principal Secretaries of State in this Act referred to as the Secretary of State, as is in this Act mentioned, and in the case of a person holding such conditional license as is herein-after mentioned, or of experiments performed for the purpose of instruction in a registered place; and

(3) The animal must during the whole of the experiment be under the influence of some anaesthetic of sufficient power to prevent the animal feeling pain; and

(4) The animal must, if the pain is likely to continue after the effect of the anaesthetic has ceased, or if any serious injury has been inflicted on the animal, be killed before it recovers from the influence of the anaesthetic which has been administered; and

(5) The experiment shall not be performed as an illustration of lectures in medical schools, hospitals, colleges, or elsewhere; and

(6) The experiment shall not be performed for the purpose of attaining manual skill. Provided as follows; that is to say, . . .

[The law continues with certain circumstances under which section (6) does not apply. It then concludes with provisions for the administration of the law.]

Source: Chapter 77. "An Act to Amend the Law Relating to Cruelty to Animals (15th August 1876)." http://web.archive .org/web/20061214034848/http://homepage.tinet.ie/~pnowlan/ Chapter-77.htm. Accessed July 3, 2012.

Statement Opposed to Animal Experimentation (1895)

Individuals have been objecting to the practice of animal experimentation for well over a century. Of the untold number of documents that could be cited in this regard, the following takes a somewhat unusual view. The writer claims that the main point about animal experimentation is not the medical benefit it may bring but the harm it does to animals. The writer has prepared this essay in response to a series of articles about animal experimentation in the Manchester *Guardian*:

Sir,

It is interesting to notice in the correspondence on vivisection that is going on in your columns, how the argument tends to rage round the point that is really unessential : viz., whether or not certain scientific knowledge has been obtained by means of experiment on living animals.

To rivet attention on this side issue, as if it were the main principle at stake, is the natural policy of the vivisector, for on the moral ground what can possibly be urged by him which does not at once open the door to the justification of all crime that can boast an important object? It is well to keep in mind the fact that if the point at issue were once admitted to be simply: whether the gain in knowledge is great enough to counterweigh all the vast expenditure of time and public money and talent involved in it, and the loss to research of other kinds, then we should all be committed to the following theorem :—"Atrocious cruelty may be perpetrated if it can be shown to be for the advancement of science; but this special licence for cruelty is granted only when the object is scientific, and in no other case whatever—for reasons (as Mrs. Carlyle says), 'which it would be interesting not to state.' "

It would certainly not be interesting to vivisectors to attempt to explain why science should thus be selected for particular favour by the State, and why that favour should be the permission to practise terrible cruelties under certain (very lax) conditions. That the cruelties of vivisection are terrible can, of course, be proved up to the hilt from the works of the vivisectors themselves.

Source: Mona Caird. "Vivisection." Reprint of a letter to the Manchester *Guardian*, September 11, 1895. http://ia700805 .us.archive.org/25/items/vivisectionlette00cair/vivisectionlette 00cair.pdf. Accessed June 30, 2012.

Statement in Favor of Animal Experimentation (1914)

Researchers have been arguing their case for animal experimentation for more than 200 years. The following statement is just one example of the many that have been announced in this regard:

1. We, the members of the Federation of American Societies for Experimental Biology,—comprising the American Physiological Society, the American Society of Biological Chemists, the American Society for Pharmacology and Experimental Therapeutics, and the American Society for Experimental Pathology,—in convention assembled, hereby express our accord with the declaration of the recent International Medical Congress and other authoritative medical organizations, in favor of the scientific method designated properly animal experimentation, but sometimes vivisection.

2. We point to the remarkable and innumerable achievements, by means of animal experimentation in the past, in advancing the knowledge of biological laws and devising methods of procedure for the cure of disease and for the prevention of suffering in human beings and lower animals. We emphasize the necessity of animal experimentation in continuing similar beneficent work in the future.

3. We are firmly opposed to cruelty to animals. We heartily support all humane efforts to prevent the wanton infliction of pain. The vast majority of experiments on animals need not be and, in fact, are not accompanied by any pain whatsoever. Under the regulations already in force, which reduce discomfort to the least possible amount and which require the decision of doubtful cases by the responsible laboratory director, the performance of those rare experiments which involve pain is, we believe, justifiable.

4. We regret the widespread lack of information regarding the aims, the achievements, and procedures of animal experimentation. We deplore the persistent misrepresentation of these aims, achievements, and procedures by those who are opposed to this scientific method. We protest against the frequent denunciations of self-sacrificing, high-minded men of science who are devoting their lives to the welfare of mankind in efforts to solve the complicated problems of living beings and their diseases.

Source: Quoted in Keen, William Williams. *Animal Experimentation and Medical Progress*. Boston: Houghton Mifflin, 1914, xvi–xvii. http://ia600502.us.archive.org/9/items/animalexperiment00keenuoft/animalexperiment00keenuoft.pdf. Accessed June 30, 2012.

A Compromise on Vivisection (1914)

As shown above, there has never been a lack of calls for or against animal experimentation from opposite ends of the spectrum, from those who argue that researchers should be essentially free to use the practice as they fit to those who insist that the use of animals in research should be strictly outlawed. Throughout history, however, there have been individuals who seek a middle road, one that would allow the continued use of animals in research, but under closely controlled humane conditions. An entirely statement of this middle-of-the-road position is the following:

> For myself, I believe no permanent or effective reform of present practices is probable until the Medical Profession generally concede as dangerous and unnecessary that freedom of unlimited experimentation in pain, which is claimed and practiced to-day. That legislative reform is otherwise unattainable, one would hesitate to affirm; but it assuredly would be vastly less effective. You must convince men of the justice and reasonableness of a law before you can secure a willing obedience. Yielding to none in loyalty to the science, and enthusiasm for the Art of Healing, what standpoint may be taken by those of the Medical Profession who desire to reform evils which confessedly exist?
>
> I. We need not seek the total abolition of all experiments upon living animals. I do not forget that just such abolition is energetically demanded by a large number of earnest men and women, who have lost all faith in the possibility of restricting an abuse, if it be favored by scientific enthusiasm. "Let us take," they say, "the upright and conscientious ground of refusing all compromise with sin and evil, and maintaining our position unflinchingly, leave the rest to God." *[citation omitted]* This is almost precisely the ground taken by the Prohibitionists in national politics; it is the only ground one can occupy, provided the taking of a glass of wine, or the performance of any experiment,—painless or otherwise,—is of itself an "evil and a sin." There are those, however, who believe it possible to oppose and restrain intemperance by other methods than legislative prohibition. So with the prohibition of vivisection. Admitting the abuses of the practice, I cannot yet see that they are so intrinsic and essential as to make necessary the entire abolition of all physiological experiments whatsoever.

II. We may advocate (and I believe we should advocate)—the total abolition, by law, of all mutilating or destructive experiments upon lower animals, involving pain, when such experiments are made for the purpose of public or private demonstration of already known and accepted physiological facts.

This is the ground of compromise—unacceptable, as yet, to either party. Nevertheless it is asking simply for those limitations and restrictions which have always been conceded as prudent and fair by the medical profession of Great Britain. Speaking of a certain experiment upon the spinal nerves, Dr. M. Foster, of Cambridge University, one of the leading physiological teachers of England, says: "I have not performed it and have never seen it done," partly because of horror at the pain necessary. And yet this experiment has been performed before classes of young men and young women in the Medical Schools of this country! Absolutely no legal restriction here exists to the repetition, over and over again, of the most atrocious tortures of Mantegazza, Bert and Schiff.

Source: Leffingwell, Albert. *An Ethical Problem; Or, Sidelights upon Scientific Experimentation on Man and Animals.* London: G. Bell and Sons; New York: C. P. Farrell, 1914. http://archive.org/stream/vivisection32033 gut/pg32033.txt. Accessed July 1, 2012.

Cruelty to Animals Act (India) (1960)

One of the first nations in the world to adopt comprehensive legislation dealing with the care of animals in research was India, which adopted the Cruelty to Animals Act in 1960. The following selection contains some of the major substantive provisions of the act:

CHAPTER IV
EXPERIMENTATION OF ANIMALS

14. Experiments on animals : Nothing contained in this Act shall render unlawful the performance of experiments (including) experiments involving operations) on animals for the purpose of advancement by new discovery of physiological knowledge or of knowledge which will be useful for saving or for prolonging life or alleviating suffering or for combating any disease, whether of human beings, animals or plants.

[Sections 15 through 17 provide that committees are to be formed for the supervision of experiments on animals and outline the memberships, powers, and duties of such committees.]

(lA) [Numbering revised in later amendments to the act] In particular, and without prejudice to the generality to the foregoing power, such rules may provide for the following matters namely:

(a) the registration of persons or institutions carrying on experiments on animals;

(b) the reports and other information which shall be forwarded to the Committee by persons and institutions carrying on experiments or, animals.]

(2) In particular, and without prejudice to the generality of the foregoing power, rules made by the Committee shall be designed to secure the following objects, namely:

(a) that in cases where experiments are performed in any institution, the responsibility therefore is placed on the person in charge of the institution and that, in cases where experiments are performed outside an institution by individuals, the individuals, are performed outside an institution by individuals, the individuals, are qualified in that behalf and the experiments are performed on their full responsibility;

(b) that experiments are performed with due care and humanity and that as far as possible experiments involving operations are performed under the influence of some anaesthetic of sufficient power to prevent the animals feeling pain;

(c) that animals which, in the course of experiments under the influence of anaesthetics, are so injured that their recovery would involve serious suffering, are ordinarily destroyed while still insensible;

(d) that experiments on animals are avoided wherever it is possible to do so; as for example; in medical schools, hospitals, colleges and the like, if other teaching devices such as books, models, films and the. like, may equally suffice;

(e) that experiments on larger animals are avoided when it is possible to achieve the same results by experiments upon small laboratory animals like guinea-'pigs, [*sic*] rabbits, frogs and rats;

(f) that, as far as possible, experiments are not performed merely for the purpose of acquiring manual skill;

(g) that animals intended for the performance of experiments are properly looked after both before and after experiments;

(h) that suitable records are maintained with respect to experiments performed on animals

(3) In making any rules under this section, the Committee shall be guided by such directions as the Central Government (consistently with the objects for which the Committee is set up) may give to it, and the Central Government is hereby authorised to give such direction.

(4) All rules made by the Committee shall be binding on all individuals performing experiments outside institutions and on persons incharge [*sic*] of institutions in which experiments are performed.

Source: The Prevention of Cruelty to Animals Act, 1960. (59 of 1960). http://www.envfor.nic.in/legis/awbi/awbi01 .pdf. Accessed August 13, 2012.

Animal Welfare Act of 1966

The U.S. Congress adopted a set of regulations in 1966 outlining provisions for the proper care of animals used in experimentation and for "other purposes." That legislation became known as the Animal Welfare Act of 1966, although that term is not used anywhere in the act itself. The act is of great importance in U.S. history because it is the only federal legislation devoted solely and entirely to the topic. Other legislation about animal welfare exists, but it all refers to the fundamental principles outlined in this act. The law authorizes the secretary of agriculture to regulate the transport, sale, and handling of dogs, cats, nonhuman primates, guinea pigs, hamsters, and rabbits intended for use in research and "other purposes," and requires the licensing and inspection of dealers in these animals. Some of the main provisions of the act are listed below. (Also see an important change in this act made in the Farm Security Act of 2002, below.)

§ 2131. Congressional statement of policy

The Congress finds that animals and activities which are regulated under this chapter are either in interstate or foreign commerce or substantially affect such commerce or the free flow thereof, and that regulation of animals and activities as provided in this chapter is necessary to prevent and eliminate burdens upon such commerce and to effectively regulate such commerce, in order—

(1) to insure that animals intended for use in research facilities or for exhibition purposes or for use as pets are provided humane care and treatment;

(2) to assure the humane treatment of animals during transportation in commerce; and

(3) to protect the owners of animals from the theft of their animals by preventing the sale or use of animals which have been stolen.

The Congress further finds that it is essential to regulate, as provided in this chapter, the transportation, purchase, sale, housing, care, handling, and treatment of animals by carriers or by persons or organizations engaged in using them for research or experimental purposes or for exhibition purposes or holding them for sale as pets or for any such purpose or use.

[Section 2132 provides definitions for terms used in this act.]

§ 2133.   Licensing of dealers and exhibitors

The Secretary shall issue licenses to dealers and exhibitors upon application therefor in such form and manner as he may prescribe and upon payment of such fee established pursuant to 2153 of this title: *Provided*, That no such license shall be issued until the dealer or exhibitor shall have demonstrated that his facilities comply with the standards promulgated by the Secretary pursuant to section 2143 of this title: *Provided*, however, That any retail pet store or other person who derives less than a substantial portion of his income (as determined by the Secretary) from the breeding and raising of dogs or cats on his own premises and sells any such dog or cat to a dealer or research facility shall not be required to obtain a license as a dealer or exhibitor under this chapter. The Secretary is further authorized to license, as dealers or exhibitors, persons who do not qualify as dealers or exhibitors within the meaning of this chapter upon such persons' complying with the requirements specified above and agreeing, in writing, to comply with all the requirements of this chapter and the regulations promulgated by the Secretary hereunder.

§ 2134.   Valid license for dealers and exhibitors required

No dealer or exhibitor shall sell or offer to sell or transport or offer for transportation, in commerce, to any research facility or for exhibition or for use as a pet any animal, or buy, sell, offer to buy or sell, transport or offer for transportation, in commerce, to or from another dealer or exhibitor under this chapter any animals, unless and until such dealer or exhibitor shall have obtained a license from the Secretary and such license shall not have been suspended or revoked.

§ 2135.   Time period for disposal of dogs or cats by dealers or exhibitors

No dealer or exhibitor shall sell or otherwise dispose of any dog or cat within a period of five business days after the acquisition of such animal or within such other period as may be specified by the Secretary . . .

§ 2136.   Registration of research facilities, handlers, carriers and unlicensed exhibitors

Every research facility, every intermediate handler, every carrier, and every exhibitor not licensed under section 2133 of this title shall register with the Secretary in accordance with such rules and regulations as he may prescribe.

§ 2137.   Purchase of dogs or cats by research facilities prohibited except from authorized operators of auction sales and licensed dealers or exhibitors

It shall be unlawful for any research facility to purchase any dog or cat from any person except an operator of an auction sale subject to section 2142 of this title or a person holding a valid license as a dealer or exhibitor issued by the Secretary pursuant to this chapter unless such person is exempted from obtaining such license under section 2133 of this title.

§ 2138.   Purchase of dogs or cats by United States Government facilities prohibited except from authorized operators of auction sales and licensed dealers or exhibitors

No department, agency, or instrumentality of the United States which uses animals for research or experimentation or exhibition shall purchase or otherwise acquire any dog or cat for such purposes from any person except an operator of an auction sale subject to section 2142 of this title or a person holding a valid license as a dealer or exhibitor issued by the Secretary pursuant to this chapter unless such person is exempted from obtaining such license under section 2133 of this title.

[Sections 2139 through 2141 deal with housekeeping issues, such as enforcement and record keeping.]

[Perhaps the key section of the act is Section 2142, which says that:]

§ 2143.   Standards and certification process for humane handling, care, treatment, and transportation of animals

(a) Promulgation of standards, rules, regulations, and orders; requirements; research facilities; State authority

(1) The Secretary shall promulgate standards to govern the humane handling, care, treatment, and transportation of animals by dealers, research facilities, and exhibitors.

(2) The standards described in paragraph (1) shall include minimum requirements—

(A) for handling, housing, feeding, watering, sanitation, ventilation, shelter from extremes of weather and temperatures, adequate veterinary care, and separation by species where the Secretary finds necessary for humane handling, care, or treatment of animals; and

(B) for exercise of dogs, as determined by an attending veterinarian in accordance with general standards promulgated by the Secretary, and for a physical environment adequate to promote the psychological well-being of primates.

(3) In addition to the requirements under paragraph (2), the standards described in paragraph (1) shall, with respect to animals in research facilities, include requirements—

(A) for animal care, treatment, and practices in experimental procedures to ensure that animal pain and distress are minimized, including adequate veterinary care with the appropriate use of anesthetic, analgesic, tranquilizing drugs, or euthanasia;

(B) that the principal investigator considers alternatives to any procedure likely to produce pain to or distress in an experimental animal;

(C) in any practice which could cause pain to animals—

(i) that a doctor of veterinary medicine is consulted in the planning of such procedures;

(ii) for the use of tranquilizers, analgesics, and anesthetics;

(iii) for pre-surgical and post-surgical care by laboratory workers, in accordance with established veterinary medical and nursing procedures;

(iv) against the use of paralytics without anesthesia; and

(v) that the withholding of tranquilizers, anesthesia, analgesia, or euthanasia when scientifically necessary shall continue for only the necessary period of time;

(D) that no animal is used in more than one major operative experiment from which it is allowed to recover except in cases of—

(i) scientific necessity; or

(ii) other special circumstances as determined by the Secretary; and

(E) that exceptions to such standards may be made only when specified by research protocol and that any such exception shall be detailed and explained in a report outlined under paragraph (7) and filed with the Institutional Animal Committee.

[The act then provides additional details about animal care in research facilities.]

(b) Research facility Committee; establishment, membership, functions, etc.

(1) The Secretary shall require that each research facility establish at least one Committee. Each Committee shall be appointed by the chief executive officer of each such

research facility and shall be composed of not fewer than three members. Such members shall possess sufficient ability to assess animal care, treatment, and practices in experimental research as determined by the needs of the research facility and shall represent society's concerns regarding the welfare of animal subjects used at such facility.

[The act then provides details as to the required compensation of the committee.]

(c) Federal research facilities; establishment, composition, and responsibilities of Federal Committee

In the case of Federal research facilities, a Federal Committee shall be established and shall have the same composition and responsibilities provided in subsection (b) of this section. . . .

(d) Training of scientists, animal technicians, and other personnel involved with animal care and treatment at research facilities

Each research facility shall provide for the training of scientists, animal technicians, and other personnel involved with animal care and treatment in such facility as required by the Secretary.

[The act then provides details as to the topics to be included in training sessions. The remaining portions of this section deal with related details, such as creation of an information service on animal welfare, cut off of funding for facilities that do not follow these regulations, shipment of animals, and veterinary certificates.]

Source: U.S. Code. Title 7—Agriculture. Sections 2131–2158, pages 1267–1283. http://www.gpo.gov/fdsys/pkg/USCODE -2011-title7/pdf/USCODE-2011-title7-chap54-sec2131.pdf. http://www.gpo.gov/fdsys/pkg/USCODE-2011-title7/ pdf/USCODE-2011-title7-chap54-sec2158.pdf.

Council Directive of 27 July 1976 on the Approximation of the Laws of the Member States Relating to Cosmetic Products (76/768/EEC) (1976)

As early as 1976, the European Union had begun to deal with the problem of the use of experimental animals in the testing of cosmetics. In that year, the European Council adopted a directive to member states on this issue. After an introductory section dealing with the use of harmful substances in cosmetics designed for human use, the directive focuses on the use of experimental animals in testing such products (text since updated).

Article 4a

1. Without prejudice to the general obligations deriving from Article 2, Member States shall prohibit:

(a) the marketing of cosmetic products where the final formulation, in order to meet the requirements of this Directive, has been the subject of animal testing using a method other than an alternative method after such alternative method has been validated and adopted at Community level with due regard to the development of validation within the OECD;

(b) the marketing of cosmetic products containing ingredients or combinations of ingredients which, in order to meet the requirements of this Directive, have been the subject of animal testing using a method other than an alternative method after such alternative method has been validated and adopted at Community level with due regard to the development of validation within the OECD;

(c) the performance on their territory of animal testing of finished cosmetic products in order to meet the requirements of this Directive;

(d) the performance on their territory of animal testing of ingredients or combinations of ingredients in order to meet the requirements of this Directive, no later than the date on which such tests are required to be replaced by one or more validated methods listed in Commission Regulation (EC) No 440/2008 of 30 May 2008 laying down test methods pursuant to Regulation (EC) No 1907/2006 of the European Parliament and of the Council on the Registration, Evaluation, Authorisation and Restriction of Chemicals (REACH) (1) or in Annex IX to this Directive.

Source: COUNCIL DIRECTIVE of 27 July 1976 on the approximation of the laws of the Member States relating to cosmetic products (76/768/EEC). http://eur-lex.europa .eu/LexUriServ/LexUriServ.do?uri=CONSLEG:1976L0768:201 00301:en:PDF.

Since its original adoption, this document has been updated on a number of occasions, usually to reflect technological changes that have occurred in testing procedures or the risks posed by certain chemicals. For a list of all amendments to the document, see http://ec.europa.eu/consumers/sectors/cosmetics/ documents/directive/index_en.htm#h2-technical-adaptations -and-amendments-already-incorporated-in-the-consolidated-text.

Primate Protection League v. Tulane Educ. Fund (500 U.S. 72 [1991])

Animal welfare activists hail this court case as the first victory for animals used in experiments. The facts of the case are some-what more complicated than that. In September 1981, Dr. Edward Taub of the Institute of Behavioral Research at Silver Spring, Maryland, was charged with 119 incidents of cruel and unusual use of animals in his experiments on the use of limbs in which nerves had been cut. Of those charges, 113 were dismissed in the first court case, 5 more in the second court case, and the last, two years later. By 1990, the case had reached the U.S. Court of Appeals for the Fifth District with the question as to whether a number of animal rights groups had standing to sue for custody of the two remaining monkeys from the original research. The court of appeals ruled that the groups did not have standing for the reasons outlined below. That case was *International Primate Protection League, et al., v. Administrators of the Tulane Educational Fund, and National Institutes of Health*, 895 F.2d 1056 (1990). In 1991, the animal rights groups appealed to the U.S. Supreme Court, which eventually ruled that the court of appeals had been in error and that the groups did, in fact, have standing in the case. It ordered the case returned to a district court in New Orleans. That case soon became moot, however, as the last two monkeys were euthanized shortly after the Supreme Court issued its decree.

The primary elements of the appeal court's decision were as follows:

In the present case, the plaintiffs have advanced three separate claims of injury.

10 The plaintiffs' first claim is that:

11 Plaintiffs, plaintiff organizations and individual members thereof would suffer a permanent disruption of their personal relationships with the monkeys, relationships which were established prior to any previous litigation in related matters and which continued during such litigation.

12 This claim of injury to the plaintiffs' "personal relationships with the monkeys" is one which, within the context of this case, is insufficient to meet [the relevant legal] requirements. . . .

17 The plaintiffs' second claim of injury is that:

18 Plaintiffs, plaintiff organizations and individual members thereof maintain a long-standing, sincere commitment to preventing inhumane treatment of animals, especially as concerns the monkeys now at Delta, and their aesthetic, conservational and environmental interests would be particularly, severely, and detrimentally affected. . . .

22 The plaintiffs' claim of harm to their "aesthetic, conservational and environmental interests" fails for the same reason that their "personal relationship" claim fails. The plaintiffs neither allege facts which demonstrate that they

have any aesthetic, conservational or environmental interests in the laboratory monkeys, nor allege facts which would demonstrate that the destruction of the laboratory monkeys would impair the plaintiffs' interests in monkeys living in the wild. Were the plaintiffs to allege, for example, that the species of monkey here involved was endangered and that the destruction of the laboratory monkeys would therefore impair conservation efforts to preserve or restore such an endangered species to its wild habitat, their claims of injury might be more cognizable. As they have not (and likely could not credibly) make such an allegation, the plaintiffs second claim of injury is insufficient to confer standing.

23 The plaintiffs' third claim of injury is that:

24 Plaintiffs' mission as advocates for the rights of the Silver Spring Monkeys, who have no means of protecting themselves, would be severely impaired.

25 As discussed above, the Supreme Court in *Sierra Club* has ruled this kind of "special interest" insufficient to confer standing. Implicit in the plaintiffs' third claimed injury, however, is the contention that the plaintiffs should be allowed standing because to deny it would leave the monkeys unprotected. The Supreme Court rejected a similar contention in *Valley Forge Christian College v. Americans United for Separation of Church and State*:

26 The assumption that if respondents have no standing to sue, "no one would have standing, is not a reason to find standing." ... Accordingly, the mere fact that the monkeys would be left without an advocate in court does not create standing where it otherwise does not exist.

The Supreme Court decided that it was confronted with a somewhat different issue. The case had originally reached the Federal Court of Appeals at the request of a defendant, the National Institutes of Health, as it was allowed to do under federal law. By so doing, however, the Supreme Court held, the animal rights groups had lost the right to have their case heard in local and state courts first. The Court ruled that that process was illegal. It explained that:

> Petitioners have standing to challenge the removal of the case. They have suffered an injury—the lost right to sue in the forum of their choice—that can be traced to NIH's action—the removal. And, if they prevail, their injury will be redressed because the federal courts will lose subject matter jurisdiction and the case will be remanded. Although the Court of Appeals ruled that petitioners lacked standing to seek protection of the monkeys, the adverseness required for standing to contest the removal is supplied by petitioners' desire to prosecute their claims in state court. . . .
>
> We therefore reverse the decision of the Court of Appeals and remand the case to the District Court with instructions that the case be remanded to the Civil District Court for the Parish of Orleans, Louisiana.

Source: *Primate Protection League v. Tulane Educ. Fund*, 500 U.S. 72 (1991). Justia.com. http://supreme.justia.com/cases/federal/us/500/72/case.html. Accessed August 13, 2012.

NIH Revitalization Act of 1993 (Public Law 103-43; 107 Stat. 122)

In 1993, the U.S. Congress passed an extensive reorganization plan for the National Institutes of Health, which included a section on the treatment of animals used in scientific and biomedical research. The core of that section is reprinted here:

SEC. 205. PLAN FOR USE OF ANIMALS IN RESEARCH.

(a) IN GENERAL.—Part A of title IV of the Public Health Service Act, as amended by section 204 of this Act, is amended by adding at the end the following section:

"PLAN FOR USE OF ANIMALS IN RESEARCH

"SEC. 404C. (a) The Director of NIH, after consultation with the committee established under subsection (e), shall prepare a plan—

"(1) for the National Institutes of Health to conduct or support research into—

"(A) methods of biomedical research and experimentation that do not require the use of animals;

"(B) methods of such research and experimentation that reduce the number of animals used in such research;

"(C) methods of such research and experimentation that produce less pain and distress in such animals; and

"(D) methods of such research and experimentation that involve the use of marine life other than marine mammals);

"(2) for establishing the validity and reliability of the methods described in paragraph (1);

"(3) for encouraging the acceptance by the scientific community of such methods that have been found to be valid and reliable; and

"(4) for training scientists in the use of such methods that have been found to be valid and reliable.

[Remaining parts of this section deal with administration aspects of these requirements, one of which is the following:]

"(d) The Director of NIH shall take such actions as may be appropriate to convey to scientists and others who use animals in biomedical or behavioral research or experimentation information respecting the methods found to be valid and reliable under subsection (a)(2)."

Source: Public Law 103-43. 103d Congress. http://history.nih.gov/research/downloads/PL103-43.pdf. Accessed August 13, 2012.

Use of Animals in Testing; State of California (2000)

Over a period of more than a decade, efforts were made in the California legislature to pass bills that would protect animals from the worst excesses of testing. Bills sponsored by Senator Jack O'Connell were passed twice, in 1989 and 1991, but were vetoed in both cases by Republican governor Pete Wilson. A bill along these lines finally passed in 2000 and was signed by Governor Gray Davis. California was the first state to adopt legislation protecting animals in experiments and testing. The provisions of the O'Connell bill are now part of the California Civil Code, Section 1834.9, as given here. Note that the final section restricts the law to nonmedical research, which, to a considerable degree, means the testing of cosmetics and other beauty aids.

1834.9. (a) Manufacturers and contract testing facilities shall not use traditional animal test methods within this state for which an appropriate alternative test method has been scientifically validated and recommended by the Inter-Agency Coordinating Committee for the Validation of Alternative Methods (ICCVAM) and adopted by the relevant federal agency or agencies or program within an agency responsible for regulating the specific product or activity for which the test is being conducted.

(b) Nothing in this section shall prohibit the use of any alternative nonanimal test method for the testing of any product, product formulation, chemical, or ingredient that is not recommended by ICCVAM.

(c) Nothing in this section shall prohibit the use of animal tests to comply with requirements of state agencies. Nothing in this section shall prohibit the use of animal tests to comply with requirements of federal agencies when the federal agency has approved an alternative non-animal test pursuant to subdivision (a) and the federal agency staff concludes that the alternative nonanimal test does not assure the health or safety of consumers.

(d) Notwithstanding any other provision of law, the exclusive remedy for enforcing this section shall be a civil action for injunctive relief brought by the Attorney General, the district attorney of the county in which the violation is alleged to have occurred, or a city attorney of a city or a city and county having a population in excess of 750,000 and in which the violation is alleged to have occurred. If the court determines that the Attorney General or district attorney is the prevailing party in the enforcement action, the official may also recover costs, attorney fees, and a civil penalty not to exceed five thousand dollars ($5,000) in that action.

(e) This section shall not apply to any animal test performed for the purpose of medical research.

Source: California Civil Code. Section 1834.9. http://www .leginfo.ca.gov/cgi-bin/displaycode?section=civ&group=010 01-02000&file=1833-1840. Accessed July 2, 2012.

Farm Security Act (2002)

In the massive omnibus Farm Security Act of 2002, the U.S. Congress made an interesting change in the original Animal Welfare Act of 1966, removing birds, rats, and mice from the list of protected animals. In reality, therefore, only mammals are now protected by the 1966 act in the United States.

Subtitle D—Animal Welfare
SEC. 10301.   DEFINITION OF ANIMAL UNDER THE ANIMAL WELFARE ACT.

Section 2(g) of the Animal Welfare Act (7 U.S.C. 2132 (g)) is amended in the first sentence by striking "excludes horses not used for research purposes and" and inserting the following: "excludes (1) birds, rats of the genus Rattus, and mice of the genus Mus, bred for use in research, (2) horses not used for research purposes, and (3)".

Source: Public Law 107–171—May 13, 2002. http://www
.gpo.gov/fdsys/pkg/PLAW-107publ171/pdf/PLAW-107publ171
.pdf. Accessed July 4, 2012.

New Jersey Exemption from Dissection Law (2006)

Ten states in the United States currently have laws that allow
students in elementary and/or high school to opt out of school
exercises that involve the dissection of animals. An example of
those laws is one adopted in New Jersey in 2006. That law is
reprinted in full here:

1. As used in this act:

"Alternative education project" means the use of video
tapes, models, films, books, computers, or any other tools
which provide an alternative method for obtaining and
testing the knowledge, information, or experience
required by a course of study.

"Animal" means any living organism that is an invertebrate, or is in the phylum chordata or organisms which
have a notochord and includes an animal's cadaver or severed parts of an animal's cadaver.

2. a. A public school pupil from kindergarten through
grade 12 may refuse to dissect, vivisect, incubate, capture
or otherwise harm or destroy animals or any parts thereof
as part of a course of instruction.

b. A school shall notify pupils and their parents or
guardians at the beginning of each school year of the right
to decline to participate in the activities enumerated in
subsection a. of this section and shall authorize parents
or guardians to assert the right of their children to refuse
to participate in these activities. Within two weeks of the
receipt of the notice, the pupils, parents or guardians shall
notify the school if the right to decline participation in the
enumerated activities will be exercised.

c. Any pupil who chooses to refrain from participation in or observation of a portion of a course of instruction in accordance with this section shall be offered an alternative education project for the purpose of providing the pupil with the factual knowledge, information or experience required by the course of study. A pupil may refuse to participate in an alternative education project which involves or necessitates any harmful use of an animal or animal parts.

d. A pupil shall not be discriminated against, in grading or in any other manner, based upon a decision to exercise the rights afforded pursuant to this act.

Source: P.L. 2005, Chapter 266, §§1,2 C.18A:35-4.24 & 18A:35-4.25. http://www.state.nj.us/education/aps/cccs/science/dissection/student%20opt-out.pdf. Accessed August 14, 2012.

United States of America v. Darius Fullmer (et al.) (2009)

In the early 2000s, members of the anti-vivisection group Stop Huntingdon Animal Cruelty (SHAC-US) carried out a number of actions against officials and workers at the U.S. offices of Huntingdon Life Sciences, a testing facility with headquarters in the United Kingdom. Six members of the group were essentially found guilty of violating the Animal Enterprise Protection Act of 1992 (AEPA), as amended in 2002, and sentenced from one to six years in prison. The six men appealed the decision on the basis that the AEPA was unconstitutional in general and also unconstitutional as applied to themselves. The appeals court disagreed. Its reasoning in the case was as follows:

We do not agree with Defendants that the AEPA is void for vagueness. First, the term "physical disruption" has a well understood, common definition. Defendants argue that the term "physical disruption" could be read to proscribe legal protest activity, such as a letter-writing campaign, because that could be interpreted as an intent to cause a physical disruption resulting in economic loss to the targeted enterprise. However, the statute provides an exception that exempts legal protest activity from proscribed conduct. In this case, Defendants engaged in various "direct action" campaigns, which even SHAC's website concedes constitute illegal activity. Therefore, Defendants cannot argue that the statute was vague. The record is rife with evidence that Defendants were on notice that their activities put them at risk for prosecution, including the extensive use of various encryption devices and programs used to erase incriminating data from their computer hard drives. Because Defendants' conduct was clearly within the heartland of the statute, speculation as to the hypothetical ways that the AEPA could be unconstitutionally vague would require us to "formulate a rule of constitutional law broader than is required by the precise facts" before us. . . .

. . . Defendants next argue that we should reverse their convictions for conspiracy to violate the AEPA because the statute is unconstitutional as-applied to them. Specifically, Defendants argue that their actions constituted political speech, and that the SHAC website neither incited violence nor constituted a true threat. Moreover, Defendants argue that their protected speech cannot be converted into unprotected speech by the independent action of others who engaged in illegal conduct. . . .

. . . With regard to the individual Defendants in this case, they attribute the illegal activity of the Huntingdon protestors to "anonymous activists" or unaffiliated organizations, and now argue that they cannot be held responsible for the illegal acts of others. However, there was ample evidence at trial to demonstrate that Kjonaas, Gazzola, Conroy, Stepanian, Harper and Fullmer coordinated and controlled SHAC's activities, both legal and illegal. Direct action, electronic civil disobedience, intimidation and harassment were part and parcel of SHAC's overall campaign, and these individual Defendants employed those tactics because they were effective. The record also supports a jury inference that these individual Defendants personally participated in illegal protests, in addition to orchestrating the illegal acts of others. They personally took credit for the success of the direct action campaigns as companies discontinued their business dealings with Huntingdon, one by one. Kjonaas and Gazzola, in particular, worked the phones at SHAC headquarters, confirming that various companies had severed ties with Huntingdon. As soon as Kjonaas or Gazzola received written confirmation, the protests stopped—strongly suggesting that they, on behalf of SHAC, had substantial control over the entire campaign. In addition, the individual Defendants held up the successes of the illegal campaigns as an example to other companies they targeted, in furtherance of their conspiracy to violate the AEPA. Further, other conduct constituted "true threats," which also removes Defendants' speech from the realm of First Amendment protection. In particular, Defendants used past incidents to instill fear in future targets. For example, SHAC displayed placards with photos of Brian Cass after his beating, with his injuries highlighted in red, at protests. Indeed, they attributed the quick exit of some targets, such as Deloitte and Touche, to the past experiences of employees at companies like Stephens and Marsh. In this regard, their actions meet the standard of a "true threat" as articulated in Watts, because viewed in context, the speeches, protests, and web postings, were all tools to further their effort. Moreover, given the success of the campaign in the past, including the destruction of private property and the telecommunication attacks on various companies, the implied threats were not conditional, and this speech rightly instilled fear in the listeners.

We therefore conclude that some of the speech on SHAC's website, viewed in context, is not protected by the First Amendment. Likewise, we find that any Defendant who created or disseminated that speech, or who personally participated in illegal activity, is likewise not protected by the First Amendment.

Source: United States Court of Appeals for the Third Circuit. No. 06-4211, et al. http://www.ca3.uscourts.gov/opinarch/064211p.pdf. Accessed August 14, 2012.

S. 810: Great Ape Protection and Cost Savings Act of 2011

Legislation to eliminate the use of great apes in scientific research in the United States was first introduced into the U.S. Congress in 2008. If failed to receive consideration in that year and when it was again introduced in 2009 and 2011. Important sections of the most recent of these bills are presented here:

S. 810
SECTION 1. SHORT TITLE.

This Act may be cited as the "Great Ape Protection and Cost Savings Act of 2011".

[Section 2 deals with findings and purposes of the bill. Section 3 deals with definitions of terms used in the bill.]

SEC. 4. PROHIBITIONS.

(a) INVASIVE RESEARCH PROHIBITED.—No person shall conduct invasive research on a great ape.

(b) HOUSING FOR INVASIVE RESEARCH PROHIBITED.—No person shall possess, maintain, or house a great ape for the purpose of conducting invasive research.

(c) FEDERAL FUNDING FOR INVASIVE RESEARCH PROHIBITED.—No Federal funds may be used to conduct invasive research on a great ape or to support an entity conducting or facilitating invasive research on a great ape either within or outside of the United States.

(d) BREEDING FOR INVASIVE RESEARCH PROHIBITED.—No person shall knowingly breed a great ape for the purpose of conducting or facilitating invasive research.

(e) TRANSPORT FOR INVASIVE RESEARCH PROHIBITED.—No person shall transport, move, deliver, receive, lease, rent, donate, purchase, sell, or borrow a great ape in interstate or foreign commerce for the purpose of conducting or facilitating invasive research on a great ape.

(f) TRANSFER OF OWNERSHIP PROHIBITED.— No Federal agency may transfer ownership of a great ape to a non-Federal entity unless the entity is a suitable sanctuary.

(g) EXEMPTION.—Nothing in this Act limits or prevents individualized medical care performed on a great ape by a licensed veterinarian or physician for the well-being of the great ape, including surgical procedures or chemical treatments for birth control.

SEC. 5. RETIREMENT.

Notwithstanding any other provision of law, not later than 3 years after the date of enactment of this Act, the Secretary of Health and Human Services shall effectuate the permanent retirement of all great apes owned by the Federal Government that are being maintained in any facility for the purpose of breeding for, holding for, or conducting invasive research.

Source: S. 810. To Prohibit the Conducting of Invasive Research on Great Apes, and for Other Purposes. http://www.gpo.gov/fdsys/pkg/BILLS-112s810is/pdf/BILLS-112s810is.pdf. Accessed July 5, 2012.

6 Resources

Humans have been talking and writing about animal experimentation for at least two thousand years. Today, there are countless number of books, articles, reports, Internet websites, and other written and electronic resources on this topic. No list of such resources can possible be complete in the limited space available here. However, the items provided here offer a sample of the biological, medical, social, ethical, moral, economic, and other arguments that have been brought to bear on the topic of animal experimentation. The resources in this chapter are arranged into four general categories: books, articles, reports, and electronic resources. In many instances, a book, article, or report is also available in electronic form and where that is the question, the comparable reference is also provided.

Books

Bateson, Sir Patrick, et al. *The Use of Non-human Animals in Research: A Guide for Scientists*. London: The Royal Society, 2004.

Dogs await experimentation in a French toxicology lab in 1989. Beagles are the main breed of dog used in animal testing. (Yves Forestier/Sygma/Corbis)

This publication offers a philosophical basis for the use of animals in research along with practical suggestions for the practice. The second half of the publication provides seven case studies in the use of experimental animals in research in fields such as polio vaccine, kidney dialysis, cystic fibrosis, and gastric acid secretion.

Beauchamp, Tom L., et al. *The Human Use of Animals : Case Studies in Ethical Choice*. 2nd ed. Oxford: Oxford University Press, 2008

This excellent volume reviews the human use of animals in a wide variety of contexts that includes the raising of farm animals, the use of animals for entertainment, the role of animals as companions and helpers, religious use of animals, endangered species, biomedical research and cosmetic testing, behavioral research, wildlife research, and educational uses of animals.

Best, Steven, and Anthony J. Nocella, eds. *Terrorists or Freedom Fighters?: Reflections on the Liberation of Animals*. New York: Lantern Press, 2004.

This anthology presents a collection of papers dealing with the history, philosophy, strategy and tactics, and moral basis of the animal liberation movement.

Burgess, Colin, and Chris Dubbs. *Animals in Space: from Research Rockets to the Space Shuttle*. New York: Springer, 2007.

The authors consider a form of animal experimentation that is perhaps not discussed so commonly, the use of animals in space projects. They present complete and detailed descriptions of such experiments and argue that the results of these experiments have been of incalculable value in the progress of human space travel.

Carbone, Larry. *What Animals Want: Expertise and Advocacy in Laboratory Animal Welfare Policy*. Oxford: Oxford University Press, 2004.

The author begins with a review of the history of animal experimentation, but then turns to the main focus of the book: the role of the veterinarian in maintaining and operating a laboratory in which animals are used for experimentation.

Conn, P. Michael, and James V. Parker. *The Animal Research War*. New York: Palgrave Macmillan, 2008.

The authors, a medical researcher (Conn) and an ethicist (Parker), review the attack on animal experimentation at the end of the twentieth century and the beginning of the twenty-first century. They discuss the strategies and methods used by animal rights activists and describe some of the most egregious events conducted by these individuals. They point out the direction for some type of compromise between those who favor and those who oppose animal experimentation.

Croce, Pietro. *Vivisection or Science?: An Investigation into Testing Drugs and Safeguarding Health*. 2nd ed. (English translation). London: Zed Books, 1999.

This book is one of the classic studies in the field of animal experimentation, written by a man who long used animals in his own research. Croce eventually came to the conclusion that this practice was morally and scientifically incorrect. In this book, he explains the reasons that using animal models can produce erroneous and dangerous results when applied to human biology and health issues. He also outlines for researchers a number of alternative methods that avoid the use of live animals in their experiments.

Francione, Gary L. *Animals as Persons : Essays on the Abolition of Animal Exploitation*. New York: Columbia University Press, 2008.

Francione presents a theory of animal rights that argues that all animals need to be acknowledged as having their own inherent value and not treated simply as "property" by humans, to be used only for human purposes.

Francione, Gary L. *Introduction to Animal Rights: Your Child or the Dog?* Philadelphia: Temple University Press, 2000.

The author points out that the majority of Americans agree with most basic principles of the animal rights movement, such as the impropriety of wearing fur coats, but that most Americans still eat meat and wear materials made from animals. He attempts to resolve this "moral schizophrenia."

Fraser, David. *Understanding Animal Welfare: The Science in Its Cultural Context.* Oxford: Wiley-Blackwell, 2008.

The author reviews the historical background of concern over the health and well-being of animals and indicates how that history has led to the growth of the new and modern field of animal welfare science.

Garrett, Jeremy R., ed. *The Ethics of Animal Research: Exploring the Controversy.* Cambridge, MA: MIT Press, 2012.

The four sections of this book contain papers on "The Ethics of Animal Research: An Overview of the Debate"; "Bringing Moral Theory to Bear on Animal Research"; "The Ethics of Animal Research in the New Age of Biotechnology"; and "Making Progress in the Debate: Alternative Paths Forward."

Greek, C. Ray, and Jean Swingle Greek. *Specious Science: How Genetics and Evolution Reveal Why Medical Research on Animals Harms Humans.* New York: Continuum, 2002.

The authors argue that the use of animals in biological and medical research is unwarranted and dangerous because findings obtained from such research are generally not applicable to humans and, in fact, their use in medical science can lead to harmful effects.

Guerrini, Anita. *Experimenting with Humans and Animals: From Galen to Animal Rights.* Baltimore: Johns Hopkins University Press, 2003.

> The author provides a well-researched review of the way biological and medical researchers have used both humans and nonhuman animals in their research. She includes an excellent review of the philosophical, moral, and theological arguments that have been used to defend such practices over a period of more than two thousand years.

Guither, Harold D. *Animal Rights: History and Scope of a Radical Social Movement.* Carbondale: Southern Illinois University Press, 1998.

> The author presents a review of the history of the debate over animal testing from what he describes as his own "middle of the road" view.

Hau, Jann, and Steven J. Schapiro, eds. *Handbook of Laboratory Animal Science.* Vol. 2, *Animal Models.* 3rd. ed. Boca Raton, FL: CRC Press, 2011.

> This book is regarded as an essential resource by scientific and biomedical researchers. It makes conscientious use of the three Rs in determining the best procedures to be used in selecting animals for various types of experimentation.

Haugen, David M. *Animal Experimentation.* Detroit, MI: Greenhaven Press, 2007.

> This book is part of Greenhaven's Opposing Viewpoint series, which attempts to present all sides of controversial issues for readers aged 13 years and up.

Hawthorne, Mark. *Striking at the Roots: A Practical Guide to Animal Activism.* Winchester, UK: O Books, 2008.

> As the title suggests, this book is a "how-to" manual for individuals who are opposed to the use of animals for biological, medical, and other kinds of research.

Hedich, Hans J., ed. *The Laboratory Mouse.* 2nd ed. Amsterdam: Academic Press, 2010.

This book is probably the ultimate authority on all aspects of the laboratory mouse. It is divided into six sections that cover history and genetics, anatomy and normative biology, neoplasms and infectious diseases, husbandry and maintenance, procedures, and legal regulations.

Hester, R. E., and Roy M. Harrison, eds. *Alternatives to Animal Testing.* Cambridge, UK: Royal Society of Chemistry, 2006.

This book deals with many aspects of alternatives available for the use of animals in scientific and biomedical research, including the safety evaluation of chemicals, international validation of alternative tests, barriers to such validation systems, in vitro testing for endocrine disruptors, intelligent approaches to safety evaluation of chemicals, and the regulatory framework for development and use of alternative methods.

Lankford, Ronald D. *Animal Experimentation.* Detroit, MI: Greenhaven Press, 2009.

This book is part of Greenhaven's At Issues series, which presents all sides of controversial issues, designed primarily for young adults but suitable for readers of all ages.

Leffingwell, Albert. *An Ethical Problem; Or, Sidelights upon Scientific Experimentation on Man and Animals.* London: G. Bell and Sons; New York: C. P. Farrell, 1914.

This book is one of the classic analyses of the morality of using animals, including humans, in biological and medical experiments. The book is now available in a modern edition from Filiquarian Publishing, Minneapolis, Minnesota, 2010.

Maguire, Timothy J., and Eric Novik, eds. *Methods in Bioengineering: Alternatives to Animal Testing.* Boston: Artech House, 2010.

This book consists of 15 scientific papers dealing with various technologies that have been developed as alternatives to the use of animals in experimentation, including brain cell cultures for neurotoxicity tests, in vitro skin substitutes, and alternatives for absorption testing.

Mason, Peter. *The Brown Dog Affair: The Story of a Monument That Divided the Nation*. London: Two Stevens Press, 1997.

This book retells the story of a violent nationwide battle over vivisection that took place in Great Britain in the first decade of the twentieth century over the use of a mongrel dog in a laboratory demonstration by the eminent English physiologist William Bayliss.

Monamy, Vaughan. *Animal Experimentation: A Guide to the Issues*. 2nd ed. Cambridge, UK: Cambridge University Press, 2009.

An outstanding general introduction to the topic of animal testing with chapters on history of the movement, current issues, alternatives to animal testing, the moral status of animals, and the regulation of experiments.

Morrison, Adrian A. *An Odyssey with Animals: A Veterinarian's Reflections on the Animal Rights & Welfare Debate*. New York: Oxford University Press, 2009.

The author is a veterinarian and sleep researcher who has been attacked for his work by animal rights advocates. In this book he describes the "in-between" position of some who loves animals but believes that animal experimentation is absolutely essential to the progress of medical science. He outlines some of the ways in which compromises have been reached, and perhaps could be reached again in the future, between animal rights advocates and researchers.

Newkirk, Ingrid. *Free the Animals: The Amazing True Story of the Animal Liberation Front*. New York: Lantern Books, 2000.

Newkirk is founder of People for the Ethical Treatment of Animals. Her book is a collection of stories about the actions of animal rights activists and the lessons that can be learned from these stories.

Orlans, F. Barbara. "History and Ethical Regulation of Animal Experimentation: An International Perspective." In *A Companion to Bioethics*. Edited by Helga Kuhse and Peter Singer. Oxford: Blackwell, 2004, 399–410.

The author provides an excellent historical background to the use of animals in research with a discussion of the elements of controversy that underlie current debates over the practice.

Phillips, Allie. *How Shelter Pets Are Brokered for Experimentation: Understanding Pound Seizure*. Lanham, MD: Rowman & Littlefield, 2010.

The author focuses on the special problem of the use of animals taken from shelters for experimentation, providing a historical background for the practice and a discussion of some of the ways individuals can act to avoid losing their own pets in such a process.

Regan, Tom. *The Case for Animal Rights*. 2nd ed. Berkeley: University of California Press, 2010.

This book is one of the classic studies animal rights, with an analysis of the way in which animal experimentation violates those rights.

Regan, Tom. *Defending Animal Rights*. Urbana: University of Illinois Press, 2006.

The author updates and revises some of the basic concepts presented in his original groundbreaking work, *The Case for Animal Rights* (above), with consideration of issues such as patterns of resistance; understanding animal rights violence; and work, hypocrisy, and integrity.

Rollin, Bernard E. *Animal Rights and Human Morality*. 3rd ed. New York: Prometheus Books, 2006.

> This book is one of the classics in the literature of animal experimentation. It was written by a man who has been described as the father of veterinary ethics. The four main sections of the book deal with moral theory and animals, animal rights and legal rights, the use and abuse of animals in research, and morality and pet animals.

Rollin, Bernard E. *Farm Animal Welfare: Social, Bioethical, and Research Issues*. Ames: Iowa State University Press, 2003.

> After an introductory section on the social and bioethical background of animal experimentation, the author focuses specifically on such issues involving farm animals, with chapters on the beef, swine, poultry, dairy, and veal industries in particular.

Rudy, Kathy. *Loving Animals: Toward a New Animal Advocacy*. Minneapolis: University of Minnesota Press, 2011.

> Rudy argues that the debate over animal testing often ignores, usually quite intentionally, the intense emotional bonds that many humans feel for their pets and other animals. She suggests that this debate can proceed in a more realistic way if both antivivisectionists and researchers acknowledge the power of these bonds and incorporate those feelings into reaching a solution satisfactory to everyone involved.

Russell, William Moy Stratton, and Rex Leonard Burch. *The Principles of Humane Experimental Technique*. London: Methuen, 1959.

> One of the classic texts in the history of animal experimentation, outlining the variety of methods that are available and that could be developed to reduce the harm and distress to animals that results from testing. The book introduced the now-classic concept of the three Rs in

animal experimentation: replacement, reduction, and refinement. The book is now available online in its entirety at http://altweb.jhsph.edu/pubs/books/humane_exp/het-toc.

Russell, W. M. S., R. L. Burch, and Michael Balls. *The Three Rs and the Humanity Criterion*. Nottingham, UK: FRAME, 2009.

This book is a modern adaptation and review of the two senior authors' classic text on the principles of humane experimental technique, originally published in 1959. (See above.)

Scully, Matthew. *Dominion: The Power of Man, the Suffering of Animals, and the Call to Mercy*. New York: St. Martin's Press, 2002.

The author chooses as the title of this book the biblical admonition that man is to have dominion over the animals. He shows how humans over the ages have used this passage to justify unspeakable horrors against nonhuman animals and pleads for a more humane and enlightened use of animals by humans in the future.

Singer, Peter. *Animal Liberation: The Definitive Classic of the Animal Movement*. New York: Harper Perennial, 2009.

This book is a revised and updated version of perhaps the most famous single work on the animal rights movement in modern history. The latest version includes the prefaces to the original 1975 edition as well as the 1990 and 2002 editions.

Sunstein, Cass R., and Martha Craven Nussbaum, eds. *Animal Rights: Current Debates and New Directions*. Oxford: Oxford University Press, 2004.

The papers presented in this collection present a diversity of views about the philosophical, ethical, legal, and political aspects of the debate over the use of animals in biological and medical experiments.

Twine, Richard. *Animals as Biotechnology: Ethics, Sustainability and Critical Animal Studies*. London: Earthscan, 2010.

> Twine discusses the way in which humans use animals as a critical element in our food supply, focusing on the methods used by growers to maximum their return on their investment. He raises questions as to how a changing world that must adjust to climate change and the challenge of sustainability can resolve moral and ethical questions related to humans' relationship to other animals within these contexts.

Wolfe, Cary. *Animal Rites: American Culture, the Discourse of Species, and Posthumanist Theory*. Chicago: University of Chicago Press, 2003.

> The premise of this book is that philosophers have been thinking about the moral status of animals for centuries. She shows how these musings have contributed to today's debate over the use of animals in experiments that can cause pain and fear in animals.

Yari, Donna. *The Ethics of Animal Experimentation: A Critical Analysis and Constructive Christian Proposal*. Oxford: Oxford University Press, 2005.

> The author argues that the fundamental issue in the use of laboratory animals is whether such animals have any moral standing. She takes principles from Christian theology to argue that the answer to that question is "yes."

Articles

Abbott, Alison. "Animal Testing: More than a Cosmetic Change." *Nature* 438, no. 7065 (2005): 144–146. http://ethics .ucsd.edu/journal/2006/readings/Animal_Testing_More_than _a_cosmetic_change.pdf. Accessed July 8, 2012.

> The author reviews new recommendations and requirements in the European community and suggests that they

are likely to have a radical effect on the use of animals in biomedical and basic research.

Andre, Claire, and Manuel Velasquez. "Of Cures and Creatures Great and Small." *Issues in Ethics* 1, no. 3 (1998). http://www .scu.edu/ethics/publications/iie/v1n3/cures.html. Accessed July 2, 2012.

Basketter, David A., et al. "A Roadmap for the Development of Alternative (Non-animal) Methods for Systemic Toxicity Testing—T4 Report." *ALTEX* 29, no. 1 (2011): 3–91.

This article consists of five white papers on ways of moving whole-body cosmetics testing to an entirely animal-free status, with commentaries on the five papers by members of a conference called to consider this issue.

Bryant, Taimie L. "Similarity or Difference as a Basis for Justice: Must Animals Be Like Humans to Be Legally Protected from Humans?" *Law and Contemporary Problems* 70 (2007): 207–254.

The author considers the circumstances under which animals must be similar to humans in order for them to be treated in the same way that humans are treated from the standpoint of justice.

Buettinger, Craig. "Antivivisection and the Charge of Zoophil-psychosis in the Early Twentieth Century." *The Historian* 55 (1993): 277–283.

The author describes the efforts by the medical and psychiatric community to label excessive concern for the welfare of animals, particularly those used in research, to be a form of mental illness that was given the name of zoophil-psychosis. The author provides an excellent history of the development of the antivivisection movement in the United States, and explains how the backlash by medical researchers probably brought greater harm than good to this movement.

Couto, Marcelo. "Laboratory Guidelines for Animal Care." *Methods in Molecular Biology* 770 (2011): 579–599.

> The author reviews the practical issues involved in planning and conducting biomedical research in which animals are to be used and points out the steps that need to be taken to make sure that such research follows all relevant regulations and guidelines. He suggests ways of dealing with instances of noncompliance in research.

Daneshian, Mardas, et al. "A Framework Program for the Teaching of Alternative Methods (Replacement, Reduction, Refinement) to Animal Experimentation." ALTEX 28, no. 4 (2011): 341–352.

> This article summarizes recommendations made at a three-day workshop on "Teaching Alternative Methods to Animal Experimentation" sponsored by the Center for Alternatives to Animal Testing in Europe (CAAT-Europe) and the Transatlantic Think Tank for Toxicology (t(4)).

De Wever, Bart, et al. "Implementation Challenges for Designing Integrated In Vitro Testing Strategies (ITIS Aiming at Reducing and Replacing Animal Experimentation." *Toxicology in Vitro* 26, no. 3 (2012): 526–534.

> This article reviews the discussions held at the November 26, 2009, meeting on "Toxicology in the 21st Century," with special consideration given to the practical challenges of putting into practice a number of the ideas for alternatives to animal testing presented at that meeting.

Donnellan, Laura. "Animal Testing in Cosmetics: Recent Developments in the European Union and the United States." *Animal Law* 13, no. 2 (2007): 251–280.

> This article reviews the current status of laws dealing with animal experimentation in the field of cosmetics research in the European Union and the United States.

Ferdowsian, Hope R. "Human and Animal Research Guidelines: Aligning Ethical Constructs with New Scientific Developments." *Bioethics* 25, no. 8 (2011): 472–478.

> The author reviews the history of the development of guidelines dealing with human and nonhuman animal research and points out the way in which these guidelines have evolved over time as research has provided better information on the physical, mental, emotional, and other characteristics of all types of animals.

Foëx, Bernard A. "The Ethics of Animal Experimentation." *Emergency Medicine Journal* 24, no. 11 (2007): 750–751.

> The author provides a general overview of the moral and ethical issues involved in the use of animals in medical and biological research.

Glaholt, Hayley Rose. "Vivisection as War: The 'Moral Diseases' of Animal Experimentation and Slavery in British Victorian Quaker Pacifist Ethics." *Society and Animals* 20, no. 2 (2012): 154–172.

> The author reviews the process by which Quakers in Great Britain between 1870 and 1914 attempted to deal with the issue of vivisection within their moral philosophy. They concluded that the procedure was a "moral disease" similar to slavery and war.

Gruber, F. P., and T. Hartung. "Alternative to Animal Experimentation in Basic Research." ALTEX 21, Suppl. 1 (2004): 3–31.

> The authors outline the arguments for using alternatives to animals wherever possible in biological research and discuss some of the options that have been developed for this purpose.

Hood, Ernie. "Agreement Could Speed Reductions in Animal Use." *Environmental Health Perspectives* 117 (2009): A347.

This article reports on a Memorandum of Agreement signed by the United States, Canada, Japan, and the European Union on advancing the use of alternatives to animal testing.

Kolar, Roman. "Animal Experimentation." *Science and Engineering Ethics* 12, no. 1 (2006): 111–122.

The author reviews the fundamental issues involved in the use of animals in research and points out the problems involved in putting into practice certain ethical principles that should direct such research, namely "unclear conditions and standards for ethical decisions, insufficient management of experiments undertaken for specific (e.g. regulatory) purposes, and conflicts of interest of ethics committees' members."

Lane-Petter, W. "The Ethics of Animal Experimentation." *Journal of Medical Ethics* 2 (1976): 118–126. The author discussed the work of the Littlewood Committee, appointed to review the Cruelty to Animals Act of 1876, as a basis for commenting on the general issue of the ethical status of animal testing.

Lauerman, John F. "Animal Research." *Harvard Magazine*, January–February 1999, 49–57. Also available online at http://harvardmagazine.com/1999/01/mice.html. Accessed July 2, 2012.

The author provides a balanced overview of the issues involved in the use of animals for laboratory research.

Liebsch, Manfred, et al. "Alternatives to Animal Testing: Current Status and Future Perspectives." *Archives of Toxicology* 85, no. 8 (2011): 841–858.

This article provides a comprehensive and detailed review of the history of concerns about and development of technologies for alternatives to animal testing, with some predictions as to the future directions of the field.

Loukianov, Anatoly S. "Is a Compromise Possible in Russia between Animal Advocates and Researchers Who Use Animals in Harmful Experiments?" *Alternatives to Laboratory Animals* 39, no. 3 (2011): 227–231.

> The author explains that no federal legislative exists in Russia to control the use of animals in biomedical research and that, as a result, vigorous debates have developed in the country about the need for developing alternatives to animal experimentation. He suggests that the quality of biomedical research has suffered significantly in Russia because of this disagreement.

Paixão, Rita Leal, and Fermin Roland Schramm. "Ética e experimentação animal: o que está em debate?" ("Ethics and Animal Experimentation: What Is Debated?") *Cadernos de Saúde Pública* 15, Suppl. 1 (1999). http://www.scielosp.org/scielo.php?script=sci_arttext&pid=S0102-311X1999000500011 (Portuguese and English). Accessed July 3, 2012.

Pound, Pandora, et al. "Where Is the Evidence That Animal Research Benefits Humans? *BMJ* 328, no. 7438 (2004): 514–517. Also available online at http://www.ncbi.nlm.nih.gov/pmc/articles/PMC351856/. Accessed July 8, 2012.

> The authors note that it is axiomatic that research using laboratory animals has brought great benefit to the treatment of human illness. Yet, they say, there is very little experimental evidence to support that claim and that, in fact, much animal research "is wasted because it is poorly conducted and not evaluated through systematic reviews."

Tacium, Debbie. "A History of Antivivisection from the 1800s to the Present." *Veterinary Heritage: Bulletin of the American Veterinary History Society* 31, no. 1 (May 2008): 1–9; 31, no. 2 (November 2008): 21–25; 32, no. 1 (May 2009): 1–5.

In this three-part series, the author traces the main events in the history of the antivivisectionist movement from the nineteenth century to the present day.

Tsolis, Renée, et al. "How to Become a Top Model: Impact of Animal Experimentation on Human Salmonella Disease Research." *Infection and Immunity* 79, no. 5 (2011): 1806–1814.

The authors discuss specific events in the history of attempts to find alternatives to animal testing in research on the effects of salmonella on human health.

Reports

Animal Experimentation and Clinical Studies: Ethical Recommendations to Ensure Participants' Safety in Early Drug Development. http://www.efgcp.be/Downloads/confDocuments/Final%20Report%20-%20EFGCP%20Workshop%2008-06-11%20Part.pdf. Accessed July 7, 2012.

This is a report of a meeting held in Brussels on June 11, 2008, of the European Forum for Good Clinical Practice (EFGCP) to consider the ethical issues involving in using research animals in the testing of drugs for human use.

Becker, Geoffrey S. "The Animal Welfare Act: Background and Selected Legislation." Congressional Research Service. http://crs.ncseonline.org/nle/crsreports/10Jan/RS22493.pdf. Accessed August 14, 2012.

This report provides a concise but complete summary of the original Animal Welfare Act of 1966, its amendments, and related legislation.

Committee on Toxicity Testing and Assessment of Environmental Agents. National Research Council. *Toxicity Testing in the 21st Century: A Vision and a Strategy.* Washington, D.C.: National Academies Press, 2007.

This report notes that recent advances in systems biology, testing in cells and tissues, and related scientific fields has the potential to produce a dramatic revolution in the way that chemicals are tested for their effects on humans, largely replacing the need to use animals in experimental research.

Committee to Update Science, Medicine and Animals. National Research Council. *Science, Medicine and Animals*. Washington, D.C.: National Academies Press, 2004.

This report is designed to help the average person understand and make decisions about issues such as the way in which animal models fit into the larger scheme of biomedical research, some of the advances in biomedical research that have resulted from animal experimentation, and the laws and regulations that protect animals and manage their use in research.

The Ethics of Research Involving Animals. London: Nuffield Council on Bioethics, 2005.

This excellent report covers virtually all aspects of the controversy over the use of animals in research, including a review of the history of such research, a summary of the arguments for and against animal research, some accomplishments that have resulted from the research, possible alternatives to the use of animals, and the use of animals in specific types of research, such as basic physiological studies and research on a variety of medical conditions.

Institute for Laboratory Animal Research. *International Perspectives: The Future of Nonhuman Primate Resources*. Washington, D.C.: National Academies Press, 2003.

This document is the report of a workshop held on April 17–19, 2002, on the future of the use of nonhuman primates in scientific research. It deals with topics such as conservation and supply of animals nutritional needs, genetics, microbiology, genetics, transportation, and unresolved issues.

Institute for Laboratory Animal Research. Committee on Recognition and Alleviation of Distress in Laboratory Animals. *Recognition and Alleviation of Distress in Laboratory Animals.* Washington, D.C.: National Academies Press, 2008.

Institute for Laboratory Animal Research. Committee on Recognition and Alleviation of Pain in Laboratory Animals. *Recognition and Alleviation of Pain in Laboratory Animals.* Washington, D.C.: National Academies Press, 2009.

> These two reports are updates on a 1992 report by the National Research Council, *Recognition and Alleviation of Pain and Distress in Laboratory Animals.* The authors of the reports note that significant progress has been achieved in the years since the original research in understanding, documenting, and alleviating the pain and distress experienced by animals used in research. They also note that a number of new alternatives are available so that additional progress can be made along these lines in the future.

Langley, Gill. *Next of Kin: A Report on the Use of Primates in Experiments.* London: British Union for the Abolition of Vivisection, June 2006.

> The author provides a thorough review of the rationale behind and practice of using primates in research experiments. The report includes sections on the moral status of primates and their evolutionary relationship with humans, statistics of experiments on primates in Britain and the European Union, the regulation of primate experiments, the supply and transport of primates to laboratories, causes of primate suffering and its impact on research, primates in medicines testing, and primates in fundamental research.

Report from the Commission to the Council and the European Parliament. Sixth Report on the Statistics on the Number of Animals used for Experimental and other Scientific Purposes in the Member States of the European Union. http://eur-lex .europa.eu/LexUriServ/LexUriServ.do?uri=COM:2010:0511:FIN :EN:PDF. Accessed July 5, 2012.

> This report is the sixth in a series mandated by a 1986 directive on assessing the status of animals used in scientific experimentation in the European Union. The report provides detailed statistics on the number and types of animals used in experimentation, and the purposes for which they were used over the time period covered by the report.

Select Committee on Animals in Scientific Procedures. *Animals in Scientific Procedures.* London: Her Majesty's Stationery Office, 2002.

> This document is the report of a special committee appointed by the British Parliament "to conduct an inquiry into the use of animals in scientific procedures in the United Kingdom." The committee reviewed written submissions from more than 100 organizations and 35 individuals interested in the topic, along with oral testimony from an additional 40 organizations and individuals.

Taylor, Katy. *Still Dying of Ignorance: 25 Years of Failed Primate AIDS Research.* London: British Union for the Abolition of Vivisection, n.d.

> This report explores the history of research on AIDS treatments that have used primates and finds that that research has, over a period of 25 years, produced essentially no useable results.

U.S. Congress. Office of Technology Assessment. *Alternatives to Animal Use in Research, Testing, and Education.* Washington,

D.C.: U.S. Government Printing Office, OTA-BA-273, February 1986.

> This well-researched review of alternatives to animal experimentation is now quite dated, but still of some historical interest.

Internet Sources

"@ltweb." Johns Hopkins Bloomberg School of Public Health. http://altweb.jhsph.edu/. Accessed July 4, 2012.

> This website was created as a gateway to news about alternative to the use of animals in research. It is designed to serve biomedical researchers, industry, the international alternatives community, international regulatory community, institutional groups that review animal protocols, the animal welfare community, individuals and groups who work with laboratory animals, educators, students, and the general public. It offers a number of print and electronic publications, including the online newsletter *Altweb News*, and *Altex*, the official journal of the Johns Hopkins Center for Alternatives to Animal Testing. It also provides a number of other online resources, such as information on alternatives for all target groups, a history of alternatives, a database on alternative resources, and a glossary of important terms.

"Alternatives to Animals." British Union to Abolish Vivisection. http://www.buav.org/humane-science/alternatives-to-animals. Accessed August 14, 2012.

> This web page provides a concise review of the types of technologies available for use in place of animals in scientific and biomedical research.

Anderegg, Christopher, et al. *A Critical Look at Animal Experimentation*. http://mrmcmed.org/Critical_Look.pdf. Accessed August 14, 2012.

The authors review 238 published articles on the use of animals in research and come to the conclusion that "the value of animal experimentation has been grossly exaggerated by those with a vested economic interest in its preservation."

"Animal Consciousness." *Stanford Encyclopedia of Philosophy.* http://plato.stanford.edu/entries/consciousness-animal/. Accessed July 3, 2012.

This article discusses in detail the variety of theories proposed throughout human history for the ability of animals to think, reason, and carry on other mental activities generally associated with humans. It provides an extensive bibliography on the topic.

"Animal Experimentation." Bright Hub. http://www.bright hub.com/science/medical/articles/16237.aspx. Accessed August 14, 2012.

A series of six online articles dealing with the history of animal experimentation, how animals are used in research, practical and ethical issues, alternatives to the use of animals in research, and regulations for the use of animals in research.

"Animal Experimentation—Indispensable or Indefensible? Speakers' Corner Trust. http://www.speakerscornertrust.org/forum/forum-for-debate/. Accessed August 14, 2012.

Tom Holder, from Speaking of Research, and Michelle Thew, of the British Union for the Abolition of Vivisection, debate the question as to whether animals should be used in scientific and biomedical research.

Animal Experimentation: A Student Guide to Balancing the Issues. ANZCCART. http://www.adelaide.edu.au/ANZCCART/resources/AnimalExperimentation.pdf. Accessed July 3, 2012.

ANZCCART, the Australian and New Zealand Council for the Care of Animals, has prepared and published this excellent curriculum on the topic of animal experimentation. It includes chapters on the history of animal experimentation, issues relating to the topic, opposition to the use of animals in experiments, the moral status of animals, animal use and regulation of experiments, and alternatives to the use of animals in research.

"Animal Experimentation: Suffering on the Name of Science." Philosophical Investigations. http://www.philosophical-investigations .org/Animal_Experimentation:_Suffering_on_the_Name_of_Science. Accessed July 9, 2012.

This website provides a broad, general review of the issue of animal experimentation including sections on history, recent medical and scientific advances, and alternatives to the use of animals in research.

Animal Legal and Historical Center. Michigan State University College of Law. http://animallaw.info/. Accessed August 14, 2012.

This enormously valuable website contains detailed information on virtually every aspect of animal experimentation legal issues, including laws in all of the 50 U.S. states and many foreign countries, as well as information on a host of specific topics, such as animal rights, dog issues, ecoterrorism, horse issues, and research and testing.

"Animal Research Is Poor Science." http://www.youtube.com/ watch?v=G-ksdubxkZo Accessed December 22, 2012.

This video is a recording of a conversation between interviewer Peter Tatchell and Dr. Gill Langley, scientific director of the Dr Hadwen Trust for Humane Research. Langley argues that the differences in human physiology and that of experimental animals is so great that data obtained from laboratory animals is essentially useless in understanding and solving human medical problems.

"Animal Rights History." http://www.animalrightshistory.org/. Accessed July 3, 2012.

> A very important Internet source with information on laws, historical archives, a history timeline, quotations, archives of primary sources, vegetarianism, and other useful resources.

"Animal Testing." Buzzle.com. http://www.buzzle.com/articles/animal-testing/. Accessed July 1, 2012.

> This web page contains sections on topics such as how to stop animal testing, why animal testing should be banned, using animals for research, animal-testing arguments, history of animal testing, animal experimentation statistics, alternatives to animal testing, animal-testing pros and cons, and animal-testing facts.

"Animal Testing." Vegan Peace. http://www.veganpeace.com/animal_cruelty/animal_testing.htm. Accessed July 4, 2012.

> This web page is part of the Vegan Peace website that argues in general against the use of animals in research. One of the page's most valuable sections provides links to a number of other organizations that hold similar views to those expressed on this page.

"Animal Testing and Animal Experimentation Issues." Physicians Committee for Responsible Medicine. http://www.pcrm.org/research/animaltestalt/animaltesting/. Accessed July 2, 2012.

> This web page provides access to a number of papers dealing with topics such as "A New Scientific Understanding of Animals," "When Animal Tests Fail," "Nonanimal Methods in Research and Education," and "Regulatory Issues."

Bailey, Jarrod. "How Well Do Animal Teratology Studies Predict Human Hazard?—Setting the Bar for Alternatives."

AltTox.org.   http://alttox.org/ttrc/toxicity-tests/repro-dev-tox/way-forward/bailey/. Accessed August 14, 2012.

> The author reviews the experimental evidence for the use of alternatives to animal testing to traditional methods for testing for teratogenic effects using laboratory animals.

"The Basel Declaration." http://www.basel-declaration.org/. Accessed July 4, 2012.

> The Basel Declaration is a document calling for greater transparency and communication with regard to the use of animals in laboratory research. The document was released to the public on November 30, 2010, and has since been signed by more than 1,400 individuals. This page provides details about the declaration and its underlying philosophy.

"The Basics." About Animal Testing. http://www.aboutanimaltesting.co.uk/thebasicscategory.html. Accessed June 29, 2012.

> This useful website has separate sections on animal testing myths, the history of animal testing, background of animal testing, facts about animal testing, and other related topics.

"Biomed for the Layperson." Laboratory Primate Advocacy Group.   http://www.lpag.org/layperson/layperson.html#history. Accessed July 5, 2012.

> This somewhat dated (February 2005) website is a composite of reports from people who work with primates in laboratory settings across the country. It includes sections on the history of animal experimentation, statistics on laboratory research involving animals, laboratory practices involving the use of animals, "a typical day for a laboratory chimpanzee," opposition to nonhuman animal research, and a list of references.

"End Animal Testing." Humane Society International. http://hsi.org/campaigns/end_animal_testing/. Accessed July 4, 2012.

This web page describe the Humane Society International's (HSI) special project on animal experimentation. Its primary focus is the Be Cruelty Free campaign through which it hopes to achieve its goal of greatly reduced use of animals in research. The page also has links to other similar HSI projects, such as Advancing Humane Science, which promotes the development and use of alternatives to animal testing; Chemical and Product Testing, which encourages the use of existing chemicals as substitutes in animal research; Cosmetics: Be Cruelty Free, which focuses on the use of animals in cosmetics testing; and Lethal Dose Animal Testing, which results in the death of millions of experimental animals in determining the lethal dose for new chemicals.

"Experimenting on Animals." BBC Ethics Guide. http://www
.bbc.co.uk/ethics/animals/using/experiments_1.shtml.   Accessed
July 2, 2012.

This excellent website provides an unbiased and comprehensive introduction to the topic of animal experimentation, with accessed to a number of other valuable Internet sites.

Francione, Gary L. "Vivisection." Animal Rights: The Abolitionist Approach. http://www.abolitionistapproach.com/ vivisection-part-one-the-necessity-of-vivisection/. Accessed July 10, 2012.

This long essay consist of two parts, the first on "The 'Necessity' of Vivisection" and the second on "The Moral Justification of Vivisection."

"Harvey and Vivisection." Kickoff. http://fx.damasgate.com/ harvey-and-vivisection/. Accessed July 3, 2012. This excellent article discusses in some detail the role that dissection and vivisection played in the research by William Harvey that led to the downfall of the Gallean principles of medicine. Harvey is generally known as the Founder of Modern Medicine.

"How Mice Helped Combat Childhood Leukemia." Animals in Research. http://science.education.nih.gov/animal research.nsf/Story1/How+Mice+Helped+Combat+Childhood +Leukemia#Q7. Accessed August 11, 2012.

> This National Institutes of Health website provides a detailed explanation of the way in which laboratory animals were used in research on acute lymphocytic leukemia.

The Humane Care and Use of Laboratory Animals. National Association for Biomedical Research. http://www.google.com/ url?sa=t&rct=j&q=&esrc=s&source=web&cd=1&ved=0CFE QFjAA&url=http%3A%2F%2Fwww.nabr.org%2FWorkArea %2Flinkit.aspx%3FLinkIdentifier%3Did%26ItemID%3D346 %26libID%3D367&ei=Fv_1T6_POoyCqQHd_fGKCQ&usg =AFQjCNE1DZGD1L4_NEqsYRMy4LzuYfVL3w&sig2=xYL -0nRokEew3ZR0-CuAEQ. Accessed July 5, 2012.

> This publication begins with a section that purports to present the facts "about the realities of animal research and researchers' strong motivations to protect animals from harm." It then provides a number of guidelines for the humane use of laboratory animals in research projects.

Lahanas, Michael. "Dissections and Vivisections." Hellenica World. http://www.mlahanas.de/Greeks/Dissection.htm. Accessed July 3, 2012.

> The author reviews animal experimentation practices (including some with living humans) about which we have information from the ancient Greek world and its contemporaries, predecessors, and successors.

Lin, Doris. "Why It's Wrong to Test on Animals." http:// animalrights.about.com/od/vivisection/a/VivisectionFAQ.htm. Accessed July 4, 2012.

> The author, who specializes in animal rights law, offers a succinct and thoughtful argument as to why animals should not be used in research.

Medical Advances and Animal Research. Understanding Animal Research and Coalition for Medical Progress, 2007. http://www.pro-test.org.uk/MAAR.pdf. Accessed August 14, 2012.

This glossy pamphlet describes in some detail the many areas of medical science in which animal experimentation has played a critical role, such as the development of vaccines, treatments for cancer, blood transfusion, anesthesia, and gene therapy.

Member Society Manual. World Society for the Protection of Animals. http://www.oaba.fr/pdf/WSPA%20members%20manual%20interactive%20pdf.pdf. Accessed August 14, 2012.

This invaluable resource has chapters on topics such as animals in entertainment, working animals, animal experimentation, animal protection legislation, humane education, lobbying, using the media, and project management.

Munro, Lyle. "Contesting Moral Capital in Campaigns against Animal Liberation." Society & Animals Forum, 1999. http://www.societyandanimalsforum.org/sa/sa7.1/munro.html. Accessed August 14, 2012.

The author explores the socio-dynamics of the interaction between animal liberationists and research-based and -oriented groups who contest against them.

Pharmboy, Abel. I Am Pro-Test: Responsible Animal Testing Improves Lives of Humans, Pets. http://scienceblogs.com/terrasig/2010/04/08/i-am-pro-test-responsible-anim/. Accessed July 4, 2012.

This blogger describes a pro-testing rally held at the University of California at Los Angeles in 2010 to explain the position of a number of organizations and individuals about the value of animal testing in basic and applied scientific and medical research.

"Research Using Animals." University of Oxford. http://www
.ox.ac.uk/animal_research/research_using_animals_an_overview/
index.html. Accessed August 12, 2012.

> This website provides a fascinating detailed look at the
> animal-testing procedures at one major university that
> includes the philosophy behind using animals, data on
> the numbers of animals used, and information about the
> procedures for which animals are employed.

"Resources." New England Anti-Vivisection Society. http://www
.neavs.org/resources/suggested-reading. Accessed August 14,
2012.

> This website provides an unusually good list of readings
> dealing with vivisection from the antivivisection standpoint.
> Articles are classified according to topics, such as Vivisection
> and Non-Animal Alternatives; Dissection Alternatives;
> Human and Non-Human Animal Connection; Law;
> Non-Human Animal Protection; and Animal and Human
> Rights.

"Speaking of Research." http://speakingofresearch.com/news/.
Accessed July 4, 2012.

> This website supports the use of animals in certain types
> of research in a humane and respectful way. The website
> has separate sections on links to blogs consistent with its
> views, policy statements about the use of animals in
> research, information about the use of experimental ani-
> mals, corrections for erroneous statements made about
> animal testing for antitesting individuals and groups, and
> ways of getting involved in pro-testing organizations and
> activities.

"This House Would Ban Animal Testing." International
Debate Education Association. http://idebate.org/debatabase/
debates/science-technology/house-would-ban-animal-testing. Accessed July 2, 2012.

This website offers an extended number of pro and con choices about animal testing for use in debate contests.

"The Truth about Vivisection." In Defense of Animals. http://www.vivisectioninfo.org/index.html. Accessed on July 2, 2012.

This website provides some basic information on vivisection, describes some alternative forms of research, and suggests some modes of action for those interested in the topic.

"Welcome to AnimalResearch.Info." http://www.animalresearch.info/en/. Accessed June 29, 2012.

This website claims to focus on the scientific and technological aspects of animal research, exploring current developments in the field, reviewing the history of research in this area, and determining when animal experimentation is appropriate, and when it is not.

Introduction

Humans have used animals for biological and medical experiments at least since the third century BCE. Since that time, a remarkable number of discoveries have been made and intense disagreements have been exposed about the scientific, ethical, and economic justifications, or lack of them, for this practice. This chapter provides a timeline of some of the most important events that have occurred over the past 2,500 years in the field of animal experimentation. An important aspect of the chronology of animal research and animal rights debates is the proliferation of groups that have been organized to argue for all sides of this issue. The chronology cannot provide a complete listing of all such groups, although most of the major groups are listed here.

ca. 450 BCE   The early Greek natural philosopher Alcmaeon of Croton is credited with being the first person to practice dissection and, perhaps, vivisection. In a search for the seat of human intelligence, he discovered the optic nerve, which carries visual impulses from the eyes to the brain.

Rabbits are prepared for a test at a chemical research center. Rabbits have been secured in this fashion for chemical and allergen testing since the introduction of the Draize test in 1944. (Sherman/Getty Images)

Third century BCE Greek physicians Herophilus and Erasistratus are known to have conducted experiments on living animals, including condemned human prisoners, to learn new details of anatomy and physiology.

Second century CE Galen, a Roman physician and perhaps the most famous physician of the ancient world, describes animal experiments conducted by his Greek predecessors as well as vivisections he performed himself.

1543 Andreas Vesalius uses dissection to learn more about human anatomy and physiology and as a teaching tool for his students. He acknowledges that vivisection is of greater value in accomplishing his objectives than is dissection of dead bodies.

Early seventeenth century French philosopher René Descartes argues that animals are mere automata, with no thoughts, feelings, emotions, sensations, language, or other qualities associated with human life. This philosophy justifies the use of animals in experiments (which Descartes may have conducted himself) because they experience no "feelings" with regard to their treatment.

Early seventeenth century English physician William Harvey conducts a series of experiments on animals using dissection and vivisection that largely refutes the fundamentals of medical science originally laid down by the Roman physician Galen 1,500 years earlier.

Early nineteenth century French physiologist François Magendie uses vivisection for research and instruction on the physiology of the human body. He is generally regarded as one of the most inhumane of all early experimentalists and is thought to have been responsible to a considerable degree for the rise of the antivivisectionist movement in England and parts of Europe.

1809 The British Parliament adopts a Cruelty to Animals Bill. The bill is extended and strengthened in 1810.

1810 British Cruelty to Animals Bill. *See* **1809**.

1822   The British Parliamentary passes the Cruel and Improper Treatment of Cattle Act. The bill is revised and expanded on later occasions, including 1825 and 1826.

1824   Irish member of Parliament Richard Martin founds the Royal Society for the Prevention of Cruelty to Animals (RSPCA).

1824   Medical student Franz Riesinger performs a successful corneal transplant on his pet gazelle, solving for perhaps the first time a medical challenge that had defeated medical researchers for almost 2,000 years.

1826   A bill is introduced into the British Parliament to criminalize cruelty to dogs. It is withdrawn when the proposer is convinced that dogs are already protected by existing laws. A colleague meanwhile hopes that the proposer will include cats in the bill because it is well known that cats are "worried" by dogs.

1835   The British Parliament passes the Cruelty to Animals Act, which combines a number of existing laws into one piece of legislation protecting against mistreatment of cattle, dog, and bullfighting, improper impounding of horses, slaughtering of horses and cattle, and other matters. From this point on, the Cruelty to Animals Act was regularly amended and updated in 1837 (Ireland), 1849, 1850, and 1854.

1866   American philanthropist Henry Bergh founds the American Society for the Prevention of Cruelty to Animals (ASPCA).

1873   The U.S. Congress adopts the first animal welfare law in the nation, the so-called Twenty-Eight Hour Law, which requires anyone handling animals in transit to provide food, water, and release from cages at least once every 28 hours.

1875   A group of individuals concerned with animal welfare, led by Francis Power Cobbe, forms the Victoria Street Society for the protection of Animals from Vivisection to campaign against cruelty to animals in all settings, including scientific and biomedical research. The society is later renamed the Anti-Vivisection Society in 1929.

1876 The British Parliament passed another version of the Cruelty to Animals Act, this one dealing specifically with the issue of animal experimentation. The act remained the guiding principle behind the use of experimental animals for more than a hundred years, when it was replaced by the Animals (Scientific Procedures) Act of 1986.

1881 French scientist Louis Pasteur proves that *Bacillus anthracis* is the causative agent for anthrax by culturing the pathogen from the blood of infected sheep and then inducing the disease in healthy sheep using the cultured product.

1883 American philanthropist Carolyn Earle White founds the American Anti-Vivisection Society.

1895 The New England Anti-Vivisection Society (NEAVS) is founded.

1898 British physician and medical research Ronald Ross discovers the mode of transmission for malaria in four sparrows and a weaver bird that have been bitten by the Anopheles mosquito.

1898 A splinter group from the National Anti-Vivisection Society (UK) forms the British Union for the Abolition of Vivisection (BUAV), which takes an absolutist position on the abolition of animal experimentation.

Early twentieth century English physician Albert Leffingwell takes a leading position in the antivivisectionist movement, producing a series of pamphlets and books on the topic that include *Vivisection in America* (1895), *The Vivisection Question* (1901), *Illustration of Human Vivisection* (1907), *The Vivisection Controversy* (1908), *American Meat* (1910), and *An Ethical Problem* (1914).

1900 The U.S. Congress adopts the first law protecting wildlife, the Lacy Act, which prohibits the trade in plants and wildlife that have been collected illegally.

1902 French biologist Lucien Cuénot conducts what are probably the first medical experiments with mice when he identifies three genes that are responsible for the development of coat color and the production of certain enzymes in laboratory mice.

1911   The British Parliament adopts the Protection of Animals Act.

1926   Major Charles Hume founds the University of London Animal Welfare Society, whose name is later changed to Universities Federation for Animal Welfare (UFAW).

1929   The Victoria Street Society (1875) is renamed the National Anti-Vivisection Society (NAVS).

1944   A test for determining the allergic properties of a substance, the so-called Draize test, is first announced.

1946   A group of American researchers concerned about the attacks of antivivisection groups founds the National Society for Medical Research (NSMR).

1951   A group of individuals who believe that there is a middle way between researches who use animals in their studies and antivivisectionists who oppose all use of animals for experimentation form the Animal Welfare Institute (AWI).

1952   The National Research Council establishes the Institute for Laboratory Animal Resources (ILAR) to serve as a source of information and a coordinator of information on the use of animals in research.

1954   Four advocates for animal welfare issues—Fred Myers, Helen Jones, Larry Andrews, and Marcia Glaser—found the National Humane Society, later renamed the Humane Society of the United States (HSUS), reputedly now the largest animal advocacy organization in the world.

1955   The Animal Welfare Institute creates a division, the Society for Animal Protective Legislation, whose sole responsibility it is to develop and lobby for legislation dealing with animal rights and animal welfare issues.

1959   U.S. researchers William M. S. Russell and Rex L. Burch introduce the three Rs of animal experimentation: reduction, refinement, and replacement.

1959   Helen Jones, one of the founders of the National Humane Society (1954) founds a new breakaway group, the Catholic Society for Animal Welfare, later renamed the International Society for Animal Rights.

1960   India passes one of the first animal welfare acts in the world requiring that individuals take "all reasonable measures" to avoid causing pain and suffering among animals.

1961   The British Medical Research Council establishes the Lawson Tait Memorial Fund to provide grants to researchers who use or study the use of alternatives to animal testing.

1963   Cosmetician and animal welfare activist Katherine Long and her friend Noel Gabriel found Beauty Without Cruelty, an organization committed to developing cosmetic products without the use of animal experimentation.

1963   A group of veterinarians known as the Animal Care Panel (ACP) publishes "The Guide for the Care and Use of Laboratory Animals," a set of guidelines for the care of animals used in scientific and biomedical research. The guide is currently in its eighth edition.

1965   In the United Kingdom, the Littlewood Committee makes its report on changes it deems to be necessary in the nation's animal welfare laws. The report includes 83 recommendations, 49 of which will require new legislation.

1965   A group of scientific, education, and industrial organizations combine to establish the American Association for the Accreditation of Laboratory Animal Care (AAALAC), whose purpose it is to develop standards for the proper care of laboratory animals. Institutions who voluntarily join the organization are inspected regularly to see if they are maintaining their animals according to standards published regularly by the AAALAC.

1966   The U.S. Congress passes the Laboratory Animal Welfare Act, later to be called simply the Animal Welfare Act.

1968   Belton P. Mouras and Kenneth E. Guerrero of the Humane Society of the United States found the Animal Protection Institute (API) to advocate for animals against exploitation and cruelty. In 2007, it was reorganized as Born Free, USA.

1969   The National Anti-Vivisection Society creates the International Association against Painful Experiments on Animals (IAAPEA), which is entirely opposed to all use of animals in scientific and biomedical research.

1969   In the United Kingdom, Dorothy Hegarty and Charles Foister create a charity whose goal it is to find alternatives to animal testing, the Fund for the Replacement of Animals in Medical Experiments (FRAME).

1970   The U.S. Congress amends the Animal Welfare Act to extend its provisions to all warm-blooded animals and to make other provisions for animals used in research.

ca. 1971   Militant animal activists Ronnie Lee and Cliff Goodman organize the Band of Mercy, a British group willing to use violent means to liberate animals from experimental settings. The group later takes the name Animal Liberation Front (ALF).

1972   West Germany adopts its first animal welfare act, the Tierschutzgesetz, or Animal Protection Act.

1975   Peter Singer's *Animal Liberation* is published. It becomes one of the iconic publications in the history of animal welfare.

1976   The European Union adopts a Cosmetics Directive (76/768/EEC) that introduces limitations on the use of live animals in the testing of cosmetics. (*See also* **2004**.)

1976   The Animal Welfare Act is amended to include "sport" fighting among animals and the transport of animals.

1976 Animal rights activist Henry Spira founds Animal Rights International.

1977 A group of scholars at England's Oxford University known as the Oxford Group holds the first international conference on the emerging issue of animal rights, later known as the Cambridge Conference on Animal Rights.

1977 The first action taken in the United States under the name of the Animal Liberation Front (ALF) involves the release of two dolphins from the University of Hawaii Marine Mammal Laboratory.

1978 Scientists Center for Animal Welfare (SCAW) is founded by concerned scientists interested in finding a reasonable balance between the need for animal testing in some forms of research with the rights and needs of experimental animals.

1979 A group of attorneys interested in legal issues related to the use of animals in research and a variety of other settings creates the Animal Legal Defense Fund.

1979 A group of individuals and corporations interested in ensuring researchers access to an adequate supply of research animals forms Research Animal Alliance, an organization that is later to become part of the modern National Association for Biomedical Research (NABR).

1980 People for the Ethical Treatment of Animals (PETA) is formed.

1981 The Silver Spring monkeys case brings to the attention of the American public in dramatic fashion the issue of the use of animals in scientific and biomedical research.

1981 An anonymous donor provides funds for the establishment of the Center for Alternatives to Animal Testing at the Johns Hopkins University.

1981 The Foundation for Biomedical Research (FBR) is founded for the purpose of promoting "public understanding and support for humane and responsible animal research."

1983   The organization Californians for Responsible Research is formed to protest inhuman use of animals for research at the University of California at Berkeley. The group soon changes its name to In Defense of Animals.

1985   The National Association for Biomedical Research (NABR) is formed through the merger of the National Society for Medical Research, the Association for Biomedical Research, and the Foundation for Biomedical Research.

1985   The Health Research Extension Act requires that researchers using animals in their work must provide statements indicating that alternatives to animals have been considered in their research.

1986   The British Parliament adopts the Animals (Scientific Procedures) Act, which largely replaced the century-old Cruelty to Animals Act of 1876, which had provided guidelines for the use of animals in scientific experiments.

1986   The European Union adopts its first directive (Directive 86/609/EEC) on the use of animals in scientific and biomedical research.

1988   California becomes the first state to adopt student choice legislation, allowing students to opt out of dissection experiments in biology classes.

1990   An estimated 25,000 people take part in the March for the Animals in Washington, D.C., sponsored by a coalition of animal rights groups that take the name National Alliance for Animal Legislation (later, National Alliance for Animals).

1990   The Animal Welfare Act is amended to protect the taking of pets for use in experimental research projects.

1991   Americans for Medical Progress (AMP) is founded for the purpose of "protecting society's investment in research by nurturing public understanding of and support for the humane and necessary use of animals in medicine."

1992   The European Center for the Evaluation of Alternative Methods is established.

1992 The U.S. Congress passes the Animal Enterprise Protection Act, designed to deal with violent acts against research institutions by groups such as the Animal Liberation Front.

1993 The first World Congress on Alternatives to Animal Testing is held.

1993 The NIH Revitalization Act requires the National Institutes of Health to develop research methods that implement the three Rs concept.

1994 The Animal Legal Defense Fund sues the USDA in an effort to force it to include rats, mice, and birds among animals covered by the Laboratory Animal Welfare Act of 1966. The district court rules in favor of the plaintiffs, but two years later that decision is overturned by the Third District Court of Appeals based on lack of standing by the plaintiffs. Rats, mice, and birds remain outside the protection of the Animal Welfare Act as of late 2012.

1996 The Corporate Standard of Compassion for Animals is adopted. The standard is a voluntary agreement by cosmetics and other companies not to use animals in their testing procedure unless no satisfactory substitute is available.

1997 The U.S. National Institutes of Health establishes the Interagency Coordinating Committee on the Validation of Alternative Methods (ICCVAM).

1998 All use of animals in the testing of cosmetics is banned in the United Kingdom.

2000 The U.S. Congress passes the Chimpanzee Health Improvement Maintenance and Protection (CHIMP) Act making provisions for sanctuaries to which chimpanzees that are "no longer needed" in scientific and biomedical research can be returned.

2004 The European Union adopts the 7th Amendment to the Cosmetics Directive of 1976, which lays out a road map for the elimination of animal testing of cosmetics.

2006   Oxford theologian and author of *Animal Rights: A Christian Assessment* Andrew Linzey establishes the Oxford Centre for Animal Ethics.

2006   The U.S. Congress passes the Animal Enterprise Terrorism Act, a comprehensive law prohibiting any action that threatens the operation of an animal enterprise or that places any individual in "reasonable fear of injury."

2006   Six members of the Stop Huntingdon Animal Cruelty (SHAC) U.S. organization are convicted of violating the Animal Enterprise Terrorism Act and sentenced to one to six years in federal prison.

2007   The National Research Council releases a report, *Toxicity Testing in the 21st Century: A Vision and a Strategy*, suggesting that advances in a number of fields should soon make it possible to eliminate a large fraction of the animal research currently used to test toxic chemicals.

2008   Based on the 2007 National Research Council report, *Toxicity Testing in the 21st Century: A Vision and a Strategy*, the Environmental Protection Agency, National Toxicity Program, and National Institutes of Health sign a memorandum of understanding to develop and implement new high-throughput, in vitro methods for testing chemicals and drugs.

2010   The Center for Alternatives to Animal Testing establishes its first non-U.S. center, CAATY-EU, at Konstantz University, in Germany.

TOOLS

 Pins

 Marker

 Scissors

 Scalpel

Forceps

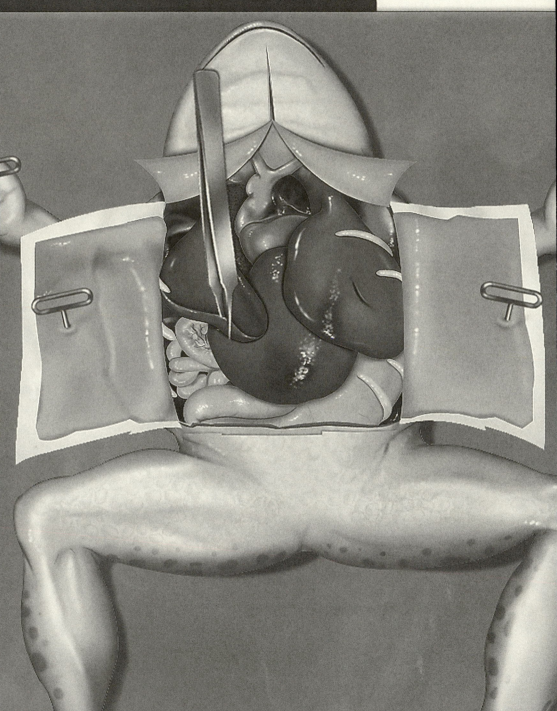

Introduction

This chapter defines a number of words and terms commonly used in discussion about animal experimentation, animal rights, and related activities.

Acute toxicity   The short-term effects of a onetime exposure to a chemical substance.

Alternative   Any method that can be used to replace the use of animals in a test, that minimizes distress caused an animal by a test, or that reduces the number of animals needed in an experiment.

Analgesic   A substance that reduces pain level without also reducing consciousness in an animal.

Animal assurance   A protocol that describes the care and use of animals in an institution's research program.

Animal model   An animal that is used to study the way a human body system functions or a human disease.

Behavioral research   Experiments designed to study the way in which an animal responds to its environment.

Screen view of Frog Dissection, an interactive computer simulation program designed for use by K-12 students on computers or tablets. Programs that provide a virtual dissection experience are promoted by animal welfare groups as humane alternatives to traditional classroom exploration. (Courtesy of mLab Emantras/Punflay)

Biomedical research   Experiments designed to understanding the function of human biological processes with the aim of ameliorating, preventing, and/or curing diseases in humans.

Carcinogen   Any substance that causes cancer or tends to increase the risk of developing cancer.

Chronic toxicity   Any effect caused by long-term or repeated exposure to a substance.

Clinical trial   A type of research conducted with humans using a substance or procedure that has already been tested in animals or other nonhuman settings (such as cell cultures) to determine whether that substance or procedure is safe and efficacious for use with human.

Computer simulation   A computer program designed to replicate the behavior of biological molecules, cells, tissue, organs, or other components of living systems, usually developed as a substitute for the use of animals in research.

Cytotoxicity   The extent to which a chemical causes damage to or kills cells.

Dissection   A procedure that involves cutting into an animal for the purpose of study or medical treatment.

Distress   The state produced in an animal as the result of pain, suffering, anxiety, fear, or other negative emotional states.

Dose-response relationship.   *See* **exposure-response relationship**.

Draize eye irritancy test   Once a very popular test with animals (usually rabbits) in which a substance being tested is placed in the animal's eyes to determine the degree of irritation it produces.

Efficacious   Successful in producing some desired result.

Environmental enrichment   An activity or set of activities that provide captive animals with a living experience comparable to that of their natural environment.

Exposure-response relationship   The relationships that exists between the amount of a substance used in an experiment and the effect produced on an organism. Also called the dose-response relationship.

Etiology   The study of the conditions or materials responsible for the origin of a disease.

Euthanasia   The process of killing an animal by the most humane process possible.

Good Laboratory Practices (GLP)   A set of rules developed by the U.S. Food and Drug Administration specifying proper procedures to be used in laboratory experiments, such as those in which animals are used as subjects.

Half maximal inhibitory concentration   *See* IC_{50}.

Hepatotoxicity   The extent to which a given substance causes damage to the liver.

IC_{50} (half maximal inhibitory concentration)   The amount of a substance that will reduce the biological function of molecules, cells, tissues, or other biological entities by one-half.

Inbred strain   A type of animal produced through brother-sister breeding in order to produce a population of organisms that are genetically identical or, at least, very similar.

In vitro testing   Studies done with cells or tissues cultured in petri dishes. The term *in vitro* comes from the Latin expression for "in glass."

In vivo testing   Studies done in a living organism. The term *in vivo* comes from the Latin expression for "in life."

Knockout   The process by which one or more genes in an organism are inactivated.

LD_{50} (median lethal dose)   The amount of a substance that results in the death of one-half of a population of experimental animals.

Median lethal dose   *See* LD_{50}.

Mutagen   Any substance that causes a mutation, a genetic change, in an organism or that tends to increase the likelihood of such a change.

Neurotoxicity   The tendency of a substance to cause death of nerve cells.

Peer-reviewed publication   Any scientific paper that has been reviewed and approved by the author's colleagues in the field.

Placebo   An inactive substance that has all the outward appearance of some other substance that is being tested in laboratory or clinical research.

Pound seizure   The transfer of animals from an animal shelter to a research facility where they are used as subjects of a scientific or biomedical experiment.

Protocol   A detailed plan of a projected scientific experiment.

Reduction   One of the three Rs in animal experimentation (q.v.) that calls for the use of fewer numbers of animals in scientific research.

Refinement   One of the three Rs in animal experimentation (q.v.) that calls for the provision of more comfortable and less stressful living conditions for animals used in scientific research.

Replacement   One of the three Rs in animal experimentation (q.v.) that calls for the development of alternative methods of experimentation in which animals can be replaced by mechanical, computer, or other mechanisms of testing.

Sanctuary   A place of protection; for animals that have been used in research, a site similar to their natural environment to which they have been retired after no longer being used in experiments.

Speciesism   The denial of rights that should be available to all animals, based only on the species of an animal.

Teratogen   Any substance that cause malformations in an animal fetus.

Three Rs principle   A philosophy of humane animal research originally expounded in the late 1950s by zoologist W. M. S. Russell and microbiologist R. L. Burch. The three Rs stand for replacement, reduction, and refinement.

Tissue culture   A process by which cells or tissue are grown outside a living organism in, for example, a petri dish.

Vivisection   Originally, the dissection of any living animal. More recently, the term has been applied to any type of research on experimental animals.

About the Author

David E. Newton holds an associate's degree in science from Grand Rapids (Michigan) Junior College, a BA in chemistry (with high distinction) and an MA in education from the University of Michigan, and an EdD in science education from Harvard University. He is the author of more than 400 textbooks, encyclopedias, resource books, research manuals, laboratory manuals, trade books, and other educational materials. He taught mathematics, chemistry, and physical science in Grand Rapids, Michigan, for 13 years; was professor of chemistry and physics at Salem State College in Massachusetts for 15 years; and was adjunct professor in the College of Professional Studies at the University of San Francisco for 10 years. Previous books for ABC-CLIO include *Global Warming* (1993), *Gay and Lesbian Rights: A Reference Handbook* (1994, 2009), *The Ozone Dilemma* (1995), *Violence and the Mass Media* (1996), *Environmental Justice* (1996, 2009), *Encyclopedia of Cryptology* (1997), *Social Issues in Science and Technology: An Encyclopedia* (1999), *DNA Technology* (2009), and *Sexual Health* (2010). Other recent books include *Physics: Oryx Frontiers of Science Series* (2000), *Sick!* (4 volumes; 2000), *Science, Technology, and Society: The Impact of Science in the 19th Century* (2 volumes; 2001), *Encyclopedia of Fire* (2002), *Molecular Nanotechnology: Oryx Frontiers of Science Series* (2002), *Encyclopedia of Water* (2003), *Encyclopedia of Air* (2004), *The New Chemistry* (6 volumes; 2007), *Nuclear Power* (2005), *Stem Cell Research* (2006), *Latinos in the Sciences, Math, and Professions* (2007), and *DNA Evidence and Forensic Science* (2008). He has also been an updating and consulting editor on a number of books and reference works, including *Chemical Compounds* (2005), *Chemical Elements* (2006), *Encyclopedia of Endangered Species* (2006), *World of Mathematics* (2006), *World of Chemistry* (2006), *World of Health* (2006), *UXL Encyclopedia of Science* (2007), *Alternative Medicine* (2008), *Grzimek's Animal Life Encyclopedia* (2009), *Community Health* (2009), and *Genetic Medicine* (2009).